Sensory Integration and Learning Disorders

by A. Jean Ayres, Ph.D.

Published by

WESTERN PSYCHOLOGICAL SERVICES
PUBLISHERS AND DISTRIBUTORS
12031 WILSHIRE BOULEVARD
LOS ANGELES, CALIFORNIA 90025

A DIVISION OF MANSON WESTERN CORPORATION

Sensory Integration and Learning Disorders

Library of Congress Catalog Card Number: 72-91446

International Standard Book Number: 0-87424-303-3

Second Printing . . . . . October, 1973

To

Franklin

Table of Contents

Chapter   *Page*

LIST OF FIGURES viii

PREFACE ix

1. OVERVIEW 1
   Background 2
   Basic Premises 4
   Limitations in Applying Animal Research to Human Beings   7
   Principles of Brain Development 8

2. SOME GENERAL PRINCIPLES OF BRAIN FUNCTION.... 13
   Functional Interdependence of Brain Structures 13
   The Concept of Brain Mechanisms 14
   Plasticity of Neural Function 16
   The Neural Synapse 17
   Sensory Stimulation 20
   Organism-Environment Interaction 22

3. THE INTEGRATIVE PROCESS 25
   The Nature of Integration 25
   Intermodality Association 28
   Centrifugal Influences 31
   Sensory Feedback 32
   Inhibitory Processes 34
   Integration through Movement 36

4. LEVELS OF FUNCTION OF THE CENTRAL NERVOUS
   SYSTEM 38
   The Spinal Cord 39
   The Brain Stem 40
   The Cerebellum 46
   The Basal Ganglia 48
   The Old Cortex and/or Limbic System 49
   The Neocortex 52
   Principles Relating to Levels of Function 53

5. THE SENSORY MODALITIES 55
   The Vestibular System 55
   The Tactile System 61
   Proprioception 66
   The Auditory System 70
   Olfaction 72
   Vision 73

6. POSTURAL RESPONSES AND RELATED FUNCTIONS.... 75
   The Role of Gravity 76
   Neural Level of Organization 77
   The Developmental Sequence 79
   Muscles and Their Major Receptor 83
   Postural Mechanisms and Extraocular Muscle Control 85
   Extraocular Muscle Responses and the Development of
   Visual Space Perception 88

7. FACTORS, SYNDROMES, AND NEURAL SYSTEMS 89
   The Concept of Syndromes or Neural Systems 89
   The Syndromes or Neural Systems Identified 94

8. CLINICAL EVALUATION OF SENSORY INTEGRATIVE
   DYSFUNCTION 96
   Primitive Postural Reflexes 98
   Cocontraction of Antagonistic Muscles 107
   Muscle Tone 109
   Extraocular Muscle Control 110
   Assessment of Vestibular System Function 110
   Integration of Function of the Two Sides of the Body 111
   Choreoathetoid Movements 112

9. GENERAL PRINCIPLES AND METHODS OF
   INTERVENTION 113
   Influencing Sensation and Response 114
   Tactile Stimulation 115
   Vestibular Stimulation 119
   Other Proprioceptive Stimuli 123
   The Adaptive Response 125
   Precautions 129

10. DISORDER IN POSTURAL AND BILATERAL
    INTEGRATION 134
    Description of the Syndrome 134
    Research Related to the Neural System 140
    The Remedial Program 145

11. DEVELOPMENTAL APRAXIA 165
    The Development and Nature of Praxis 166
    Description of the Syndrome 171
    Neurological Considerations 174
    Treatment Plan and Principles 177
    Suggested Activities to Develop Praxis 181

Chapter   *Page*

12. FORM AND SPACE PERCEPTION 190
    Description of Disorder in Form and Space Perception 191
    Some Aspects of Neuroanatomy Subserving Visual Percep-
    tion 192
    The Development of Visual Perception in Man 194
    Hypothesized Dual Modes of Vision 199
    Treatment to Develop Form and Space Perception 201

13. TACTILE DEFENSIVENESS AND RELATED
    BEHAVIORAL RESPONSES 207
    Neuroanatomical and Physiological Considerations 210
    Developmental Considerations 215
    The Therapeutic Program 217

14. UNILATERAL DISREGARD AND FUNCTIONS OF
    THE RIGHT CEREBRAL HEMISPHERE 221
    Definition of the Syndrome 222
    Theoretical Discussion 226
    Other Functions of the Right Cerebral Hemisphere 229
    The Intervention Program 232

15. AUDITORY-LANGUAGE DISORDERS 235
    Nature of the Syndrome 236
    Some Neural Bases of Audition and Language 237
    The Intervention Program 242

16. HAND DOMINANCE AND LATERALIZATION OF
    CEREBRAL FUNCTION 247
    Lateralization as a Developmental Process 248
    Failure to Establish Hand Dominance 250
    Considerations in Selecting a Dominant Hand for a Child.... 252
    Case Studies 253

17. THE ART OF THERAPY 256
    The Internal Drive toward Sensory Integration 256
    Factors Promoting Self-Direction 258
    The Child's Response to Guided Exploration 260
    Disadvantages of Structured Exploration 264
    Similarities between Psychotherapy and Sensory Integra-
    tive Therapy 265

    LIST OF REFERENCES 267

    INDEX 288

List of Figures

Figure   *Page*

1. Normal posture when riding a scooter board at a rapid rate.... 99

2. Posture assumed when the tonic labyrinthine reflex is poorly integrated 101

3. Arm position elicited by poorly integrated tonic neck reflex.... 103

4. Normal reaction to test of degree of integration of the tonic neck reflex 104

5. Spinning in a net hammock 105

6. Positions for inhibition of the tonic neck reflex 106

7. Activating the neck righting reflex 153

8. Use of a large therapy ball 154

9. One use of the platform swing. A commercial version of this and some of the other equipment illustrated is available from Developmental Design, P. O. Box 55, Carpinteria, California 93013 157

10. Quadruped balancing board 158

11. A sitting equilibrium board 159

12. Use of a one leg stool 160

Preface

This book presents a neurobehavioral theory. Theory is not fact but a guide for action. In this case the action is sensory integrative therapy to assist children with learning deficits. Therapy may be carried out by educators, psychologists or health related professionals.

The theory is supported by factual data selected and interpreted in a manner that has been found helpful in hypothesizing about neurobehavioral events. Selections and interpretations of basic brain research have been made with the intention of relating the data to observations of behavior of children with sensory integrative deficits. Since the relevancy is not always obvious, the reader must be somewhat dependent upon his own ability to make interpretations that go beyond the facts and make them meaningful. The more information the reader brings to perusal of the book, the more he will gain from the book.

Just as the continued production of research results in constantly changing neurological concepts, so also will this theory need to undergo frequent revision.

Each theory grows on the work of others, and to those other individuals I am very much indebted. The degree of obligation is fairly well indicated by the list of references with one exception. The contribution of Margaret S. Rood is far greater than appears from citations alone. The following authors and publications have kindly permitted fairly extensive citations of their work: George H. Bishop, Ronald Melzack, *Journal of Nervous and Mental Disease, Psychologische Forschung,* and *Science.*

I especially thank Anne Henderson for her helpful suggestions regarding the manuscript and Marcella Curtright and Florence A. Sharp for other assistance.

A. Jean Ayres
Torrance, California
September, 1972

Chapter 1

Overview

Learning is a function of the brain; learning disorders are assumed to reflect some deviation in neural function. This underlying assumption has led to constructing a theoretical model which provides guidance for an intervention program to ameliorate the neurological dysfunction and promote learning ability. The theory has been built on both brain and behavioral research. Knowledge and theory arising from basic research alone are not sufficiently advanced to provide direct guidelines for treatment and education; many inferences must be made.

Essentially, the theory holds that disordered sensory integration accounts for some aspects of learning disorders and that enhancing sensory integration will make academic learning easier for those children whose problem lies in that domain. Sensory integration, or the ability to organize sensory information for use, can be improved through controlling its input to activate brain mechanisms.

More specifically, sensory integration has been studied both in the manner in which it develops and possibly functions and the ways in which it deviates in the learning disabled child. Sensory integrative processes result in perception and other types of synthesis of sensory data that enable man to interact effectively with the environment. Disorders of perception have been reasonably well established as concomitants of early academic problems. Other aspects of brain physiology, such as biochemistry, are recognized

1

as equally important to learning and its disorders but lie outside the scope of this work.

A sensory integrative approach to treating learning disorders differs from many other procedures in that it does not teach specific skills such as matching visual stimuli, learning to remember a sequence of sounds, differentiating one sound from another, drawing lines from one point to another, or even the basic academic material. Rather, the objective is to enhance the brain's ability to learn how to do these things. If the brain develops the *capacity* to perceive, remember, and motor plan, the ability can then be applied toward mastery of all academic and other tasks, regardless of the specific content. The objective is modification of the neurological dysfunction interfering with learning rather than attacking the symptoms of that dysfunction.

This type of therapy — therapy being defined as any intervention with an intent to remediate given by educator, psychologist, speech pathologist, physical or occupational therapist, or other professional person — does not necessarily eliminate the need for the more symptomatic approach. Therapy is considered a supplement, not a substitute, to formal classroom instruction or tutoring. It reduces the severity of the difficulty and allows specifics, such as the sum of two and two or reading the word "cat," to be learned more rapidly.

It is not claimed that sensory integrative therapy eliminates the underlying causes of inadequate neural organization and resultant learning disorder. Rather this therapy is seen as mitigating some of the conditions, usually arising from unknown causes, that directly interfere with learning. It is supposed that normalizing these conditions through therapy comes closer to altering the underlying neurological dysfunction (regardless of cause) than do typical academic procedures. Only some and not all of the different types of neurological dysfunction are thought to be influenced by this therapeutic approach.

Background

Before any domain of knowledge becomes a science it must go through a long period of informal exploration of a subjective nature. This stage has been called a proto-science, "proto" referring to the first or earliest form. The field of learning disorders appears to be in that stage, with actual scientific exploration just beginning to emerge.

Until very recently, methods of understanding the perceptual process typically have been derived from behavioral observations of the mature subject, either animal or man. Additional information was derived from introspection on the part of various authors and a resultant presentation of their arguments. Generally, there was more concern with such perceptual phenomena as optical illusions than with the nature of the development necessary to enable perception (cf. Dember, 1964). Perceptual abnormalities have long been recognized in the brain-damaged adult whose neurological dysfunction was evident, but only within the last decade has exploration of the causes of learning disorders brought a focus of attention to perceptual-motor development in children.

Theoretical models, like children, follow a developmental sequence. The sequence, unlike that of children, may never be completed. Early efforts to intervene in perceptual development were directed through eye-hand manipulative tasks involving the very perceptual-motor components where deficiencies lay. The approach was largely cognitive, i.e., the child was expected, with the help of the therapist, to "figure things out" intellectually, usually employing primarily the auditory or visual channels. In observing the child's response to this type of intervention program, it soon became apparent that there was a larger underlying sensory integrative problem, probably related to previous developmental steps, that had not matured properly. These developmental gaps seemed to be interfering with further maturation, including that which makes possible academic learning. A deeper search into the problem was required.

Scientific facts regarding the neurological development of sensory integrative processes in the human child are insufficient in quantity to provide guidance in developing methods of promoting perceptual development in disabled learners. This lack of information on the human brain leads to relying on basic brain research, especially that carried on during the past twenty years. Brain research has provided some bases for understanding certain aspects of sensory integration, including perception and other phenomena. Although the data were gathered on vertebrates lower on the phyletic scale than human beings, they have provided guidance in understanding man.

Results of basic brain research have been interwoven with those of behavioral observations and research and the answers placed in a theoretical framework from which treatment procedures have been devised. Unifying the concepts to provide a heuristic guide for therapeutic intervention required filling the holes of the theory with a number of guesses, a process which assists the human mind in utilizing unorganized and isolated details. While a relatively complete theoretical framework is essential to planning remediation, it is important to always keep in mind what is assumption and what is fact. Assumptions are constantly under test and subject to change.

That the treatment based on this theory can bring about statistically significant increases in academic learning among young disabled learners with certain types of sensory integrative dysfunction has been demonstrated (Ayres, 1972a). While one study does not by itself establish the validity of any theory or method, it does indicate that the direction of development of the body of knowledge is probably correct in some respects. At this stage, learning disorders present a situation in which one must base one's action on theoretical reasoning rather than on decisive experimental evidence.

In many instances the theory falls short of its goals, but a useful purpose will have been served if a new focus on the problem of learning disorders stimulates further search for an even more effective and comprehensive theory that will yield procedures that may enhance central nervous system integration and, consequently, ameliorate associated learning and behavior problems. Truth, like infinity, is to be forever approached but never reached.

Basic Premises

Man's brain learned how to perceive and learn; similarly, each child's brain is designed to follow an orderly, predictable, interrelated sequence of development that results in the capacity for learning. In this context, elementary learning might be defined as acquiring the capacity to interpret the environment and to respond appropriately to it. The concept of sequential development holds a central position in the theory. The rationale followed in determining processes and events in the early life of the child which are critical to his later development of the capacity for academic learning deserves considerable explanation as orientation for the material in subsequent chapters.

The early developmental steps, determined by evolutionary history, have been "pre-programmed" into the human brain at conception, but ontogenetic experience is necessary for the full expression of the inherent developmental tendencies. It is generally held that each developmental step is in some way dependent upon a certain degree of maturation of previous steps, a concept that will be expressed in many different ways throughout the book. This contention is generally accepted by child psychologists and exemplified particularly well in statements of some of the leading child developmentalists.

The world's best-known current observer of the child's developmental sequence, Piaget (1952), has stressed the early sensorimotor, including reflex, stage of the infant. This stage makes possible meaningful experiences for the child who makes associations which become the source of sensorimotor intelligence. This then extends itself into reflective intelligence through processes of "accommodation" and "assimilation." Each developmental stage assimilates part of the previous one. Piaget emphasizes sensory integration and response to it as critical to the early origins of intelligence. Symbolic action, according to Piaget, is based on assimilation of prior sensorimotor intelligence. Action is the point of departure for intelligence.

Ames and Ilg (1964) also emphasize the patterned, lawful, and sequential manner of child development. They have observed "reciprocal interweaving" or "a spiral process reflecting a reincorporation of sequential forms of behavior." The description of the process is remarkably similar to that expressed by Piaget.

A child's development is generally inferred from his motor actions, for that is the human dimension which is most easily available for observation. From these observations, however, one can only draw broad inferences as to the underlying sequence of development of sensory integrative processes upon which the motor manifestations are dependent. It is the nature and sequence of sensory integration that is the *sine qua non* to understanding perception and the requirements of early academic learning.

In the absence of objective data on the sequence of sensory integrative development in man, reliance must be placed on inferences drawn from data obtained from study of the brains of subhuman vertebrates, the animals that in some way resemble those from which man evolved and inherited his central nervous system, its mode of development, and its function. This type of study has been rewarding. The possible reasons why it has been productive are worth exploring.

According to Herrick (1956), the higher intellectual functions are just as much a product of the evolutionary development as is the human skeleton. It is not possible, then, to say when man's brain began to learn how to learn. Acquiring the capacity to learn has been a continually evolving process ever since life on earth began. Similarly, a child's development of the capacity to learn begins with conception and continues to evolve until it approaches an asymptote.

While the major determinants of the acquisition of the capacity to perceive and learn lie within each individual, these determinants

are the summation and final product of a series of changes, processes, and reactions. Billions of years have been required for the
brain to develop the potentiality seen in it today. Man's cognitive
ability did not spring suddenly into existence; it developed into
what it is just as each human being develops into what he is. His
previous phyletic steps are assumed to hold similarities to the brains
of other vertebrates living today.

It is *not* assumed that each child recapitulates his own evolutionary history. The concept oversimplifies a complex arrangement.
Although the very early ontogenetic process is not unrelated to
the phylogenetic process, the extent of that relationship is not yet
known. Some hint as to its extensiveness is shown in a study by
Gordon (1956) in which he found biochemical recapitulation of
phylogeny in the chicken. Gordon's study suggests that a continuing presence of an appropriate substrate may be a necessary re-
quirement for continued enzyme development.

One recognized reason why the concept of evolution of the
brain has meaning is that, with each evolutionary step, the brain
retained some of its older organization and incorporated it into the
reorganized state, just as this occurs in the developing child. The
carrying over of part of the organization from one phyletic stage to
the next implies that the brain of man holds remnants of each of
these stages.

Green (1958) has stated that "The impression is gained that by
surgery one can somewhat reverse the evolutionary tide of development" by sectioning the brain at progressively more caudal levels.
The statement grows out of the practice, formerly quite prevalent,
of studying the brain of lower vertebrates by sectioning the brain
at various levels and observing the results. The implication made
by Green is that the evolutionary past is still reflected in successively lower levels of the brain.

Even though man inherits some innate adaptive behavioral patterns, their individual maturation and expression are dependent
upon ontogenetic experience. Environment acts upon the innate
tendencies which each individual brings into his world and molds
and modifies them. The innate potential for development of sensory
integration and related adaptive behavior is a substrate for individual development. That substrate must be understood.

When the brain of a child develops within normal expectations,
his phyletic heritage "appears" less important because the innate
programming directs the child through the early experiences of
swallowing, lifting the head, rolling over, grasping, ambulating in

a quadruped position, and eventually rising to a bipedal position. The environment need only allow the child to express these sensorimotor patterns and, barring any abnormality, the child usually develops them without much guidance or attention. The lack of attention required has led to a tendency to overlook the significance of the early developmental steps to the maturation of perceptual and cognitive functions.

When the development of the brain has deviated from the norm, the resultant behavior is often reminiscent of lower levels of the phyletic scale, with interference in the sequential expression of these developmental patterns. For example, primitive reflexes often are present, the sense of touch is apt to be diffuse rather than well differentiated, and some children are overly ready with a fight or flight reaction in response to some tactile stimuli. This is one of the reasons why knowledge of more primitive function is helpful in understanding current dysfunction and assisting in its remediation.

It is for these reasons, and not for any direct interest in neurobiology of either current or prehistoric vertebrates, that the evolution of the brain and current mode of function of subhuman vertebrate brains are significant to the theory. It is the deviations in maturation of the child's brain today and what to do about them that are the focus of attention in this book.

Limitations in Applying Animal Research to Human Beings

Seeking hypotheses to help understand human development and function from the study of lower animals has many limitations which must be recognized. Not only are there interspecies differences, but the progenitors of man are extinct. Brain research is based largely on those animals which are the closest current approximations of those earlier animals. In addition, once a structure of the brain appeared, its evolution did not cease. Changes have continued at all levels of the nervous system, including the spinal cord, reducing even further the similarity between man's brain and that of lower vertebrates.

Generalizations from lower animals applied to man are probably safest where the brains of the two species are most similar. Of the brain's structures, the brain stem and possibly cerebellum show the least amount of interspecies difference. A large part of elementary sensorimotor functions are regulated within these neural structures and differ less between man and other vertebrates than do cognitive functions. Three sensorimotor patterns that appear to be species specific to man are his bipedal locomotion, his skilled hand use, and his speech.

Possibly one of the more important errors resulting from use of research data from subhuman species results from attributing certain functions to certain areas of the brain. The phyletic trend has been toward corticalization of function, i.e., to transfer control of an activity from subcortical up to the cortical level where elaboration could and did occur. The educators' error has been in the direction of considering all sensation, perception, and cognition as exclusively cortical, overlooking the probability that some subcortical function may still be critical to that which evolution has tended to move toward the cortex. Perhaps to err in the direction of stressing the subcortical will balance the matter.

Principles of Brain Development

If the brain learned how to learn, by what means did it do so? As a working hypothesis, it is proposed that the principles that determined the direction of evolutionary development are manifested in the principles that govern the development of the capacity to perceive and learn by each child today. These principles are discussed to help establish a manner of conceptualizing that aspect of human behavior which has failed to develop in a neurologically normal manner. They may also facilitate understanding of the treatment process.

Exploration of the general direction of phylogenesis of the brain has yielded premises which have been demonstrated to hold heuristic value. One of the most basic demands of existence is interpreting sensory stimuli and responding to them. The process is mediated by the nervous system. A reflex exemplifies the function in simple form; reading exemplifies it on a complex level. Both types of responses are adaptive responses representing greatly different levels of complexity. Adaptive behavior is the ability to adjust one's action upon environmental demand. It may be considered a manifestation of intelligence, especially of a very fundamental nature or low on the cognitive scale.

As the nervous system of the vertebrates evolved, growth at the cephalic end added structures which increased the organism's adaptive capacity, including the capacity for sensory interpretation and effective motor response. At each stage of phylogenesis, regardless of the size and complexity of the nervous system, the animal had a well integrated although simplified repertoire of neural structure with which to interpret the environment and to react to it. When it had only, essentially, a cord (analogous to the

spinal cord) it was capable of integrated, albeit simple, environmental interpretation and reaction. Similarly, when the spinal cord
of man is traumatically severed from the higher portion of the
nervous system, the spinal cord can continue to function in an
autonomous manner, although that function is restricted to spinal
reflexes and the loss of higher control drastically changes the
quality of spinal function.

The addition of the brain stem vastly increased the capacity of
the organism for interpreting sensory stimuli and responding to
them. This control was *added to* spinal control and influenced
spinal control but did not substitute for it. The principle of adding
control with a new structure but not substituting for the older
control is not dissimilar to the ontogenetic principle of one stage
of development reincorporating a prior stage. For a very long
period of time the brain stem, including its upper end, the thalamus, functioned as the highest center of neural processing, integrating sensorimotor activity in a competent although elementary
mastery of the perceptual-motor world. The mechanisms that enabled that well-integrated although simple life are still present,
although in modified form, in man today.

Just as man would not function adequately without spinal
reflexes, for which there is no substitute, he would function even
less well without the complex sensory integrative and motor responses mediated by the brain stem. The cerebral hemispheres,
when they were added, did not provide function that substituted
for that of the brain stem but added abilities that enabled it to
modify brain stem function and to deal with the world on an ever
more complex level. The increase in the extent and type of adjustment potential resulted in more effective behavior and better control of the environment (Herrick, 1956). The function of each
human cortex today is still strongly dependent upon brain stem
functions.

With the expansion of the cortex the parietal lobe, which
especially subserves somatosensory functions, and the visual cortex
showed steady expansion. Auditory centers developed into speech
centers, a sequence which may help to explain some of the effectiveness of sensory integrative therapy on language development.
Lassek (1957) links the emphasis on these functions with the
development of motor and sensory aspects of hand function, an
evolutionary direction that enabled man's survival as *Homo sapiens,*
distinct from other primates. Lassek further points out that during
the major portion of a man's existence as man, his survival was
closely dependent upon acts of the hand. Only very recently, he

stresses, have the abstract processes so characteristic of the last few centuries been the most reliable source of survival. Lassek's comments place emphasis on the importance of precognitive development of the brain, the same locus of stress of sensory integrative therapy.

It has been argued that abstract intellectual capacity, such as that required in reading and interpreting that which is read, is in part a product of development involving a steady increase in the quantity as well as the quality of informational transaction between organism and environment. Treatment principles are in accord with that argument.

The significance of additional but not substitute control through encephalization of function is central to this theory. As the nervous system evolved to meet the expanding needs of existence, the newer structures tended to duplicate older structures and functions and improve upon them rather than to devise different functions. Nature, like some people, hesitates to throw anything away; instead it will modify the function of the older structure. Thus the same kinds of function are repeated at several levels of the brain. The higher levels, as they developed, also remained dependent upon the lower structures. As the young child plays with blocks, then, the cerebral hemispheres direct the action which is implemented with the brain stem and spinal cord assuming essential roles. Similarly, the cerebral hemispheres would not be able to interpret sensations that carry information from the environment if it were not for the transmission and processing of the spinal cord and brain stem.

Because they are pertinent to the rationale underlying therapeutic efforts, the questions are submitted: "What *caused* the brain to evolve and to do so in the direction in which it did?" and "Could the same forces influence each child's maturation?" It is proposed that the answer to the first question lies in great and prolonged "stress" from the environment acting upon an organism with an urge to respond and the capacity for change. Environmental stress is defined as an imposing of information and a demanding of a response that favors survival.

The fact that the forebrain was first a sensory organ to which motor control then migrated — probably to better integrate sensory and motor performance—suggests that the evolution of the nervous system was molded by an environment full of information that consistently and relentlessly pounded upon the nervous system, bringing about a marked increase in the capacity to receive information and developing the organism's capacity to respond.

This premise is consistent with the observation of Lassek (1957) that one of the outstanding events in the evolution of the nervous system was the almost one-sided development of additional sensory — as opposed to motor — neurons to enable effective perception of the environment, which in turn led to additional new and more complex adaptive responses. This structural expansion occurred especially in the modalities of discriminative touch, hearing, and sight. These modalities developed later than, and were therefore somewhat dependent upon, the earlier modalities, which were served by mechanoreceptors — those responding to touch, gravity, and movement.

If the same forces that directed the phyletic development of the human brain assume a role in its ontogenetic development, then the sensations that act upon the nervous system have a profound effect upon its development. Second to that importance is the manner in which that same nervous system reacts to the sensations. The events between the sensation and the response and the manner of influencing those events comprise the topic of this book, for it is in these events that some of the problems of learning disability lie.

This same process of the environment impinging upon a sensitive, receptive, growing nervous system is seen in the normally developing child. Gravity, sounds, sights, tactile stimuli, and those arising from the muscles and related structures impose themselves upon the child, making demands upon him that help determine the nature of growth of the nervous system. The child's innate drives and neural capacity lead him to an abundance of responses, many of them involving maximal effort, that enable him to master those demands and result in experiences that foster his development. It is the child whose central nervous system has not developed in a normal manner, leaving him unable to organize a response to these demands, who becomes the learning disabled child. It is the organizing of successful or adaptive responses to environmental demands that has pushed the progress of evolution of the brain to the point where it is now. The therapeutic situation attempts to modify both the child's capacity and the environmental demands to make it possible for the child to succeed in organizing a response and thus to proceed with the developmental sequences that eventually result in the capacity for academic learning.

As the brain evolved, adding more complex structures to deal with the environment more effectively, a change in the potential for motor output also occurred. The brain stem is primarily concerned with total massive patterning involving overt responses of the entire body, determined by a relatively simple integration. The advent of the cerebral hemispheres enabled more discrete, individualistic motor patterns based on more precise interpretation of sensory information.

The course of therapy follows a similar progression. Enhancing maturation at the lower, less complex levels of environmental-response function enables a child to become more competent at the higher, more complex levels.

Because many of the symptoms seen in children with learning disabilities suggest dysfunction in the brain stem, much therapy centers around organizing sensory integrative mechanisms there. The brain stem is particularly concerned with gross or total body sensorimotor function, such as that involved in simple space perception or in riding a scooter board. The cortex is better prepared to handle specialized and discrete actions such as reading and the use of tools, including the pencil, but it cannot do so well without adequate function at the brain stem level. Accordingly, therapy emphasizes the gross before the fine and specific function.

Cognitive function has its tap root in the spinal cord, most of the rest of its roots in the brain stem and other subcortical structures, and the cortex assumes a mediating role over all.

Chapter 2

Some General Principles of Brain Function

It is man's brain that allows him to know his environment and to interact with it. Academic learning is part of that environment and is one of the brain's functions — a function not isolated from the other functions. Given the assumption that academic learning is a function of the brain and that some interference with brain function is at the root of learning disabilities, it then follows that attempting to understand how the brain normally functions and in what way it is failing to function in the learning disabled child provides an appropriate approach to remediation of the problem. This chapter reviews some of the general principles by which the brain is believed to function and which are germane to the objective of treating learning disorders. Subsequent chapters deal with neural functions more specifically related to the sensory integrative processes that are believed critical to learning.

Functional Interdependence of Brain Structures

Although it is heuristically helpful to categorize different aspects of brain function, the brain is believed to function essentially as a whole, and academic learning appears to be dependent upon the totality of function. Perception and elementary cognition may be customarily attributed to cortical activity, and sometimes even isolated aspects of the cortex, but the cortex does not function independently of the lower parts of the brain, nor does one part of the cortex perform independently of other cortical structures. No locus of the brain, no nucleus, not even a single neuron is sufficient unto itself or isolated from another neuron. Every area of the brain is dependent upon other areas, and yet not completely dependent. While evolution has favored increased localization of the functions of the brain, it has not eliminated the dependence of each part of the central nervous system on other parts, especially on lower or more caudal structures. The result of dependence is not so much a matter of either functioning or failing to function but a matter of efficiency of function. The greater the opportunity for interaction among parts of the brain, the greater the adaptive capacity. The primary sensory areas of the brain have become highly competent, and this competence has been enhanced with increasing localization. By the same evolutionary process, the capacity for interaction among the localized areas has been increased through the association areas. Each primary sensory area of the cerebral cortex is surrounded by integrating areas which overlap integrating areas of other sensory modalities. The overlapping topography presumably facilitates coordination and totality of function. The well-known Russian psychologist Luria (1966a) is among those adhering to this type of conceptualization.

In studying the intercorrelations of electrical activity of different cortical regions of the human brain, Livanov, Gavrilova and Aslonov (1964) found that under conditions of rest or easy mental activity, about half of the recorded areas of the brain showed a slight tendency toward correlated biopotential changes. During difficult mental work, however, there was a marked augmentation in both the degree of intercorrelation and the number of paired areas responding in a similar manner. The authors suggested that the correlations reflected, to some extent, functional connections of the cortex. It seems likely that, when a child is struggling with language or mathematics or any other classroom subject, he is calling upon many parts of the cerebral cortex as well as upon all of the rest of the brain upon which cortical function is dependent. In short, a child studies with his entire brain.

The Concept of Brain Mechanisms

Much of the brain's activity occurs through what have been termed "mechanisms." The frequency of use of this term requires a reasonable understanding of its meaning. When used in connection with the central nervous system, "mechanism" refers to a transformation process whereby information, often of a sensory nature, is utilized to determine an act, usually of a motor nature. A mechanism illustrates one of the most fundamental principles of brain function, the processing of sensory information in order to formulate and execute an appropriate and survival-serving action. Herrick (1956) has likened a mechanism to a machine for obtaining a product, the most characteristic feature of a machine being described in terms of its product or "the end for which the means are adapted."

Mechanisms involve feedback systems, reverberating circuits, and other inherent structural devices for translating information into action. For example, postural mechanisms utilize proprioceptive discharge to elicit, without conscious effort, sustained contraction of muscles, especially those acting on or from the trunk and concerned with extension of the limbs, that results in an anatomical posture with functional meaning. The concept of mechanism also provides a rather convenient means of dealing verbally with that which cannot be well explained structurally. In these instances the mechanism should be considered a construct of man's thinking.

Activity in the brain does not occur intermittently if and when its owner decides to use it. Rather, it is a "hive of activity" (Brazier, 1952) directing and receiving directions from its owner with varying degrees of organization. Whenever understanding of activity in any one neuronal mechanism is sought, it must be sought not only in terms of what mechanism is involved but also in terms of how that mechanism might be processing the information in consideration of the rest of the ongoing neural activity. For example, sometimes a child will find tactile stimuli comfortable and desirable; at other times the same type of stimulus will be interpreted as uncomfortable and definitely to be avoided. Fortunately, the constantly ongoing neuronal discharge is self-organizing—or is intended to be—through a multitude of self-regulating neural mechanisms. The learning disabled child often demonstrates a malfunction of the brain's self-organizing mechanisms. The objective of the therapeutic intervention program is the normalization of these mechanisms.

The importance of interpreting the function of one mechanism in terms of ongoing neural activity was expressed in the sensory-tonic field theory of the early perceptual theorists, Werner and Wapner (1949). They held that sensory stimuli continually arose from a state of organic tension, including that from the viscera and musculoskeletal system. Superimposed and interacting with the sensory input from continuous sources was the immediate sensory input from a visual object. In their words, "the state of the organism is part and parcel of perceptual events." Perception and learning, then, are not isolated neural events but functions of a number of neural mechanisms involving most if not all of the entire brain to varying degrees.

Plasticity of Neural Function

Perceptions are built through successful interactions with the world, the self being the center or reference point. Several innate qualities of man's brain make it possible for him to develop or enhance the capacity for successful interaction, even when neural dysfunction is present. Plasticity of neural function is one of the qualities upon which man's phylogeny, his ontogeny, and the success of an intervention program directed toward ameliorating sensory integrative dysfunction are dependent.

Plasticity refers to the ability of a structure and resultant function to be influenced by ongoing activity without loss of the function. Plasticity refers to a gradual change in the neural state; lability refers to a rapid change. The latter is seen frequently in the disabled learner; the former quality sometimes seems diminished. An analogy between skeletal and neural function may help to clarify the nature of plasticity, a concept which is important to conceptualizing the entire therapeutic process.

Both the skeleton and the brain are immature at birth, with various parts of both not even very well connected structurally. As either system matures, the various parts become more firmly connected functionally and structurally to enable interaction among the various parts of each structure (cf. Scheibel and Scheibel, 1964). Plasticity and flexibility, while typical of early life, diminish with age. The direction of growth and the firmness of the functional connection are dependent upon the kind of experiences encountered as well as upon innate maturational tendencies. Bones grow and are formed in relation to muscles contracting against them and weight bearing on them. Similarly, neurons grow and become interconnected in relation to the kind of electrical and chemical impulses which are directed over them in connection with either afferent, internuncial, or efferent activity. Motor activity occurring during growth modifies skeletal development; sensorimotor activity modifies neural growth.

The past and continued evolutionary changes in the brain are dependent upon plasticity. Similarly, it is upon this capacity to alter the central nervous system of each child's brain that the success of a sensory integrative approach to remediation of learning disabilities rests. Since the plastic capacity diminishes with maturation, the longer the delay in employing sensorimotor experience to modify the interconnections of the functional system of the brain, the harder it is to modify the maturational process. Neurological organization is virtually completed within the first decade of life.

One of the more exciting and promising general principles of brain function to emerge in the past decade from a considerable quantity of research with lower animals is the remarkable capacity of the brain to reorganize after ablations of portions of it, providing the animal with a response often differing very little from pre-ablation behavior. Judging by the research methodology, it is not inconsistent to hypothesize that the demands of the environment greatly assist in bringing about reorganization, but the inherent plasticity of function must be there. The more immature the brain of the experimental animal, the greater is the equipotentiality for function. The fact that every neuron is in constant communication with every other neuron, through one route or another, may contribute to the ability to reorganize. The implication is not made that loss of a portion of the brain makes no difference in the animal's function. The more neural structure interacting with other structures, the richer the output and the higher the adaptive function. The new classical work of Lashley (1929) demonstrated that the quantity of neural structure available for use has a direct relation to the rat's ability to form maze habits.

The human brain, of course, is far more complex than that of rats and cats, and the brain function required for academic learning is not comparable to tasks used in basic brain research to test effects of ablation. Furthermore, it is *not* implied that sensory integrative dysfunction in children is necessarily due to damage to the brain. It *is* implied that a child's brain has considerable potential for change. Perhaps the extent of that potential is not yet known.

The Neural Synapse

The synapse is the structural and functional basis of neural connection. Temporary as well as permanent changes in the brain can occur structurally and biochemically at this connection. A synapse between any two neurons is subject to considerable change and modification, not only from moment to moment but also from day to day and year to year. Likening a synapse to a muscle clarifies the principle. A muscle's strength varies with use. If used consistently in demanding tasks, it hypertrophies; if it is not used, it atrophies. Use of a muscle alters the biochemistry of the muscle; it also alters the ease or degree to which other related muscles can be caused to contract through activation by a nerve impulse. In a way, use of a muscle affects all of the rest of the body.

Similarly, use of a neural synapse increases the ease by which the fundamental connection is made; disuse of a synapse reduces the probability that the connection will be made (cf. J. C. Eccles, 1961). Both biochemical and neuroanatomical changes can result from frequent use of a synapse. Part of the plasticity of the brain lies in the capacity for dendritic growth. Scheibel and Scheibel (1964) have demonstrated the extensive dendritic arborization in the early weeks of the cat's life. It is not unreasonable to suppose that dendritic growth is influenced by early environment; thus the greater the use made of the neuronal synapses, the greater the arborization of dendrites, with resultant greater learning capacity of the organism. That something of this nature might happen during sensory integrative therapy with the young child should not be overlooked.

The degree of relatedness between any one neuron and all other neurons varies as a function of use and with varying degrees of permanence. Some neuronal synapses, particularly certain types involved in cortical discharge, are dependent upon a prolonged (a matter of seconds or less) barrage of impulse flow. The resultant gradually increasing neuronal discharge, called recruitment, presumably enables the focusing of attention on the information. The positive response of some children to an amount of stimuli that would overwhelm other children has led to speculation whether certain synapses in some children were made available through recruitment resulting from such sensory bombardment.

Some pertinent hypotheses about the possible functional nature of synaptic relay stations of neurons have been put forth by Barlow (1961). He suggests that the relays detect, in the incoming messages, information of survival significance. The synapses also serve as a kind of filter or recoding center, with the filter altering the degree or kind of information it lets pass according to the needs of the rest of the nervous system. If success is signaled, transmission characteristics are unchanged, but if success is lacking, the filter changes the nature of its filtering to assure greater success. The transmission characteristics that have been effective in allowing survival throughout the evolutionary changes are the ones present today.

Barlow further submits that coding at the synapse reduces redundancy and thereby organizes sensory information in a concise way so that learning is simplified. Reduction of redundant information is dependent, however, upon prior sensory information having established an internal model of the environment. Nature, notes Barlow, has not been interested in enriching the subjective experience of the world but simply in ensuring the survival of the species.

The important premise upon which Barlow's hypotheses stand is that the structure and function of the synaptic relay center have been molded and shaped according to the environmental demands placed on the organism and the intent of that organism to survive. That sensory information of survival value holds primacy and is more readily transmitted to action centers will be seen as significant in understanding the learning disabled child and planning his therapy. For these purposes, survival must be perceived in its most primitive terms, such as righting oneself into a position for ambulation, and not in such culturally derived survival values as learning to read.

That biochemical as well as structural brain changes can occur as a result of certain types of repeated synaptic transmission has been demonstrated in rats by a group at the University of California at Berkeley (Bennett, 1964; Rosenzweig, 1962, 1966). The rats were provided toys and equipment which essentially encouraged sensorimotor exploration and development. In addition, the rats had daily experience in a maze and in a large pen in which barriers were changed each day. Following such a regimen resulted in increased weight and thickness in the cerebral cortex and decreased subcortical weight when compared with control rats. The effect was not due to over-all acceleration of brain growth. The greatest relative alteration in the cortex was in the visual region and the least was in the somesthetic region, although in both instances the difference was statistically significant. Accompanying the cortical weight change was an increase in the cholinesterase activity of all of the brain per unit of tissue weight, which the researchers believed to be due to increased synaptic transmission in the experimental animals. Gains in problem-solving ability were concomitant with brain changes. These biochemical and neuroanatomical modifications were found in adult rats as well as in those just weaned. It is especially pertinent that the researchers felt the brain change was responsive to environmental pressure. Such pressure is not unlike that which the child encounters in sensory integrative therapy.

While the brain of man is not the same as that of rats, several aspects of the University of California experiments on rats are consistent with the theory of sensory integrative development in man. The brain's plasticity enables it to respond to demands greater than those to which a response previously has been given. The quality has enabled evolution. The continual environmental stimulation of a sensitive plastic nervous system has resulted in a brain today still flexible and able to change according to its interaction with the environment. Furthermore, even in the face of dysfunction, the brain appears to have the *capacity* to reorganize and increase its efficiency.

The plasticity of neural structure is under a certain amount of control by that structure itself. It does not inevitably respond to just any stimuli presented to it by the environment. Later it will be seen that this principle holds an important place in treatment, for the child's brain cannot respond adaptively to just any stimuli elicited by just any activity. A given stimulus has only a probability of eliciting a given response; there is no inevitability of its doing so. Determining these principles of probability of response is critical to the exploration of methods of integrating neural function.

The capacity of the brain to alter the probability that a message will be synaptically transmitted and the influence on use of that probability theoretically enables modification of the central nervous system function by means of therapeutic control of sensory input and motor demands made upon the organism. This hypothesized process is proffered as an explanation for the manner in which therapeutic intervention brings about a permanent change in a child's neural function.

Sensory Stimulation

The critical role of sensation in every individual's ongoing brain function and consequent life process has been most dramatically called to the attention of the professional and scientific world through studies on sensory deprivation, which, in adult human beings, results in emotional, perceptual, and other behavioral deterioration (cf. P. Solomon, 1961). That the effects of sensory deprivation on the young child could be structural is suggested by some of the basic brain research, such as that by Levine and Alpert (1959) and Melzack (1962). In the former study, sensory deprivation delayed development of cholesterol in infant rats. Development of cholesterol is assumed to be a good index of the myelination process. The latter study demonstrated that even mild if not complete deprivation of patterned visual stimuli during early maturation of dogs resulted later in greater difficulty in perceptual discrimination and in utilizing the discrimination in a new learning problem.

From the many studies on sensory deprivation, the following assumption has developed. For optimum brain function in man, it is necessary for it both to receive and to be able to integrate for use a constant stream of stimuli, especially from the body. Without both elements, man's ability to cope with the world diminishes.

The results of sensory deprivation appear similar to the clinical picture of the child with sensory integrative dysfunction. In both cases there is a lack of organizing, structuring, and relating of self to objects and of objects to objects. In the child with poor neurological organization, the stimuli are usually available but there is inadequate processing of them. In the sensorily deprived human research subject, the stimuli have been removed, and when again freshly supplied for testing purposes, the ability to order them is temporarily diminished.

Sensory impulses bring about biochemical changes in the brain that are critical to the learning process. The opinion has been submitted (Richter, 1962) that normal protein metabolism itself is dependent upon adequate physiological stimulation resulting from functional activity of the organism. In addition, the interaction of glial cells with neurons, a process which is basic to the biochemical change in the learning process, is greater during stimulation.

Learning is believed to involve a biochemical change in ribonucleic acid (RNA). Of the many studies in this area, that by Hydén and Egyhazi (1962, 1963) best illustrates one of the neurobiochemical results of sensorimotor function. Rats learned to walk a wire in order to obtain food. The task was sufficiently difficult to require several days to master. Following the experiment, analysis of the RNA of one of the vestibular nuclei revealed a greater quantity in the wire-walking rats than in the control rats, who were given passive vestibular stimulation. Both of those groups showed significantly different composition of RNA over rats kept in a cage. The RNA changes in these experiments were not permanent. It is pertinent that the researchers felt that the change in production and composition of RNA was effected by the establishment of a sensorimotor pattern as opposed to sensory stimulation alone.

Hydén's (1961) opinion regarding the RNA content of human nerve cells holds pertinence for the framework of principles governing sensory integration. In the motor nerve cells in the spinal cords of human beings, the RNA content increases from ages three to forty years, then remains constant before declining after age sixty. The increase during the first part of the life span is associated with sensory stimulation of the cell. Lack of stimulation will result in lack of biochemical (RNA and protein) development, although structure may be normal. It is to be noted, however, that if animals become exhausted, RNA content of nerve cells falls below normal, but the level returns with rest. Maximum effort, while desirable, may temporarily defeat its purpose of enhanced integration if the subject becomes exhausted.

Organism-Environment Interaction

Central to the concept of brain development and function is the action of the environment upon the organism and the reaction of that organism upon the environment. This interaction constitutes the essence of a sensory integrative and sensorimotor response. The primary function of the brain is to translate sensory impulses into meaningful information and to organize an appropriate motor response. The process is most direct and obvious in the young child. The sensory and integrative aspect of the process, being more subtle and covert than the motor, is often overlooked.

The environment acts upon the individual through many sensory receptors, forming a constantly changing pattern of input. W. R. Russell (1959) proposes that the pattern of afferent flow into the nervous system is the basis for a change in the organism's reaction to the environment. The process is not simple. The central nervous system selects the kind of afferent flow it will accept, and its major criterion for selection is survival value. Certain kinds of responses are favored by some feedback and facilitating mechanism. Russell (1958) considers two important determinants of brain development to be (1) the fundamental tendency of nerve cells to repeat patterns of activity, and (2) the capacity of all animals to encourage or discourage a response, based on the degree of advantage the response has for the organism. It is no coincidence that many of the activities employed in sensory integrative therapy are based on concepts of elementary survival value, especially those concerned with organizing sensory input as a basis for an adaptive motor response.

A number of scientists who have looked at brain function with perspective nurtured by years of experience have expressed views emphasizing the simple sensorimotor principle of brain function. "In both the phylogenetic and ontogenetic histories," states Sperry (1952), "mental activity develops out of, and in reference to, overt action." The fundamental operating principle does not differ radically, according to Sperry, from fish to man. The change seems to be one of gradual refinement and elaboration of brain mechanisms but no "alteration of the fundamental operating principles."

Sherrington (1955) has pointed to the reflex as the symbolic "cradle of the mind." Another succinct expression comes from Yakovlev (1948): "Behavior is thus movement." This theorist believes that behavior has evolved from the visceral to the expressive to the effective, the last mode referring to change effected by the living organism on the physical enviroment.

A concept expressed earlier deserves elaboration here. At each evolutionary stage, even when the neural structure was limited to a simple cord, the organism has a sufficiently well integrated repertoire of sensorimotor functions to enable it to interact successfully with the environment. As the brain evolved, the same functions increased in complexity. The increased complexity of sensory integrative processes was enabled by the tremendous increase in the number of sensory nerve fibers, a trend proposed by Lassek (1957) as one of the most outstanding in the brain's evolutionary course. Enlarging the scope of information supplied the brain enabled it, in turn, to develop increasingly complex adaptive responses. As each neural structure appeared, it provided for additional control but not substitute control. Each structure remained capable of receiving information, integrating it, and organizing an appropriate motor response. While the highest or youngest structure present at any one time in evolution or in any one species today (in man it is the cerebral cortex) exerted critical influence over all lower structures, the higher centers still maintained a dependence upon lower structures. It will be seen later that therapy for sensory integrative dysfunction emphasizes achieving sensory integration at lower levels as a foundation for higher brain function.

The involvement of a maximal behavioral or adaptive response, demanding effort to accomplish beyond that which has already been mastered, appears necessary for optimal central nervous system integration. Sensory stimulation and repetition of an already learned response is less helpful. That demand and response are critical to maturation of sensory integrative responses may be considered a highly significant component of the basic principle of organism-environment interaction and one that is especially pertinent to the intervention program.

In summary, amelioration of learning disorders must begin with an understanding of some of the basic principles by which the brain functions, especially those principles which are related to the sensory integrative foundations of learning. While academic and other learning certainly involve portions of the cerebral cortex, those portions are not only interdependent but dependent upon lower neural structures for normal function. For that reason remedial intervention programs must first be concerned with brain function, especially the older and lower parts. These functions are carried out through brain mechanisms.

The fact that the young brain is plastic, i.e., capable of modifying its function, makes it possible for therapy to change the brain's organization so that it is better able to perceive and to learn. Some of the change may take place by establishing more and firmer connections among neural synapses and many of these connections are made through organism-environment interaction, a process which is essential to maintaining and enhancing normalcy of brain function.

Chapter 3

The Integrative Process

If all of the sensory stimuli which enter the central nervous system were allowed to bombard the higher levels of the brain, the individual would be rendered utterly ineffective. It is the brain's task to filter, organize, and integrate a mass of sensory information so that it can be used for the development and execution of the brain's functions. Fortunately, under normal circumstances, the brain is a self-organizing system, for its enormous task would challenge the most complex machine. It seems a wonder that the organizing system does not fail more often than it seems to.

It is easily observed that man is a marvel of motor function; contemplating what he must do to organize the function of five times as many afferent neurons as efferent neurons is less easily observed and even taxes man's conceptual ability. One of the first and greatest neurophysiologists to attempt that task was Sherrington (1906, 1955), who stressed the importance of central nervous system mechanisms for sensory integration. His work serves as the source for many of the basic theoretical concepts expressed in this chapter and upon which other theorists have built.

The Nature of Integration

One of the primary concerns of the brain is integration, which may be defined as the interaction and coordination of two or more functions or processes in a manner which enhances the adap-

25

tiveness of the brain's response. Through integration a "whole" is either revised or produced from fragmented parts. Information from the environment is organized and interpreted for the planning and execution of interaction with the environment, particularly the tangible, three-dimensional, gravity-bound world.

Integration is a primordial experience, a constant experience throughout the ages, and a critical experience. How has it developed and how does it occur? Within the answer lies the key to enhancing integration in the child who shows deficits in that area. Integration is the organization of the brain into a state of equilibrium that tends to be self-perpetuating. It is as though several different spheres of function each achieved a state of active homeostasis and then integration in all of the different spheres was coordinated into an organism interrelating smoothly with the environment. The acting organism is an expression of the totality of integrative acts. Integration involves being able to put data together, but not inexorably so, into a kind of "directed flexibility."

Integrative processes occur in all domains of brain function, but those that are concerned with sensorimotor integration are of particular significance to learning disorders. According to the comparative neurologist, Herrick (1956), higher integrative functions operate through the mediation of sensorimotor experience. Herrick is not alone in his thinking.

The evolutionary trend of the integrative processes holds pertinence for understanding them. The cerebral cortex evolved out of that area of the brain — the olfactory area — which was most adept at integrating sensory information and which, as one of the more important sources of environmental information in the early vertebrates, was critical for organizing sensory information as a basis for response. Apparently it was the sensory integrative capacity of that portion of the brain rather than olfaction as a sensory modality which was important. According to Karamyan (1968), evolution proceeded from the diffuse to more local forms of neural activity. He believes this to be true of both the brain as a whole as well as the separate integrating systems. He points out that a major change in both structure and function of the brain occurred with the development of the terrestrial mode of living. At that time the distance receptors developed, changing a predominantly mesencephalic-cerebellar integration in the fish to a diencephalic-cortical integration in the quadruped. It will be seen later that this is essentially the course that therapy takes, i.e., from general sensory stimulation to specific; from emphasis on brain stem-cerebellar mechanisms to cortical ones; from focusing on the somatosensory and vestibular mechanisms to those regulating vision and audition.

The importance of sensory integration as a step in the development of cognitive abilities is reflected in anatomical structure. It is generally believed that the brain's central position in the vertebrates, as opposed to the structurally diffuse nervous system of the non-vertebrates, made possible a place for convergence of the incoming information, for its processing, and for directing the resultant behavior. The invertebrates, of course, have not shown the same evolutionary development of cognitive processes. It frequently has been fruitful to hypothesize a corollary between phylogeny and ontogeny, although a precise recapitulation does not occur. If the capacity for intersensory and sensorimotor integration allowed development of man's intellectual capacity as a species, it is probable that it also is involved in each individual's development.

The central anatomical position of man's nervous system enables the brain to provide both vertical and horizontal coordination of material brought to its different portions. Organization must and does occur vertically among the levels of the brain as well as horizontally between two structures at the same level. Thus critical integrative processes not only must occur between cortex, basal ganglia, diencephalon, cerebellum, brain stem, and spinal cord, but also between the two cerebral hemispheres, between the two sides of the thalamus, brain stem, and spinal cord. The need for horizontal integration can be brought to attention by simply imagining the neural action necessary for integrating the two sides of the body during the process of opening a jar of pickles with two hands.

Less easily recognized is the need for neural integration at each vertical level of the nervous system. Again, a check of the phylogenetic process lends some insight into the probable current mode of neural function. The vertebrate central nervous system began as a simple cord, added a brain stem and cerebellum, and finally the cerebral hemispheres. At each stage of evolution, even when the neural structure was most limited, the organism had a sufficiently well integrated inventory of sensorimotor functions to enable it to interact successfully with the environment and to fulfill its link in the evolutionary chain. For example, amphibians and reptiles both have mechanisms for integrating sight, touch, and hearing in the brain stem, although neither has a true cortex. While the behavior patterns of these lower animals are well integrated, they are still simple and relatively inflexible. The question might well arise, however, as to what characteristics the reptile-like creatures that were part of man's heritage possessed that contemporary reptiles do not have.

To a certain extent, but not completely so, each level of neural structure in man today is still capable of and, for complete neural organization, must provide a relatively self-contained sensory integrative system. As each structure evolved, the functions of the total nervous system did not change so much in kind as in degree of complexity. Each new neural structure provided additional but not substitute control. Thus each level of the nervous system today offers relatively complete sensory integration in some form. However, the structures above it exert critical influence over it, and structures below it are still dependent upon the higher structures. In the developing human brain, it is important that the brain stem integrating mechanisms, which have the capacity for directing some relatively discrete sensorimotor patterns, reach optimum maturation, for higher levels of function will be dependent upon adequate integration at the brain stem level. Not incidentally, adequate execution of sensorimotor functions at the brain stem will be dependent upon lower spinal cord functions.

Intermodality Association

An important type of sensory integration, possibly basic to all of the brain's integrative processes, is that of intermodality association, a process of particular academic importance and one known frequently to be affected in children with neurological or learning disorders (Beery, 1967; Birch and L. Belmont, 1964; Birch and **I. Belmont, 1964; Belmont, Birch and Karp, 1965**). Brain-damaged monkeys have been shown to have less tactile-visual association than do no-brain-damaged monkeys (W. Wilson, 1965).

The capacity for intersensory integration may be a major source of man's advanced adaptive ability. Sherrington (1955) stressed the emergence of mechanisms enabling intersensory integration as a major phyletic trend. It has been noted by others as well. In children, intersensory integration follows a developmental sequence, with the most rapid maturation of the function occurring before eight years of age. Birch and Lefford (1963) reported the age of eight years as an important maturation point in their study of visual, haptic, and kinesthetic sensory integration in children and approximately ten years of age for most of the maturation in audio-visual integration.

Intermodality association occurs at all levels of the brain, that at higher levels being in part dependent upon that which occurs at lower levels. At higher levels additional non-sensory processes such as memory and reasoning are involved. Because higher, more cognitive processes are more easily evaluated, they are most frequently the object of studies of intermodality association in human beings. The dependence of cortical function on brain stem function, however, requires focusing attention on intermodality association at brain stem and other subcortical levels.

Understanding the apparent effectiveness of treatment designed to bring about integration in brain mechanisms through sensory integrative activity necessitates study of the possible methods by which the brain associates sensory impulses from various sensory modalities. A major method by which the central nervous system integrates multisensory information is by directing sensory information from different sensory sources to a common integrating structure such as a nucleus or to a common neuron called a convergent or polysensory neuron. Convergent neurons respond to stimuli from several different sensory modality sources. It is assumed that convergence of input on a common neuron or larger structure allows for coordinating several different types of information.

According to Fessard (1961), the mechanisms of interaction between convergent afferent impulses can be partly explained as neuronal facilitation, inhibition, occlusion, and spatial patterns of impulses at relays. The mixture of excitatory impulses takes place and results in modulation of impulse firing.

The mere summation of stimuli, of course, does not make for integration, but the process of accepting some and rejecting other information is possible at convergent points and is basic to integration. Summation of stimuli, all relevant to the same aspect of environment, may produce a response not elicited by one source of stimuli alone, and some neurons require convergence of many impulses for discharge. These latter two conditions are of particular significance to the therapeutic process. Jung, Kornhuber and DaFonseca (1963) found occlusion of an impulse during multisensory stimulation more common than facilitation or inhibition. They have suggested that multisensory information may be important for feedback and for regulating sensory attention through providing redundant information. In this case, occlusion would be of particular importance.

Evidence indicates that multisensory convergence on single neurons occurs in all parts of the cerebral cortex as well as in subcortical centers (J. C. Eccles, 1966). Fessard (1961) has noted the prevalence of convergence in the neuronal networks, especially the mesencephalic reticular formation. He also indicates that the caudate nucleus, red nucleus, and motor cortex have similar properties. The motor cortex of the cat, according to Buser and Imbert (1961), acts as a converging center for sensory input just as do certain parts of the limbic system, thalamus, and basal ganglia.

Albe-Fessard and Fessard (1963) have shown that the convergent nuclei in the thalamus receive their somatosensory input from the spinothalamic tract, while the posterior-column-medial-lemniscal fibers project their impulses via specific thalamic nuclei. Furthermore, these authors suggest that thalamic integration is not limited to sensory input but includes information from the rest of the brain and other parts of the thalamus and that the route of cortical sensory association is not transcortical but cortical-sub-cortical-cortical. They present evidence that some thalamic cells in the cat respond to more than one sensory modality, usually sound, vision, and somesthesis, excluding muscle spindles and Golgi tendon organs, which, at the time of publication of the article, were believed not to project to the convergence areas of the thalamus. The idea of a major integrative system in the region of the thalamus will be discussed again in a later chapter, for it holds considerable pertinence for sensory integrative dysfunction, particularly if cortical integration cannot occur without it.

The most commonly reported modalities showing convergence are visual, auditory, olfactory, somesthetic, and vestibular. Because the vestibular system may be used especially effectively therapeutically in children whose primary problem is in the auditory-language domain, a research study by Jung, Kornhuber and DaFonseca (1963) of sensory convergence in the cat's cortex is of particular interest. The cats were prepared by surgery in such a manner that the incision prevented the somatic sensory input from reaching the cortex but did allow study of the cortical destinations of optic, vestibular, and acoustic stimuli. Cortical responses to visual stimuli were found in many places. Acoustic responses were most common in the auditory area but also were encountered in other areas, especially the vestibular cortex. Labyrinthine responses were concentrated in the vestibular area but also were found in the auditory area. When sufficient stimulation of the vestibular apparatus was given, some response was found over all of the cortical region. Inhibition of cortical neurons through vestibular stimulation was sometimes seen. Convergence from several sense modalities on the same neurons was found in all cortical areas investigated, including the primary receiving areas that have a preference for a specific modality. These authors suggest that the cortical neurons that are convergent for the visual and vestibular systems are pre-coordinated in the brain stem structures. They concluded that multisensory stimuli are more effective than messages from one modality only.

Although certain neurons seem to be designed especially to serve as convergent neurons, any neuron centripetal to the primary sensory neuron cannot be considered free from influence from nerve impulses from one sensory modality only, for all other neurons can theoretically impinge upon the synapse between the primary and secondary neurons and any subsequent synapses. This type of multisensory convergence of neurons occurs at all levels of the central nervous system. Spinal cord levels integrate, especially, somatosensory and vestibular information by this means.

Experiments with human beings wearing lenses demonstrates behaviorally how the central nervous system utilizes intersensory integration as a basis for adaptive action. The lenses invert the visual image, but after users wear them in action for awhile, the inverted visual field is perceived as right side up. Presumably the visual, tactile, and proprioceptive inputs are reassociated through intersensory integration in order to enable an adaptive response. It is important to note that the visual input made the change in order to be consonant with the motion and its resultant proprioceptive flow, rather than the other way around. In discussing experiments of this type, Held and Rekosh (1963) stress that visual space perception can be upset seriously by disrupting the normal relation between self-produced movement and its concurrent sensory feedback.

To the clinician these data suggest that the best way to enhance audition may not be through auditory stimuli alone and the best way to develop visual perception may not be through vision alone. Both areas of perception and most of the rest of cortical function can be influenced, one way or another, by vestibular stimulation as well as through other sensory modalities. It is no longer appropriate to think in terms of isolated sensory modality development or function. That is not the major means by which the brain functions. It functions as a whole, and one of its attributes leading to wholeness is its manner of converging sensory input. It operates through intersensory integration, and, furthermore, a great deal of that integration occurs at brain stem and thalamic levels which then influence integration at higher levels. Effective treatment can be planned accordingly.

Centrifugal Influences

One of the means by which the brain obtains and maintains an integrated state is through regulation of its own sensory input through centrifugal influences, i.e., influences operating in a direction away from the cerebral cortex and toward the periphery. One of the better known examples of this type of integrating action is that of the gamma efferent or intrafusal fiber acting on the muscle spindle. Centrifugal influence is believed to be present and acting on all integrating centers, including nuclei, as well as on each sensory receptor.

Some of the early speculations of the researchers investigating some types of centrifugal influence provide a fairly good illustration of the nature of the nervous process. French, Hernández-Peón and Livingston (1955) proposed the existence of functional mechanisms within the reticular formation operated by downward projections of the cortex. In studying monkeys they found many regions of the cortex, including the oculomotor cortex and sensorimotor cortex, had a strong influence on the brain stem reticular activating system. These scientists concluded that there was an interplay of activity between the cortex and the thalamus and brain stem, with ascending influences converging with descending ones. The descending influences acted on sensory as well as motor activity. The authors further suggested that the cortical regions may make neuronal changes through an integrating effect on the "centrencephalic system," a mechanism proposed by Penfield which will be discussed in Chapter 4. It is important to remember that regulation implies a depressant as well as a facilitatory effect and a tonic as well as phasic effect (cf. Kerr and Hagbarth, 1955).

An important function of centrifugal influences is the regulation of centripetal (toward the center) flow. Without such a regulation sensory overload would result. The descending influence "edits" the ascending influence, largely by suppressing part of it. As one observes the typical child with learning and behavior disorders, it is easy to speculate that these depressant centrifugal regulators are inadequate in their functioning. Some of the disinhibited behavior, hypersensitivity to sensation, deficient perception, and clumsiness can be linked, in one way or another, to inadequate centrifugal influences from cortical or subcortical levels. Therapeutic effort is directed toward providing sensory input which is designed to enhance centrifugal depression.

Sensory Feedback

The execution of an adaptive response is dependent upon continual sensory feedback and adequate integration or interpretation of those sensations. In addition to the more obvious process of awareness through sensory feedback from action, sensory feedback occurs through less conscious mechanisms involving reverberating circuits and networks (cf. Brazier, 1952). There is constant interaction of centrifugal influence and feedback aspects of sensation, and this interaction appears to function poorly in the learning disabled child. A common experience for a therapist is attempting to help a child balance on a piece of equipment when the child does not even know that he is off balance. Inadequate feedback was expressed by the child, who was advised by the therapist that he was falling from a large therapeutic ball and should prepare to catch himself. Although he was well on the way to the floor, he replied, "But which way am I going to fall?" Somatosensory and vestibular feedback are often inadequate in the child with dysfunction, if one can judge by objective measures of these sensory domains. The problem is not one of loss of sensation but of inadequate discrimination of the temporal and spatial qualities which, presumably, results in "hazy" or vague feedback. It is advisable to consider the probability that inadequate feedback interferes with the sensory integrative functions that enable the development of visual and other perception.

Studies with human beings demonstrate the dependence of accurate skilled motor function upon visual feedback. MacKay (1961) found that involving the hands of the subject in a perceptual experiment reduced the disparity between visually perceived apparent motion and actual motion. One individual with a poor sense of joint position was unable to resolve the disparity by hand involvement as had the more normal subjects. In a study by Smith, Ansell and Smith (1963), delaying visual feedback to motions in neurologically normal individuals resulted in severe disruption of learning and motor performance. They found that very little, if any, learning occurred under conditions of delayed sensory feedback.

It does not seem likely that the amount of limitation of motion imposed by neuromuscularly limiting conditions such as athetosis should, in itself, seriously reduce the necessary contribution of sensory stimuli to the integrative processes critical to developing the ability to perceive and learn (cf. Abercrombie, Gardiner and associates, 1964). Although quantity is not to be ignored, as seen from research cited above, the quality of the processing or integrating of them is more important. Accurate discriminative information from limited movement may contribute more to perceptual-motor function than do a large number of motor actions giving rise to many sensations over many modalities but which convey vague messages never well integrated by the brain.

Inhibitory Processes

Suppression of input is fully as important as enhancement of input in the integrative process. According to Granit (1966), if it were not for the mechanisms of attenuating and organizing sensory input, impulses from the periphery would be fatal. Inhibition can occur at any neural synapse or at the receptor, but certain structures, especially in the brain stem, thalamus, basal ganglia, and cortex are especially designed for depressing neural activity. The inhibition is often effected through centrifugal action. While inhibition and depression are not identical neural processes, they will be considered approximately the same neurologically for present purposes.

The brain's inhibitory capacity increases as the phyletic scale is ascended, suggesting the importance of the role of inhibitory processes in the development of higher brain function. A comparable ontogenetic trend is seen in the gradual raising of the cortical and perhaps subcortical threshold level in man. The neural threshold level in children with brain dysfunction often appears to be too low, but not infrequently it is abnormally high for certain sensory modalities or in general. The activity level of a child may be a rough guide to the excitatory-inhibitory level or threshold level of the brain in general. The cortex of the monkey has a threshold much lower than that of man, and monkeys are characteristically active. The cat, on the other hand, has a neural threshold that is quite high, and the adult cat is proverbially depicted as sleeping on the hearth.

One way of conceptualizing the role of inhibition in the integrative process is through the need of the central nervous system for a homeostasis of sensory flow, just as the body requires a biochemical homeostasis. Without inhibition, sensory homeostasis is lost; without sensory stimulation it is likewise lost. The excitatory and inhibitory mechanisms are interwoven into an integrative organization of homeostatic flow. In fact, many neural structures seem to have a balancing as opposed to activating function.

Inhibition within the central nervous system is as much a matter of eliciting a neural impulse as it is of increasing central excitation. Abuladze (1968) has stated it thus: "There are no special inhibitory formations in the central nervous system, but . . . the process of inhibition that occurs within it is always associated with the process of stimulation." If inhibition is one of the results of stimulation, therein lies a possible route by which a therapist can inhibit selected neural functions of the child.

Research on sensory deprivation points out the importance of sensation to the development of the mechanisms for inhibition. Inhibition does not result from deprivation of stimuli but from normal processing of stimuli. Animals experiencing sensory deprivation early in life later show signs of being more easily aroused or excited, although they lack sustained attention. Some animals are literally "overcome" by a normal amount of sensation and respond with "violent emotional storms" or even convulsive disorders when exposed to a normal amount of stimulation after experiencing early sensory deprivation (Riesen, 1961a). Melzack and Burns (1965) have shown that severe restriction of early sensory experience in dogs resulted in a shift in brain wave responses from low to high frequencies in presentation of novel situations that elicited little brain wave change in control litter mates. The authors felt that responses of the deprived dogs showed a failure to depress irrelevant information and an excessive central nervous system arousal, both of which interfered with perceptual discrimination. To these research reports might be added the comment that in the therapeutic situation mere sensory stimulation alone is not sufficient; the brain must be able to process the sensation so that the integrative mechanisms can develop and function.

A common manifestation of loss of function of a portion of the brain is "release" of neural activity through loss of normal inhibition which is mediated through that portion of the brain. The muscle spasticity that accompanies a cerebral vascular accident is one of the most common examples. In a study on monkeys, Ruch and Shenkin (1943) found that ablating part of the frontal lobe cortex resulted in an increase in locomotor activity, fear, and aggressive responses. Inhibition is an important component of function of much of the brain and if certain portions of the brain have been rendered unable to perform adequately, the resultant loss of inhibition interferes with the excitation-inhibition balance that is part of the integrative process.

It is not difficult to understand the role of inhibition in the sensory integrative process, for it seems closely related to observable behavior of the dysfunctioning child, but it is considerably more difficult to employ the principle of enhancing integration through sensory inhibition in a therapeutic setting. The fact that inhibition is an active process — a result of sensory stimulation and normal activity of the brain — provides the channel for therapeutic intervention. The difficult task for the clinician is providing the therapeutic experience which elicits the sensations that are inhibitory rather than one that produces sensory overload in a brain that is already inadequate in its inhibitory role.

Integration Through Movement

One of the most powerful organizers of sensory input is movement which is adaptive to the organism. The role of movement in integration has been best recognized by the comparative neuro-anatomists. Both Herrick (1956) and Coghill (1929) perceived the total action pattern of the evolving vertebrates as integrating. Herrick believes that it was through the total reaction, which was primarily motor, to the environmental demands which effected the evolution of the mind rather than the mind that made the body into the motor being it became. Enviromental demands are known through meaningful sensory stimuli and environmental demands helped shape the evolutionary course. The fact that the vertebrates evolved into such an advanced species as man indicates that many of their responses were adaptive.

Kephart (1968) descriptively refers to the adaptive response as the human organism's "coming to some kind of acceptable terms with the environment." Emphasis must be placed on acceptability to the survival interests of the organism when considering adaptive movement as an integrating process.

Phyletically and ontogenetically, brain structure and performance follow functional demands made on the organism. Functional demands result in purposeful or goal-directed responses. Generally, if presented with a demand for function, the brain will at least attempt an adaptive response, apparently based on the innate tendency of the brain to organize itself. It is proposed that the type of response required and made by the organism assumes a forceful role in determining integrative action, for which organization of sensation forms a prerequisite. The random, poorly planned, stereotyped, or ineffectively executed actions often found among children with sensory integrative dysfunction have low integrative power. Integration is achieved by organizing and emitting an *adaptive* response and therapy is achieved when that response represents more complex organization than previously accomplished. Riesen (1961b) considers the response to a stimulus an essential aspect of perceptual development.

It was noted above in the work of Hydén and Egyhazi (1962) that optimal gains in learning in rats came from successfully meeting a sensorimotor challenge. The motor component of a demanding and skilled visual-motor act was found by Black and Myers (1965) to be far more important than the visual component in the deposition of the memory trace in lower primates.

The integrating effect of an adaptive motor response may be seen clinically in administering sensory integrative therapy. Part of this integration may come from the fact that the motor cortex is one of the major centers for integrating convergent sensory information related to motion. The fact that there is even more sensory convergence in cells in the premotor cortex suggests the greater possibility of intersensory integration through gross and proximal motor patterns as opposed to fine, skilled actions. As cited earlier, Buser and Imbert (1961) suggest that the motor cortex of the cat functions as "some sort of common pool for sensorimotor integration," a property not shared as effectively by the primary or association areas of the cortex.

Sensory integration through motion is not limited to cortical function. It occurs at all levels of the nervous system. Therapeutic results have led to the proposal that motor actions designed to elicit reflexes or automatic reactions organized primarily at one level of the brain tend to organize sensory integration at that level. Thus the goal of sensory integration at the brain stem level is hypothesized to be facilitated by utilization of motor patterns which may have integrating centers in the brain stem.

Motion allows an active involvement of the individual with the visual experience as opposed to a passive sharing only, such as occurs during looking at pictures. It helps in the focusing of attention, which may be one of the ways in which it executes its sensory integrative properties. Motion integrates the somatosensory and visual experience. An analogy is found in talking as a means of interacting with the auditory experience.

Chapter 4

Levels of Function of the
Central Nervous System

As a whole, neurological data are complex, voluminous, rapidly changing and sometimes lacking in consistency. In order for the knowledge to have functional value in intervention programs it must be structured. Largely for that reason, the concept of "levels of function" has long been in use by students of the nervous system. It is derived mainly from the study of the evolution of the brain, for as the brain evolved, the newer structures were added to the rostral (nose) end of the central nervous system, creating successively higher levels capable of more complex functions.

This organization of the structure and function of the nervous system places the phyletically older structures at the anatomically lowest and least complex level and the newer and ontogenetically later maturing structure, the cerebral cortex, in the highest position. The levels ascend roughly in the sequence in which they are discussed in this chapter.

There is heuristic value in referring to certain neural processes as occurring at a given level of the central nervous system. When such reference is made it should be interpreted to mean that the process is especially mediated at that level or is particularly dependent upon that level. In actual human behavior, several levels function together, but it is difficult to plan treatment or evaluate

38

brain function during ongoing therapeutic activity when conceptualizing the brain as performing as a whole, although it does indeed do so.

In addition to vertical arrangement of the levels of function, the central nervous system is organized in a medial-lateral or inner-outer direction. This type of organization is also determined phylogenetically. As the brain evolved, environmental demands spurred the development of new layers of neural tissues. These layers were added as outer layers to the older central core. The cerebral cortex is the most recent layer. The central tegmentum of the midbrain, which mediates many postural reactions, is phyletically very old. Similarly, the limbic system, neatly centered within the cerebral hemispheres, is concerned with more primitive functions than is the neocortex. The significance of the medial-lateral organization will be made clear later.

As pointed out before, a general principle of brain function is that higher levels do not function optimally without adequate lower function. Although there is less attention given to the medial-lateral direction of neural development, therapeutic procedures are consistent with the view that the outer layers of the brain will not function optimally unless the inner layers are well organized. Accordingly, disorders of the neocortex may be approached therapeutically by first normalizing reticular formation or tegmentum function. The approach exemplifies stressing both medial before lateral and lower before higher structures and their mechanisms.

The Spinal Cord

Mediation of spinal cord reflexes and conduction of afferent and efferent neural impulses up and down the spinal cord constitute the major functions of the spinal cord. While the locus of difficulty in disordered sensory integration is in the brain rather than in the spinal cord, the disorder is often manifested in spinal reflexes. Furthermore, they are the basis through which much of the higher neural activity manifests itself, for all motor expression at the spinal level has a reflex base. Disorder in these reflexes or other automatic spinal processes usually represents more cephalically located disorder, and therein lies its importance. Furthermore, that neuron which is the final common path is subject to all the spinal cord reflex activity as well as every other message arriving at it from higher levels. It is in part through the spinal cord that brain function is manifested, and for that reason activity mediated by the spinal cord is pertinent to sensory integrative problems. Furthermore, sensory impulses arising from tactile, kinesthetic, bone, tendon, and muscle receptors make spinal cord connections which influence motor output.

The Brain Stem

Attention must first be directed to the level of the brain stem, for it is here that some of the brain's most significant and massive sensory integration and other events equally important to the life of man occur. At one time in the evolutionary process the brain stem, as the highest neural structure, provided sufficient organization and direction to enable the organism to interact adaptively with its environment, albeit at a primitive level. Those functions, although greatly modified, still operate in man today. It is sometimes appropriate to think of disordered function as primitive function with insufficient modification of the type that evolution brought.

Although the thalamus generally has not been considered part of the brain stem, there is an increasing tendency to refer to it as its rostral end, mainly because some of its function is a continuation of part of the brain stem function. For that reason some of the thalamic functions are included in this section.

Any major neural structure receiving sensory input from many sources is apt to have widespread influence over the rest of the brain. Multiplicity of input also usually means convergence of input and thereby integration of input. The brain stem and thalamus are good examples of these principles. The reticular formation in the brain stem and thalamus receives sensory input from every sensory modality; this structure also has widespread influence over the rest of the brain. That same neural network also provides some of the most important neural integration.

The reticular formation of the brain stem, including its projections in the thalamus, is so important that it has been considered the master control mechanism in the central nervous system (French, 1960). The reticular formation is composed of most of the brain stem mass excluding the nuclei and long tracts of the specific sensory and motor tracts. Some neurophysiologists consider certain midbrain nuclei, such as the red nucleus and substantia nigra, as specialized portions of the reticular formation, although there are differences in interpretation as to exactly what structures constitute the reticular formation.

This network of fibers was originally described by Moruzzi and Magoun (1949) and again by Magoun (1952a, 1952b) as "an ascending reticular activating system." As explained by Magoun (1961), one of its major roles and one of the first to be recognized is that of promoting general alertness and attention which, under certain conditions, tend to enhance the discriminatory power of the organism to gain more information about the stimulus and thereby be better prepared to deal effectively with it. Magoun refers to the orienting reaction of the reticular arousal as "pre-adaptive," i.e., it performs a function that must precede the adaptive or perceptive process.

The reticular formation is located somewhat like the hub of a wheel, receiving influences from all parts of the brain and extending its influence in all directions. It can be considered a "transactional" link for all parts of the nervous system (Worden and Livingston, 1961). This system assumes an extensive integrative role, organizing sensory information through inhibition, facilitation, augmentation, and synthesis to assist in interpretation of the sensory world. In the lower animals this organization is sufficient to enable the animal to act on his world in a primitive and stereotyped but adaptive manner.

The reticular system deals with sensory stimuli in a less specific manner than the sensory tracts, leading to reference to it as the unspecific or nonspecific system. Herein lies a point of considerable significance for therapy. For the arousal function of the reticular formation, each sensory stimulus is not a discrete event providing the individual with an internal model of the world but a bit of information with varying degrees of alerting potential. Its significance is based on its survival value and that significance may differ from one moment to another. For this reason the reticular system is usually referred to as nonspecific in its sensory function, although there is some sensory specificity in thalamocortical projections. It helps the brain to focus on one type of sensory input by inhibiting other types. It also performs a discriminative and differential function (Magoun, 1958). Jasper (1966) refers to the reticular formation's "remarkable and widespread interactions with more specialized neuronal systems, somehow determining which of these functional systems is to gain momentary predominance in the on-going sequence of conscious awareness." The process is accomplished by a balancing of the inhibitory and excitatory components of the brain.

While there is general tonic inhibition from the reticular formation during the waking state, special conditions elicit additional inhibition. For example, attention to information from one sensory channel may inhibit potentials arising from a sensory afferent of a different modality and from monotonous repetition of stimuli, such as from the tactile or auditory systems. The process has been well illustrated by one of the earlier but now classical studies of Hernández-Peón, Scherrer and Jouvet (1956). When electrically recording auditory responses under different conditions of attention in a cat, the auditorily evoked responses were reduced or almost abolished when the cat's attention was diverted to mice, to a nociceptive shock to the paw, or to an olfactory stimulus. It was noted that the location of the recording electrodes demonstrated that the inhibition occurred before the sensory stimuli reached the central system, suggesting a centrifugal inhibitory function.

Through this same mechanism, insufficiently inhibited sensory stimuli of one modality can interfere with learning in another modality. One of the problems frequently encountered in children with learning disorders appears to be a reticular formation that allows too many sensory stimuli to over-arouse the child and prevent attention to the stimuli which carry more relevance for the instructor than for an organism operating by primitive mechanisms.

Hernández-Peón (1961) demonstrated that the brain stem reticular formation either inhibits or facilitates sensory impulse transmission at all synapses from the first order neuron to the cortex. Specific observations have been made in the visual, somatic, auditory, and olfactory pathways. This is one of the routes through which sensations from one modality influence perception in another. This may have been the case when Fox (1965) enhanced tactile perception in blind children by having them smell oil of pine.

The reticular formation regulates incoming sensory input but always under the influence of higher or cortical processes, so there is a constant reciprocal influence. The implication for therapy is that the brain stem can and will influence the cortex, and powerfully so, but the cortex will also help determine the quality and quantity of that influence. Similarly, one sensory modality can influence perception in another, but that influence will be consistent with the therapeutic plan only if sensations from the two sources are consistent with each other as interpreted by the brain stem.

In order for any external event to be perceived, information about it must travel over the specific afferent system and be involved in interaction (presumably at the cortical level but not necessarily only there) with impulses from the nonspecific or reticular system. Many experiments have demonstrated that stimulation of the reticular afferents increases cortical response to impulses arriving from specific stimuli. For example, reticular stimulation has resulted in marked augmentation of responsiveness to somatosensory stimuli (Schwartz and Shagass, 1963). Also, using a nociceptive stimulus to activate the unspecific system, Gellhorn (1961) demonstrated increased cortical responses to optic and acoustic stimuli. Gellhorn indicated that the threshold of the conscious sensation appeared to be lowered by the activation of the unspecific afferent system. Adams (1965) enhanced kinesthetic perception in children through therapeutic measures designed to act through the reticular activating system.

In an experiment in which an electrical pulse was applied to the optic tract of monkeys who were in total darkness, the response in the optic radiation was increased several times by auditory or tactile stimuli or by stimulation to the central brain stem. The effect, considered to be a function of the centrencephalic system, was exerted predominantly on the lateral geniculate nucleus rather than the striate cortex (Wilson, Pecci-Saavedra and Doty, 1965). Lindsley (1961) found that stimulating the reticular formation improved the power of the cortex to perceive brief light flashes in quick succession. The message for the clinician is clear. Sensory input from one modality influences reception and perception in another. It can either hinder or help it.

The thalamic reticular system, also known as the unspecific thalamocortical projection system, arises from the thalamic nuclei and is closely connected with the midbrain reticular formation. It acts upon almost all areas of the cortex and, along with the brain stem reticular system, serves a general arousal and alerting function as well as a central integrative one. The thalamic system also has unique functions, one of the more important ones being the ability to act on a small portion of the cortex, facilitating activity there while inhibiting it elsewhere (Jasper, 1966).

The modulating function of the reticular formation involves a complex neuronal organization that performs more than excitatory-inhibitory regulation. It serves an integrative process that probably extends so far as to process sensory stimuli into simple perceptual information. With its pooling of sensory inflow along with cortical and cerebellar inputs, it is particularly well situated to do so. It is now believed by many that sensory integration and resultant perception and probably even more cognitive functions are not necessarily an end-product occurring in the neocortex. The cortex may be only a "relay station" for messages which must continue back to the rostral end of the reticular formation for final integration or coding.

After considerable study of the sensory neurons representing different phyletic ages, Bishop (1959) concluded that the older and newer sensory paths converge at a common "corticothalamic complex," each arriving from a different direction. The complex then functions as one organ. The higher sensory input does not necessarily dominate that mediated by smaller fibers at lower levels. Pain, Bishop points out, can predominate over other sensations. It seems likely that the "corticothalamic complex" to which Bishop refers is the same as the "centrencephalic system" referred to by Penfield (1966) and Penfield and Roberts (1959).

The concept of a centrencephalic system, located in the general region of the thalamus, was advanced by Penfield as a result of his clinical work. He attributed to this system communication with both forebrain hemispheres that allowed them to function together as an integrated unit and considered this system essential to consciousness. Some physiologists (for example, Jasper, 1966) believe the centrencephalic system is the same as a portion of the reticular system. Since the rostral (thalamic) portion of the reticular formation is particularly critical to sensory integration (Hernández-Peón, 1961), it seems reasonable to assume the two structures may be essentially the same. Furthermore, the cortical-subcortical-cortical association route hypothesized by Albe-Fessard and Fessard (1963) and referred to in Chapter 2 is likely part of the same system. The work and conclusions of Doty (1966) are also consistent with the proposed major integrating center. He hypothesized that bilateral interhemispheral integration of complex phenomena occurs in the mesencephalic reticular formation.

Later chapters propose that considerable visual form and space perception occur at the midbrain in conjunction with other brain stem structures and that brain stem mediated postural mechanisms are associated with interhemispheral integration. The relationship of these processes — which have been found to be critical to academic learning — to the major integrating center located at the upper end of the brain stem lends special importance to it in understanding integrative functions.

The functions of the reticular formation assumed increased clinical importance when it was found that the reading skills of learning disabled children with auditory-language problems were increased following activity that stressed sensory integration at the brain stem level (Ayres, 1972a). In this study language was used only to communicate, but noise in almost all dimensions in which sound varies was a natural accompaniment of the activity. The results of the study gave rise to the question: Did the activity which provided especially large quantities of proprioceptive and vestibular input assist the reticular formation and other brain stem structures in their role in processing auditory stimuli?

It is hypothesized that sensory integration at the brain stem level either results in or makes possible the translation of sensory impulses into information of far greater complexity than is presently realized and that this capacity has special significance for learning disorders. The majority of children with disordered learning show some dysfunction that can be linked to the brain stem, especially the reticular formation. Disorders of arousal state such as hyperactivity and distractibility, abnormal muscle tone, postural and extraocular muscle responses, and unusually low sensory threshold may be linked to the functions of the reticular formation and other brain stem structures. No therapist concerned with sensory integrative disorders can avoid including in his thinking and in his treatment planning concepts and procedures which include the sensory functions of the brain stem.

In addition to the sensory processes, there are a number of aspects of motor operation at the brain stem level that help establish the totality of function of this level of neural organization. The most commonly recognized brain stem influence on motor function is through the facilitatory and inhibitory influences from brain stem nuclei which constantly modify ongoing motor activity. It is through them, in part, that the therapist modifies motor activity.

In addition to influences through brain stem nuclei, some specific patterns of motor function are mediated in the brain stem. Sucking, swallowing, simple head movement, and movements of the eyes are commonly recognized as directed, in part, by brain stem mechanisms. Through basic research patterns have been identified that are related to locomotion. For example, Kuroki (1958), using electrodes implanted in the midline aspects of the cat's brain stem from thalamus to medulla oblongata, elicited rotation of the head, usually accompanied by ipsilateral flexion and contralateral extension in the forelimbs with indefinite movement of the hind limbs and occasionally concave curving of the trunk. Stimulation occasionally elicited rolling and circling movements or brought about cessation of all activity.

Comparable results in the decerebrate cat were obtained by Sprague and Chambers (1954). Stimulation of the medulla reticular formation resulted in a variety of responses, mainly reciprocal, with the homologous extremity showing the opposite response. For example, if the left front extremity was flexed, the right front was extended. The leg posture most frequently evoked was that in which both ipsilateral extremities behaved similarly, i.e., either both flexed or both extended, the movements of the contralateral legs being the opposite. This pattern, known as a homolateral pat-

tern of ambulation, was also elicited by the cerebellum, presumably
mediated through the reticular and vestibular tracts. Crossed
diagonal and homologous patterns were observed less frequently.
The head usually was turned toward the side of the flexed forelimb
and the body was concave toward that side. The forelimbs usually
responded before the hindlimbs and some of the stimuli inhibited
decerebrate extensor tone.

In addition to the cranial nerve nuclei for coordinating eye
movements, brain stem centers have been found which, when
stimulated, give rise to conjugate, goal-directed eye movements or
mid-positioning of eyes (Hyde and Eliasson, 1957). The investigators suggested that in the cat the cortex functions in association
with these brain stem centers for control over eye movements.
Further reference to motor patterns subserved by brain stem
mechanisms will be made in later chapters. The essential point for
therapists to note is the possibility that motor patterns, especially
of the eyes and of the total trunk and extremities working together,
may be organized and mediated in the brain stem of human beings.
Cortically directed motion usually occurs with a reflex basis. These
brain stem motor patterns could be therapeutically important for
this reason.

The Cerebellum

It is not quite proper to ascribe to the cerebellum an anatomical
level of function, for the structure consists of both phylogenetically
old as well as new areas, apparently evolving simultaneously with
the brain stem and higher structures. The cerebellum began as a
derivative of the fifth (trigeminal) and eighth (vestibular) cranial
nerve nuclei (cf. Bishop, 1959). This origin is significant in any
interpretation of the role of the cerebellum in man today. The
cerebellum develops late ontogenetically (cf. Noback and Moskowitz, 1963), and for that reason is sometimes felt to be vulnerable
to trauma early in life. The function of the cerebellum is best
implied in the statement of Eccles, Ito and Szentágothai (1967).
They believe the evolution of the cerebral hemispheres "called
forth the great development of the cerebellar "lobes" because "it
possessed some unique mode of processing information."

The primary cerebellar function is that of an integrating and a
regulating servomechanism. Its action has been linked most frequently to motor output, acting on descending motor impulses to
smooth and coordinate action and influence muscle tone. Its close
connection with the vestibular system, receiving information from
and sending information back to the vestibular nuclei, requires

that every reference in this book to vestibular function imply involvement of that portion of the cerebellum functioning with it, even though it is not explicitly mentioned.

The cerebellum does not initiate activity, although there is some tonic neuronal discharge. Rather, it receives input from all sensory sources over the afferent neurons and from much but not all of the cerebral cortex, processes it, and then uses it to influence ongoing neuronal activity, especially down the spinal cord, to brain stem nuclei, the thalamus, basal ganglia, and cortex. Some of the routes to the cortex are through the thalamus, reticular formation, and red nucleus (Evarts and Thach, 1969). It has been suggested by Prescott (1970) that the cerebellum may have a significant role in the modulation of functions subserved by the limbic system.

It is clear that the cerebellum is well situated to exercise an influence upon most if not all of the ongoing neural activity. Furthermore, since it is so easily influenced by sensory input, the entire nervous system can be and inevitably is influenced through the cerebellum during all sensory integrative therapy.

Other than in its influence in smoothing and regulating motor activity, investigators do not agree upon the result of the cerebellar information processing. Karamyan (1968) has reported two ascending influences of the cerebellum: (1) a "toning-up" via the phyletically older paleocerebellar-reticulocortical system resulting in an adaptive influence on cortical activity and (2) an actuating system via the younger neocerebellar-thalamocortical system. On the other hand, Eccles, Ito and Szentágothai (1967) have reported the result of cerebellar influence on the rest of the central nervous system processing to be strictly inhibitory; the more intense the excitation of the cerebellar cortex, the greater the inhibitory depression. These apparent differences in reporting neurological function are not unusual but represent different experimental methods and interpretation in a rapidly growing science. Usually the additional knowledge time brings shows both points of view compatible with a more complex explanation than previously submitted.

In implementing sensory integrative therapy it is possible to observe the end result of sensory input, but it is possible only to hypothesize the neural route. Even at best one can hope to be only partially correct. Both the "toning-up" and "inhibitory" cerebellar roles are consistent with clinical observation.

It seems likely that some of the calming of the hyperactive child through sensory integrative therapy may be attributed to cerebellar processes. It is hypothesized that certain kinds of vestibular stimulation, especially, and possibly some of the afferent flow up from the spinal column may result in lowering the excitatory state of the reticular formation through cerebellar inhibition. This also may be a route through which the vital centers of the brain stem could be inhibited beyond a desirable point, resulting in decreased breathing and heart beat and possibly an altered state of consciousness.

The Basal Ganglia

The masses of subcortical gray matter that collectively are called the basal ganglia have not been studied as exhaustively as have other structures, nor has their function been incorporated into the theoretical structure underlying the treatment procedures for disordered sensory integration.

The location of the basal ganglia in the cerebral hemispheres suggests the degree of complexity of adaptive behavior which might be mediated by them, i.e., more complex and less stereotyped than that which the brain stem makes possible but not as highly precise nor as conceptually advanced as the cortex of the cerebral hemispheres.

Recent research suggests that these structures may assume a considerable role in integration of sensorimotor activity. That they have a sensory integrative role, especially in relation to the peripheral sense organs and the cortex, has been supported by the work of Krauthamer and Albe-Fessard (1964). These investigators also demonstrated multisensory and heterotopic convergence properties for visual, auditory, and somatic stimuli. Action on the nonspecific sensory activity has also been attributed to the basal ganglia (Shimamoto and Verzeano, 1954). Of particular interest is the integrative relationship of the basal ganglia with the cortex, a function which is mediated through the diencephalon and more caudal structures. This influence may be bilateral, which directs attention again to some type of subcortical bilaterally integrating system.

Important representation of tactile and proprioceptive sensory input in the basal ganglia was shown by Segundo and Machne (1956). They found that somatic stimuli, such as from light touching or stroking, were especially effective in evoking discharges. A lesser response was found from stimulation of vestibular apparatus, whereas only rarely were any responses evoked by pain, olfaction, click, or visual flash. An important type of convergence found by these researchers, although not great in quantity, was between somatic and vestibular senses. These authors hypothesized that the function of those basal ganglia they studied was not a subjective recognition of stimuli but a regulation of posture and movements of the body in space and the production of complex motor acts.

These studies suggest the basal ganglia are involved in a type of sensory integration that allows one type of sensory input to influence the integration of another type and to utilize that input for moderately complex postural and other bodily movement.

The Old Cortex and/or Limbic System

The "old" cortex (archicortex and paleocortex) and the neocortex appeared in evolutionary development at about the same time, but the old cortex reached its final gross form long before the neocortex. The latter continued much farther with its evolutionary changes with the advent of man. The older portions of the brain have not necessarily discontinued their evolution. Green (1958) points out that the brain stem, paleocortex, and neocortex have shown a concomitant progressive development, indicating a close integration among the three parts of the brain. The old cortex is roughly synonymous with the limbic system, which is taking on considerable functional significance with increasing research emphasis. Structurally, it does not fit into the higher-lower dimension as well as the lateral-medial dimension of brain anatomy.

As would be expected from the general principles proposed earlier, the old cortex and the new cortex differ on several parameters. The limbic system is less plastic or flexible and less complex. Pribram (1961) has suggested that the limbic system is an example of a more general principle of brain development, namely, that the more medial portions (which would include the limbic system) are less complex but, in general, have a longer lasting influence. The limbic system is designed to cope in a relatively diffuse manner rather than with the precise spatial or modality specificity for which the neocortex is prepared (Pribram, 1961).

The clinician concerned with sensory integration cannot ignore the limbic system, for it is related to all sensory systems (cf. MacLean, 1955). It is concerned with primitive patterns of behavior necessary for individual and species survival, including vegetative functions, defending the body against attack, and the simple perceptual-motor functions needed to fulfill these survival functions. Its function is clarified when it is considered the primary cortical structure in a large proportion of vertebrates. Fish have no neocortex; amphibians, reptiles, and birds have little, yet all of these animals show basic but well integrated behavior including perceptual, motor, and simple learning and memory.

Herrick (1933) has provided the following perspective on some aspects of evolution of the old cortex. In the earliest animals with a cerebral cortex, the olfactory system dominated that cortex. Reptiles were the first to show an influx of somatosensory information, which, along with the olfactory stimuli, went to the older parts of the cortex. The major motor outflow from that part of the old cortex was directed into locomotion and other mass movement. Adey and collaborators (1961) have also attributed simple planned motor performance to the limbic system. It appears that a somatosensory-gross motion mediating center was established in the old cortex during the evolutionary process.

At the old cortical level of function, just as at each of the lower levels of the central nervous system, lies a motor function adaptively appropriate for the sensory input at that level. Simple mass movement and locomotor patterns not only are mediated at the midbrain level but similar motor patterns have a center for organization in the old cortical areas as well. At the limbic system level the motor patterns must be able to provide the response to the integrated sensation from which the animal is interpreting his survival-pertinent information, such as attack or flee. That which is true of lower animals may have relevance for man's ontogeny.

Another point is made by noting that the neocortex began its growth out of the area of the brain serving olfaction. It was not so much the nature of the sensory modality that gave rise to the structures that enabled man to develop such a remarkable brain but the fact that the olfactory area had the greatest capacity of all nervous structures for the integrating and associating of sensory information and using that information for an adaptive response. This capacity became greatly enlarged upon in the neocortex and presumably provided a major basis for higher cognitive function.

The close interconnections of the limbic and reticular systems has been noted (cf. G. V. Russell, 1961). Functionally both systems subserve visceromatic and emotional mechanisms as well as conscious and attentive mechanisms, although there is a tendency toward respective specialization. G. V. Russell (1961) suggests that perhaps both systems are fundamental integrative mechanisms of the central nervous system.

The old cortex is also concerned with conditioning and storage of information and reinforcement of response, such as that attempted in conventional behavioral experiments or, presumably, in operant conditioning (cf. Olds and Olds, 1961). Most of the data supporting these relationships come, of course, from animal research, and a guarded attitude is appropriate in generalizing them to man, for the limbic system mediates more species-specific behavior than lower neural levels are believed to do. Furthermore, even research on the limbic system of lower animals shows results that vary so greatly that a more complex explanation is required to account for the differences.

Some of the animal research is consistent with that of man, however. Brazier (1964) is among those who have associated recent memory with the hippocampus (a limbic system structure) in man, and Milner (1965) and Corkin (1965) have reported defects in visual and tactually guided maze learning in hippocampal lesions in man. This structure may also be involved in more permanent storage of memory (cf. Smythies, 1970).

It is fairly clear that the hippocampus is involved in the processing of events for storage, and when it functions inadequately, defects in learning or memory occur. These defects are commonly seen in children with learning disorders. To assume such a critical role in learning, most information resulting from current experience and entering the central nervous system must be available to the hippocampus. Since some of the information is made available to the old cortex through the brain stem and diencephalic routes, it is not unreasonable to hypothesize that integrating sensation at lower levels and normalizing brain stem functions as much as possible may give the old cortex a better opportunity to function in its learning and memory operations. It is also possible to interfere with memory through sensory input, especially if the sensory input is unrelated to that to be remembered or is related to a behavioral pattern of more fundamental survival value. Whether the effect is positive or negative must be determined empirically.

While the domain of emotions lies outside the focus of this book, any reference to the limbic system would be incomplete without directing attention to the predominant role that system has in the emotional life of an individual. The limbic system has a general energizing effect which appears to be under the control of exteroceptive and proprioceptive stimulation (Sheer, 1961). Such a proposed system may account for the increased drive seen in some children during sensory integrative therapy. At this time it is believed that sensory integrative therapy has a significant effect on the psyche of the child and that this effect takes place through the limbic system. The clinician need to be aware of and alert to possible emotional effects of treatment. They may be profound.

In summary, the old cortex mediates sensorimotor, cognitive, and affective functions, all interrelated, at a level of complexity less than that of the neocortex. The sensorimotor functions are more complex than those of the basal ganglia which, in turn, are more complex than those of the brain stem. The limbic and the reticular systems provide the force that "drives" the individual. They are the "energizers" of the organism. A more significant statement cannot be made.

The Neocortex

The neocortex, in a way, provides the "advice and consent" for all lower central nervous system structures. The neocortex might be conceived of as a consultant to the brain stem and limbic system, providing information of a more specialized nature than that available at those lower levels so that the latter can utilize their drive in implementing mechanisms for optimal adaptation. At least, that is the intent of the brain's organization. In children with dysfunction, primacy of the neocortex has not completely developed and the child often is driven by lower level activity and more primitive function.

The neocortex, as the youngest of the integrating levels, not only organizes sensory activity at its own level but influences integration at lower levels. At the same time, it is inexorably acted upon by lower structures. The interaction is so great that perception cannot be considered to be a process performed at any particular level of the brain but a function of all levels simultaneously. The cortex can be both a facilitator and an inhibitor of all less complex levels. Furthermore, the neocortex provides a far more extended area for receipt of sensory information than did the lower centers, such as the limbic system or brain stem. It has its own nearly direct route through the thalamus from the sensory receptors, as well as receiving information through the indirect routes.

Diamond (1967) has suggested that in the higher mammals the sensory areas, such as the auditory or visual cortex, may assume an integrative role that does not exist in lower animals. Sensory integrative therapy involving purposive activity will automatically involve this level of sensory integration, for all complex perceptual processes are dependent upon the cortex. Sensory integrative therapy does not emphasize the neocortical sensory integrative process, but neither does it ignore it. Therapy is generally directed toward enhancing neocortical functions through achieving better integration at lower, subserving levels. It is believed that this approach is, in the long run, more effective than one stressing cortical activity alone. If integration at lower levels has been achieved to the maximal ability of the therapist, then emphasis on the neocortical sensory integrative processes would seem the most logical next step. As long as subcortical structures remain poorly integrated, resolution of the impairment through a cognitive approach will be limited, for neocortical processing is dependent upon subcortical processes for optimum function.

Relating the various anatomical levels to treatment philosophy is largely through the manner in which the therapist conceptualizes and implements the remediation plan. If the plan calls for involving brain stem mechanisms, they are apt to be involved to a greater extent than if the plan calls for requesting that a child move a given arm or leg. Perceptual-motor activities conducted at a desk or table are more cortically oriented; those involving the whole body moving through space involve brain stem mechanisms to a greater extent than do desk activities. Teaching a child "left" and "right" as directions or sides of his body by color or other cues on shoes or hands represents a highly neocortical approach, whereas letting a child experience direction and the sides of his body through the integration of vestibular, somatosensory, and visual stimuli and through normalizing the mechanisms of interhemispheral integration exemplifies a focus on lower levels of neural function.

Principles Relating to Levels of Function

A few of the principles of brain function described in this chapter deserve restating and further elaboration because of their importance to understanding and implementing therapeutic procedures. One of the more important principles is that any major neural structure receiving sensory input from many areas is also apt to have widespread influence over the rest of the brain. Multiplicity of input usually means convergence of input. The brain stem and thalamus are good examples of structures to which the principle is applicable. The nonspecific systems in these areas receive sensory input from all sources and in turn have a widespread influence over use of sensation by the rest of the brain. Therapy aimed at influencing the cortex must consider reaching it through the lower structures.

When behavioral functions at one level are compared to those at another level, they do not change so much in type as in complexity and degree of flexibility. The higher the level of function, the less stereotyped the behavior. The higher the level of sensory organization, the more emphasis on precise interpretation of the spatial and temporal dimensions of stimuli; the lower the level, the greater the emphasis on sensory integration as opposed to sensory analysis. Similarly, the central core of the brain stem has a more prolonged and diffuse function and is more concerned with sensory integration than, for example, the posterior column-medial lemniscal system, which is particularly concerned with carrying precise tactile and proprioceptive information to the brain.

Similarly, the quality of functioning varies according to the various levels. This principle is most easily exemplified when the same sensory function is duplicated at more than one level. It was seen above that each successively higher level of function enabled the organism to perform essentially the same basic life-supporting functions but on a more complex, more highly adaptive level.

In studying cats, Bishop (1959) found that the phyletically earlier and currently smaller fibers went to the ventral and tectal regions of the brain stem where important motor control systems were located. Later the geniculate body began sending projections to the cortex, but only the largest 10 per cent or less of the optic tract fibers relay to the geniculate body. The next larger size relay to the thalamus. A smaller size goes to the pretectal area and the smallest terminate in the colliculi. These observations, which have considerable relevance to the material in the chapter on form and space perception, are further evidence of the necessity to consider neural levels below the cortex in sensory integration. They also exemplify the evolutionary concept of adding to the existing structure and function as opposed to replacing structure and function.

These principles clearly point to the necessity for involving the brain stem and thalamus in any therapeutic efforts toward sensory integration. Such an involvement can have widespread influence on the rest of the brain.

Chapter 5

The Sensory Modalities

The objective of this chapter is to review the function of several of the sensory modalities as determined from neurophysiological research. Certain aspects especially pertinent to therapy are emphasized. These aspects contribute to an understanding of sensory integrative processes but generally are not stressed in standard neurology textbooks.

The functions explored sometimes are hypothetical as opposed to factual, although some factual data lend support to many postulates. Often the hypothetical is of more value than the factual because the former provides a tentative explanation of some of the responses of children to therapy. Furthermore, a great deal of neural functioning — especially that most closely related to human emotions, cognition, and higher adaptive functions — still lies in the realm of the postulated. Someday the accurate guesses will be separated from the non-accurate. In the meantime, hypotheses will be considered as suggestions for exploring therapeutic procedures or as providing tentative explanation for their apparent effectiveness.

The Vestibular System

The role of the vestibular system is often overlooked because many of its functions either take place largely below the level of awareness or their importance is taken for granted unless they are either disturbed or have affected the digestive tract. In spite of this lack of conscious awareness of the significance of the vestibular system, the infant likes to be rocked and the toddler enjoys being swung or tossed in the air. Older children walk curbs and higher structures, play hopscotch, jump rope, and ride merry-go-rounds. They then graduate to skiing, rides in amusement parks, and drag racing. Man is constantly enjoying stimulating his vestibular apparatus and challenging his equilibrium, pitting his skills against the earth's gravitational pull from the time he first lifts his head.

Professional individuals especially concerned with perceptual-motor training have stressed activities which directly involve the vestibular system — both in terms of eliciting sensory impulses and making demands upon the child in relation to that sensory information, as in walking a balance beam or a narrow piece of wood (cf. Kephart, 1960). The need for extensive investigation of the role of the vestibular system in the sensory integrative process arises both from the current extensive use of vestibular stimulation in perceptual-motor training and the fact that it undoubtedly does assume a significant role in the total brain's functioning.

The vestibular system includes not only the receptive apparatus but also the vestibular nuclei and tracts and each part of the brain that makes important connections with those nuclei and tracts. Some of the roles of the vestibular system probably have not yet been described by neurobiologists, yet if those roles exist they influence each human being. The vestibular nuclei in themselves are so intricate and complex in all of their connections that they are still under exploration, and the mechanisms to which the vestibular system probably is linked are too numerous to be discussed in detail. It is reasonable to assume that a system of great phyletic age and constancy, occupying many large brain stem nuclei and making many ramifying connections, would have an important role in sensorimotor function.

The vestibular system enables the organism to detect motion, especially acceleration and deceleration and the earth's gravitational pull. The system helps the organism to know whether any given sensory input — visual, tactile, or proprioceptive — is associated with movement of the body or is a function of the external environment. For example, it tells the person whether he is moving within the room or the room is moving about him. The effects of gravity and motion are not entirely separable, although their effects are usually attributed primarily but not entirely to different anatomical structures, motion being recorded chiefly by the semicircular canals and gravity by the saccule and utricle. Human subjects who had lost the use of the vestibular apparatus on one side of the head showed diminished sense of motion when in one position relative to gravity but not another (Walsh, 1960). The results were considered to indicate that the gravity receptors helped to interpret motion. Because of the interaction of the effects of gravity and motion, they are generally considered together in treat-ment and in discussion of the system.

Considerable opportunity exists for the vestibular system to exercise influence over all other ongoing sensory experiences. The large brain stem vestibular nuclei are capable of supplying inter-action with descending, ascending, and other brain stem functions. Descending fibers act at spinal cord levels to influence sensori-motor activity there. The cerebellum and pontine areas receive large amounts of input from the vestibular system and some reaches the cortex by one route or another. As was seen in an earlier chapter, the vestibular system is frequently one of the sources of influence on convergent neurons.

The extensive influence of the vestibular system on motor out-put has been one of its most well known and easily recognized effects. The appearance of nystagmus is considered a normal re-sponse following vestibular stimulation consisting of constant ac-celeration for about thirty seconds. Nystagmus serves to illustrate the close connection between the vestibule and the extraocular muscles. This relationship between the motion receptors and the extraocular muscles is critical to perceiving the correct relationship between the body's motion and that of the visual fields. The com-bination of information from the extraocular muscles, the vestibular apparatus, and the visual field itself enables the individual to tell whether his eyes are moving, his head is moving, or the visual field itself is moving.

The vestibular system has a strong influence on muscle tone, both generally and more specifically through certain neuromuscular reflexes. The influence is mediated through the lateral and medial vestibular nuclei on efferent transmission down the spinal cord (Brodal, 1964). It has a highly facilitatory effect on the gamma efferent neuron (intrafusal fiber) to the muscle spindle and also some effect on the alpha motor neuron supplying the skeletal muscles. By activating the gamma efferent neuron to the spindle, the afferent impulse flow from the spindle is maintained and regu-lated for assistance with motor function. This basic role in muscle function and motility gives it an important function in developing and maintaining the body scheme, for the development of the body scheme is in part dependent upon interpretation of movement of the limbs.

Methods used to test the integrity of the vestibular system indicate the role that the system is believed to assume in man's sensorimotor function. In addition to the usual tests of standing balance with eyes closed and the presence of nystagmus following spinning, Jongkees (1967) asks patients, with eyes closed, to lift the arm up and down, pointing to the same spot each time. If the arm moves from side to side, the influence of the labyrinthine impulse is considered abnormal. This test demonstrates the vestibular influence on muscle tone.

Some of the generalized effects on muscle function are illustrated by basic research. From their study of the human perception of verticality within a tilted field during various kinds of galvanic stimulation, Aarons and Goldenberg (1964) suggested the probability that the changed muscle tone resulting from vestibular stimulation provided internal cues utilized in the visual perception process. The mechanisms operated without awareness on the part of the individual. These results imply that the disordered muscle tone of learning disabled children may interfere with visual perception.

After severing a cat's eighth cranial nerve, which carries the nerve impulses from the vestibular apparatus to the brain, Kempinsky and Ward (1950) found that a motor response in a limb, evoked by near threshold stimulation of the cortex, was either diminished or abolished. They concluded that the vestibular system contributes afferent impulses which maintain a certain background activity in the facilitatory system. After section of the nerve, it took increased strength of cortical stimulation to compensate for diminished input. It is known that a considerable amount of afferent support is needed to elicit a motor response from the central nervous system. Apparently a considerable amount of that afferent support comes from the vestibular system. The above study suggests that the individual with insufficient afferent flow or integration from the vestibular system might have to "try harder" to perform certain movements. This may be part of the picture in the slow, hypotonic, lethargic child.

The vestibular system contributes a considerable amount to the general "energizing" properties of the reticular arousal system and it can provide one of the most highly excitatory types of sensory input. On the other hand, the same system can have a depressing effect on the brain stem, including centers for vital function in that area. Some of this effect is possibly mediated through the cerebellum's inhibitory function. J. C. Solomon (1959) observed the calming effects of train motion on the emotional condition of disturbed patients. In connection with this observation, Solomon expressed the opinion that stimulation of the vestibular apparatus was an important aspect of a mother's holding and handling a child.

Whether vestibular stimulation will have an excitatory or an inhibitory effect on human behavior through the brain stem is determined by the type of stimulation. It has been observed in the clinical situation that slow, rhythmical, passive motion with the child in a situation not demanding adaptive response can be inhibitory, whereas rapid motion is apt to be excitatory.

An example of the potentially far-reaching effects of vestibular stimulation on perceptual-motor development is demonstrated by an experiment by Young (1964). Rats stimulated by rapid rotation in a cage for three minutes on postnatal days two to five were superior to control rats in maze performance a month later. Furthermore, the harmful effect of drugs given to the mother rat during pregnancy were partially mitigated by early vestibular stimulation. These results are consistent with those reviewed and reported by Levine (1962), who consistently found rats better developed perceptually and emotionally after handling in infancy, a process which would invariably involve vestibular stimulation.

Sensory systems which appear phyletically early and mature ontogenetically early are believed to serve a critical role in the subsequent developmental sequence. The vestibular system was not only one of the earlier sensory systems to appear phyletically but the related tracts are one of the earliest to myelinate in fetal life — at about 20 weeks.

Kasatkin (1962) has stated that in the normal healthy infant the conditioned reflexes occur first in vestibular and auditory and later in tactile and visual analyzers. Since conditioned reflexes are predetermined by morphological maturity and degree of functional readiness of the brain, Kasatkin believes that the vestibular system matures before the tactile system. It is likely that Kasatkin was considering some of the phyletically and ontogenetically later tactile reflexes which are the products of specific and highly analytical tactile function. It is possible that some of the more primitive tactile functions predate the vestibular.

Using myelination as the maturational index, Norton (1970) studied neurological research to establish an hypothesis regarding the frequencies and percentage of various sensory input, motor output, and feedback from sensory stimulation that was in a position to contribute to initial awareness as a precursor of cognitive function in the early months of postnatal life. She concluded that the vestibular system contributed the greatest proportion of input and that the muscle spindle and Golgi tendon organ contributed the next greatest percentage of all possible types of sensory input affecting neurological processes providing a foundation for beginning cognitive function. When sensory input resulting from touch, pressure, and passive movement were added to that from proprioceptive input, 50 per cent of the sensory input resulting in stimulus-response function was accounted for. Norton concluded that treatment by gross motion had a valid neuroanatomical and neuropsychological basis.

It is usually helpful in placing a sensory system in theoretical perspective to hypothesize about the role of the sense in survival throughout evolution. Unlike the tactile system, which warns the organism of impending danger, either from a predator or from some object injurious to the organism, the vestibular system is more concerned with the organism's spatial relation to the earth. This relationship provides one of the most basic forms of physical and emotional security. It is far more primal than relationships with people, but may be somewhat less so than the individual's relationship with his physical body. The basic relationship of one's body is that it exists and is separate from nonself objects. The development of that awareness is assisted by the tactile as well as the vestibular systems.

The basic functions of fight, flight, and simple quadruped ambulation needed to obtain a meal are dependent upon adequate functioning of the vestibular system. That system has basic survival value at one of the most primitive levels and such significance is reflected in its role in sensory integration.

Vestibular information is constantly integrated with other sensory data at both the brain stem or cortical levels, providing widespread influence that possibly extends beyond present understanding. Research at the laboratory of Jung (Jung, 1961; Jung, Kornhuber and DaFonseca, 1963) has demonstrated in cats that neurons in the visual cortex show integration of information from the eye, the vestibular system, and the non-specific reticulothalamic system. Afferents from the three sources converged mostly on the same neuron. The vestibular information provides the stability of the visual image in accord with movements of the head and body, and a certain amount of reticular and thalamic stimulation is necessary to keep the cortex in an adequate state of excitability.

Jung's laboratory found that vestibular stimulation through labyrinthine polarization activated 90 per cent of the neurons in the cats' visual cortex. Using fairly high currents, convergent cells which responded to vestibular stimulation were found all over the superior convolutions of the cats' cortex. The investigators suggested that cortical neurons convergent for visual and vestibular stimuli were precoordinated in the brain stem, a condition which again places emphasis on brain stem function. Assuming that the human cortex probably follows some of the same principles of sensory integration as does that of the cat, it seems highly probable that optimum development of visual perception is dependent upon a certain degree of adequacy of integration of vestibular information and that enhancing sensory integration at the brain stem level is an important therapeutic goal.

Paul Schilder made many observations on the vestibular system and its role in the life of man that are consistent with those recently made during sensory integrative therapy. Schilder (1933) conceived of the vestibular system as "a coordinating apparatus for [all] sensory functions." He considered the system to have a uniting function and expressed that role thus: "The vestibular apparatus is an organ the function of which is directed against the isolation of the diverse functions of the body." To the extent the vestibular system assumes the role described by Schilder, then to that extent it is important in sensory integration.

Furthermore, there is growing evidence that some type of integration of vestibular stimuli is critical to psychosocial growth (cf. J. C. Solomon, 1959; Lebowitz, Colbert and Palmer, 1961; Schilder, 1964; Ornitz, 1970; and Prescott, 1970).

The Tactile System

The process of perception involves the continuous ordering and sorting of sensory stimuli into both temporal and spatial sequences with an ongoing intersensory relationship. Touch is one of the senses that is especially involved in the ongoing process contributing to perception of other types of sensation. Touch has been one of the predominating senses throughout evolution, is a predominant sensation at birth, and probably continues to be more critical to human function throughout life than is generally recognized. With this essential function in mind, it is of interest to note that the phyletically early neural tube evolved from the ectoderm of the animal.

The sequence of maturation of tactile functions is closely linked with general neural development and early child behavior. For example, tactile perception and motor planning in children at age four to eight years were more closely associated with quotients on the Gesell Schedules obtained early in life than were scores on tests of visual perception (Ayres, 1969b). Casler (1965) studied eight pairs of matched institutionalized babies under one year of age. Light touch-pressure stimulation enhanced the Gesell developmental quotients on the experimental group in comparison with the control group. It can be surmised from Casler's study that tactile stimulation probably made a difference in indices of maturational rates of child development.

Finding that eye-hand performance type tasks correlated most highly with general development at twenty to twenty-eight weeks of age, Blank (1964) suggested that that age period was a focal period for development of hand activities. Since tactile functions and motor planning are closely linked, it might be inferred that the age is one of considerable development of tactile discrimination.

That tactile functions are a sensitive indicator of the degree of central nervous system integration finds support in studies such as that by Zubek and Flye (1964), in which they found that tactile acuity and sensitivity to heat and pain were increased in human subjects following a week of living in the dark or exposure to unpatterned light. The effect remained for several days.

Clinical experience has led to the conclusion that in the child up to eight or nine years of age the degree of integration of the tactile system is a reasonably accurate — but not invariable — index of sensory integration in general. In adults, tactile perception has been found to be a fair measure of the general effects of brain damage (Wheeler, Burke and Rietan, 1963). A test occasionally used to test gross dysfunction of the central nervous system involves the simultaneous application of two tactile stimuli, usually one to the face and one to either the contralateral or ipsilateral hand. An abnormal response (depending upon age) is either failure to perceive one of the two stimuli, usually the one applied to the hand, or perceiving (referring) the stimuli to another part of the body. This test has been reported to reflect various kinds of abnormality including recovery from general anesthesia (Jaffee and Bender, 1952), mental deficiency (Pollack and Gordon, 1959-1960; Fink, Green and Bender, 1953; Cohn, 1951) and brain damage (Fink, Green and Bender, 1952). It has been of interest to note that it is usually the hand stimulus that is extinguished. The response is interpreted as the predominance of stimuli with greater survival value. An individual can survive longer without a hand than without a head. If this explanation is correct, it is consistent with the idea that some of the tactile mechanisms are designed to serve primitive survival functions.

Tactile functions are primal. Man's phyletic heritage involves tactile information as a major source of information about environmental conditions, telling the organism whether a given surface is appropriate for receiving the extremity or warning it that a predator may be entirely too close, requiring a flight or fight response. The latter reactions are dependent upon the close connections between the tactile system and the limbic system.

It was the work of Harlow with monkeys (1958) that called to the attention of the professional world the importance of tactile stimulation to psychosocial development in the primates, a concept introduced earlier through the idea that the skin, as the literal boundary between self and non-self, helps establish individual identity. Later chapters will demonstrate the close relationship of the tactile system not only to motor reflexes but to the capacity to motor plan. A type of sensation which influences a range of human behavior from a spinal reflex to the capacity for affectional responses may very well have a pervasive influence on all of the sensory integrative processes that occur in the brain.

Some hint as to the integrative contribution of the tactile system is seen from studies of sensory deprivation. Any experimental situation in which somatosensory input is reduced through immobilization of the body greatly restricts tactile stimulation. Even though the subject may be receiving pressure on the skin through contacts made from lying down, tactile receptors adapt quickly — more quickly than other somatosensory receptors — resulting in a reduced afferent flow from the tactile receptors as well as proprioceptors. Since this type of sensory deprivation rather quickly results in emotional and perceptual abnormalities, it is hypothesized that a continual bombardment of the brain by sensory impulses is necessary to maintain stabilization of the nervous system.

In general, research favors the presence of a widespread anatomical system mediating tactile functions as opposed to organization in more discrete and restricted areas similar to that found in the visual system (cf. Semmes and Mishkin, 1965; Neff and Goldberg, 1960). The distribution of nerve fibers responding to stimulation of tactile receptors is well suited to supply a widespread system. Bishop (1959) found that out of five afferent paths studied in the cat, three carried tactile information. He also demonstrated that fibers of different diameters tend to terminate at various levels of the brain. Thus, some of the smaller neurons subserving tactile functions primarily terminate in the reticular formation where they are enabled to command pervasive influence. The largest fibers, carrying spatial tactile information, project to the somesthetic area of the neocortex. Other fibers end in other parts of the brain. At each terminus synapses enable the tactile input to influence additional brain structures at higher levels.

The potential influence of tactile sensory input on neural structures serving other sensations was shown by a study by Melzack, Konrad and Dubrovsky (1969). After brief rubbing of a paw of moderately anesthetized cats, these investigators found prolonged changes in tonic electrical activity at several levels of the visual and somatic system, the inferior colliculus, reticular formation, and the pyramidal tract. The majority of changes lasted three to twelve minutes, but some lasted as long as thirty minutes. The visual radiations and somatic projection system typically showed prolonged decreases in activity, and the colliculus, reticular formation, and the pyramidal tract typically showed prolonged increases in activity. Either increases or decreases were found in the optic tract and lateral geniculate nucleus. Cortical responses were identical on both sides of the brain when only one paw was rubbed. Such prolonged changes were rarely seen when the cats were so lightly anesthetized that the paw rubbing resulted in withdrawal of the paw. The effect in the unanesthetized, freely moving cat was increased tonic activity in the lateral geniculate nucleus and increased cortical arousal. After subsequent studies of stimulation of different locations in parts of the reticular formation, the investigators concluded that the pervasive effects of the paw rubbing were at least in part mediated by the reticular formation. Both increases and decreases were frequently observed from different areas simultaneously.

In this study, it is of particular interest to note the consistent and reliable influence of the tactile system on the visual system and, to a lesser extent, on the auditory system. The effect on the somatosensory system and motor tracts falls more easily within the realm of expectations, for a relationship between tactile and motor system has been recognized for some time. The authors suggested that the prolonged changes elicited by the somatic stimulation may assume a role in normal integrative behavior. It is the probability of such pervasive influence of the tactile system on many levels of the brain and on several sensory systems as well as on the motor tracts of man that has led to the use of tactile stimuli as general augmentors of sensory integration.

Noting some aspects of structure of the tracts subserving tactile functions adds to the understanding of the role of tactile functions in sensory integration in general. Several afferent spinal tracts appeared over the evolutionary course to carry tactile information to the brain. The gradual shift in type of data conducted as additional tracts were added reflected changing demands.

Impulses arising from tactile receptors travel over the spinal cord to brain centers via several different tracts. The spinoreticular fibers, which are relatively small in diameter and phyletically quite old, carry rather diffuse information. The somewhat more recent spinothalamic tract developed some corticipetal projections that contribute greater discrimination. Compared to the spinothalamic system, the lemniscal system greatly increased its size during the development of the primates, suggesting that the demands made in the primate way of life required more information about the spatial and temporal nature of objects coming in contact with the skin. Mountcastle (1961) describes the phyletic development of the lemniscal system as "avalanching." Its function serves the discriminative forms of somatic sensation, particularly form, contour, position, and change in time of peripheral stimulus.

The lemniscal tract is better prepared for spatial discrimination by the presence of an inhibitory cortical field surrounding the excitatory one, an arrangement not present in the other spinal somatosensory tracts (Andersson, 1962). The spinothalamic system, on the other hand, is less concerned with the spatial pattern and temporal qualities of the stimulus and more concerned with general aspects of sensation, especially the qualitative nature of the environment. It is the spinothalamic or spinoreticular system that contributes to the reticular formation, whereas there is little evidence to date that the lemniscal system sends an appreciable number of collaterals to the reticular system.

While the lemniscal system is contralateral, portions of the spinothalamic system are ipsilateral. Ontogenetically, parts of the spinothalamic tract are myelinated before the medial lemniscus. Larger fibers are found in the dorsal columns than in the spinothalamic tract. Although the two tracts subserve slightly different functions, they perform "synergistically" (Mountcastle, 1961).

The significance of brain stem function for sensory integrative and higher cognitive factors requires that the therapist be alert to influencing neural function through activating those afferent spinal paths that carry impulses to the brain stem. Attention to the spatial qualities of tactile stimuli usually receives considerable therapeutic emphasis because of its conscious and cognitive qualities. If the spatial interpretation of tactile stimuli is to be enhanced, the more diffuse tactile functions at the brain stem must be considered simultaneously.

The spinothalamic and lemniscal system have different cortical projections. The lemniscal system projects primarily to somatic area I and does so contralaterally (excepting for the face area) while the spinothalamic system is more closely but not exclusively identified with somatic area II, providing it with both ipsilateral and contralateral representation (Mountcastle, 1961; Orback and Chow, 1959). Although the functions of the two areas overlap, they naturally tend to reflect the functions of the tracts projecting to them, somatic area I serving a more highly specific and discriminative function, as in form and roughness discrimination, than does somatic area II.

Although the most basic plan for direct representation of tactile stimuli in the brain is the contralateral projection of fibers to somatic area I, cortical neurons from many parts of the brain are activated by tactile stimuli traveling over many different multi-neuron routes, some of them over the nonspecific routes.

That the tactile cortical representation of the two sides of the body are not necessarily accurate mirror images has been demonstrated by Semmes and associates (1960). In studying human adults with brain wounds, they found a more diffuse representation of the left hand in its contralateral hemisphere than the right hand in its analogous hemisphere. Furthermore, the left hand was more often affected by lesions of the ipsilateral sensorimotor area. The difference between right and left hand cortical representation may have implications for evaluation of tactile functions, although those implications are not recognized at this time.

The subjective experience of the tactual stimulus is not solely a function of the type of receptor stimulated. What occurs within the central nervous system in relation to certain stimuli helps determine their interpretation. This is particularly true of perception of stimuli as noxious or painful. It is an important point to remember in clinical practice, where not infrequently children interpret as painful those stimuli which the therapist would experience as comfortable. The child's interpretation of the stimuli is the reality of the situation for him.

Proprioception

Proprioception refers to information arising from the body, especially from muscles, joints, ligaments, and receptors associated with bones. The vestibular sense falls within the category of proprioception, but, being a special sense, it is usually considered separately, as it has been handled in this chapter. Many of the proprioceptive sensations either do not reach consciousness, or, like vestibular information, come to awareness only when attention is deliberately focused on them. This sensory information assumes an important, albeit subserving, role in sensory integration. The function of the proprioceptors is critical to the motor action by which reflexes, automatic responses, and planned action occur. Movement in all three of these categories is the means by which man adapts himself to and acts upon the environment. Without those actions, integration of sensory impulses would not be optimum. Furthermore, the proprioceptive flow toward the brain is believed to aid in sensory perception, especially of visual impulses.

Kinesthesia, or the conscious awareness of joint position and movement, is phylogenetically more recent than the sense of touch or gravity. It is currently thought that the sense arises from stimulation of the joint receptors rather than the other proprioceptors, although the latter may serve a role not yet recognized. Behavioral research has repeatedly linked scores on a test of kinesthesia with scores on tests of visual perception and praxis, indicating a close relationship between each of these latter variables with the sense of joint position and movement. The direct route of kinesthetic impulses to the neocortical somatosensory areas via the thalamus does not allow for as much neural interaction as do the indirect routes for diffuse touch, other proprioception, and vestibular input. Until more is known of neurological connections between the sense of kinesthesia and visual perception, it is safest to assume that diminished kinesthesis limits the development of visual perception and the body scheme by limiting the amount of information entering the brain during purposeful and manipulative tasks.

One of the more important contributions to sensory integration of nonconscious proprioception from muscles and related structures is their role in providing the afferent support needed for normal muscle contraction that makes for skeletal movement. Motor activity was described above as a major means of gaining sensory integration. It is helpful to recall what is believed to be some of the basic "philosophy" of the brain regarding sensory integration. Sperry (1952) has described the primary function of the brain as "essentially the transforming of sensory patterns into patterns of motor coordination." He feels that the "fundamental anatomical plan and working principles are understandable only on these terms" and that perception merges into movement so that it cannot be said where one ends and the other begins. Finally, Sperry points out, "Motor adjustment, rather than stimulus patterns or the contents of subjective experience, figures predominantly as a proper frame of reference for understanding the organization, meaning, and significance of brain excitation."

If Sperry's conceptualization, based on many years of study of brain function, is correct, then it is proper to say, at least, that neural mechanisms are so designed that they are incomplete unless the motor component is executed satisfactorily. The motor component is not satisfactory without proprioceptive support.

Fewer basic research data were available in the time of Schilder (1964), who established his opinions on clinical observation. In his customary intuitive manner, he stressed the importance of muscle tone, its role in the postural model of the body and in psychic and motor development. With reduced muscle tone, which is a function of muscle receptors and influences acting upon them, the body scheme and motor development develop less than optimally. Hypotonia is a frequent characteristic of the child with disordered sensory integration.

Hebb (1949) suggested that the proprioceptive impulses from the eyes contributed to visual form and space perception. That there are receptors, probably muscle spindles, in the extraocular muscles that signal the static muscle tension has been shown by Breinin (1957). In his research, the mechanism allowed reciprocal innervation of the muscles and the results did not imply the existence of a conscious sense of muscle position. That a conscious awareness or cortical receipt of impulses is not necessary to sensory integration has been well illustrated. It seems likely that the proprioceptors of the eye muscles contribute at least as much as other muscle receptors to the total integrative process and that the sensory input that acts upon those receptors is accordingly important. The sensory input that acts upon the extraocular proprioceptors includes proprioceptive flow from other muscles. Proprioceptive facilitation of this type will be discussed in greater detail in a chapter on treatment.

No studies have come to attention which support the possibility of proprioceptive flow from the trunk and extremities to those mechanisms in the brain stem that mediate elementary locomotor patterns. It is difficult to imagine that mechanisms for locomotion would exist without a considerable supply of afferent impulses necessary for adequate implementation of the motor acts. If this is the case, normal proprioceptive flow is important to the integrative contribution of the total brain stem sensorimotor functions including those enhancing visual space perception.

The receptors from muscles, joints, and bones are believed not to contribute appreciably to the ascending reticular activating system, although a possible means by which proprioception can influence the general excitatory state of an individual has been proposed by Gellhorn (1964). Proprioceptive flow, determined by muscle contractions of the body, helps set the hypothalamic balance which, in turn, acts on the autonomic nervous system and exerts a tonic excitatory influence on the cortex. Through this route, according to Gellhorn, increased proprioception can enhance a positive emotional state.

Another route of influence of proprioception on the rest of the brain is through the cerebellum. Sensory impulses arising from musculoskeletal receptors, especially the muscle spindle, travel to the cerebellum to contribute to the regulation and coordination of motion. This arrangement also provides an adequate anatomical route for inhibitory influences from these receptors on the reticular activating system. The reticular activating system, in turn, modifies indirectly the ascending proprioceptive flow through its effect on cortical mechanisms. The reticular activating system may increase the arousal of the cortex; the cortex, in turn, increases the excitatory state of the descending reticular activating system and the latter system influences the muscle spindles which are a main contributor to upward proprioceptive flow.

In addition, the posterior column-medial lemniscal system can have a considerable inhibitory effect on the spinothalamic tract impulse flow and that tract is a major influence on the ascending reticular activating system. These mechanisms, probably in connection with others, would appear to help maintain the balance of the central inhibitory-excitatory state. Each of the mechanisms can be used therapeutically. The over-excited child may be calmed by increasing the proprioceptive flow through certain kinds of motor activity. On the other hand, the possibility of enhancing the excitatory state is ever-present. Often in the therapeutic situation, a temporary over-excitement is followed by a state of lower excitement and better integration.

As one of the major sources of proprioception, the muscle spindle probably makes a larger contribution to sensory integration in general than would appear on superficial perusal of its structure and function. Only recently has evidence appeared indicating that afferent discharge from the muscle spindle evokes potentials in the subhuman cortex (Albe-Fessard, Liebeskind and Lamarre, 1965; Lamarre and Liebeskind, 1965). The muscle spindle probably exerts considerable influence on lower structures, especially through its critical role in motor activity.

The gamma efferent neuron or intrafusal fiber to the muscle spindle is subject to conditioning, an elementary form of learning. Buchwald and Eldred (1961) have shown the gamma efferents to be more easily conditioned than alpha efferents and have suggested that the effect of conditioning the gamma efferents would be an increase in ventral horn cell activity because of the continued firing of the gamma system by the conditioning stimulus. The spinal and supraspinal activation of the gamma efferent system preceding an overt motor response may be an important factor in conditioned learning, according to these researchers.

The ease of conditioning of the intrafusal fiber shows that it is more subject to learning than the alpha motor neuron, activation of which is necessary before muscle fibers contract. Muscle spindle activity precedes alpha motor neuron firing to activate muscle fibers. An example of the use of this process is found in the treatment of apraxia. Planning action before actually executing it will help bias the muscle spindle in support of later alpha firing. Furthermore, concomitant afferent flow upon the gamma neuron, as through vestibular or other proporioceptive stimulation, adds to the ease of executing a given motion, whether reflex, automatic, or planned.

The Auditory System

Audition understandably has been one of the main foci of attention in reading disorders, for hearing is basic to language development and reading is a language function, usually taught in conjunction with hearing and speaking. Auditory-language problems have been a secondary focus of the research on which this book is based, and hence audition receives secondary attention. That it is considered unrelated to the processes discussed is certainly not intended, for the results of clinical research indicate that the relationship is closer than generally suspected. In that research (Ayres, 1972a), children whose primary problem was in the auditory-language domain and not in the visual-vestibular-somatosensory domain and who received sensory integrative therapy made significantly greater gains in sight reading scores over matched control subjects. Language was definitely not part of the remedial program; activation and normalization of brain stem mechanisms were. Judging by related statistical analyses, gains were probably due in large part to enhanced auditory perception and sequential memory abilities and definitely not to increased vocabulary. These results which, while tentative, are consistent with clinical observation from other sources, force consideration of the relation of audition to the total sensory integrative process. Language functions, especially as a symbolic and syntactical process and the end product of subserving auditory and other functions, are not under consideration here.

To differentiate the concepts of audition as opposed to language processes it is helpful to consider the highly effective sound processing ability of dogs and cats, animals with quite limited language skills. Without the development of the auditory capacities, language ability as it exists in man today probably would not have evolved. Children with learning problems often have trouble with language as an expression of communication; they no less frequently have trouble with nonlanguage auditory processes such as perception and memory. It is to this latter type of problem, seen as a disorder of sensory integration, to which these remarks are addressed.

The neural processing of sound can be classified as one of the primal forms of sensory integration because it has long been a major source of information regarding basic survival. The survival significance is expressed by the residual tendency for some children with disordered sensory integration to be alerted easily by auditory stimuli which often are filtered out before reaching consciousness in other better integrated brains.

Sensory systems of such primal survival significance can be expected to be served by several integrating mechanisms at the brain stem and other subcortical locations. Considerable intersensory integration sufficient to direct a simple adaptive response can also be expected. In other words, many, but not all, of the principles that apply to the other senses, especially vision, possibly apply to a certain extent to audition.

Auditory requirements consist of analyzing the different parameters of sound, such as duration, frequency or tone, intensity, and sequence. Most of the information about these auditory processes is derived from the study of cats, and that material is presented here as information on subhuman species. Auditory coding begins soon after the stimuli enter the brain stem. At that point the stimuli begin to follow a complex course, making many connections with other ongoing processes before some of them eventually reach the cortex. The number of connections is greater than that believed to take place with visual tracts. Some of these connections, such as those made at the large and complex nuclei, the inferior colliculi, provide for a great deal of sound analysis and integration. In fact, according to Ades' review of central auditory mechanisms (1959), the brain stem and thalamus offer a better neural structure for processing of sound than does the cortex, and "each [auditory] nucleus processes the information it receives from an input, complex both as to sources and patterns, in relation to events which have occurred or are occurring in centers above and below, auditory and nonauditory." It is probable that auditory coding is not completed before interaction with the cortex and that the coding occurs at some integrating center around the midbrain and/or the thalamus.

In addition to relatively direct routes for conduction of auditory stimuli to the cortex, there is also the indirect route, similar to that of the tactile system, through the reticular formation. At that location auditory stimuli probably undergo the same type of integration, including that with other senses, as is believed to occur with other senses. Auditory stimuli also contribute to the general arousal of the brain through the reticular activating system, a function easily noted subjectively.

Auditory stimuli are among those most frequently found to elicit a response in convergent neurons found throughout the brain. As with other sensory impulses, impulses elicited by sounds go to the cerebellum, thus presumably subjecting them to inhibitory functions occurring there.

The auditory system differs from the other sensory systems in that it is represented bilaterally almost as soon as it enters the brain and has many anatomical opportunities to cross from one side of the brain to the other. Ades' review (1959) indicates that bilateral representation of each ear is so close to being equal that loss of one ear is not easily detectable but, citing Rosenzweig, if sound is presented at one side, the cortical response is greater in the contralateral than in the ipsilateral hemisphere.

The fact that the auditory system evolved out of another system closely related to the current vestibular system leads to hypothesizing a closer relationship between the auditory and vestibular systems than might seem apparent judging from a casual subjective consideration of the two senses. On the other hand, clinical impression strongly suggests that vestibular stimuli have a profound effect on auditory and resultant language functions. In view of the nature of the intervention programs provided for the children with these disorders, it seems likely that the integrating interaction occurs at the brain stem level.

Olfaction

Clinicians concerned with human behavior rarely give much thought to the role of olfaction in human development and behavior, for it is considered to have a relatively minor role as a determinant of human function. There are those who would object to that statement, for fashion magazines give the impression that the human male limbic system is irresistibly vulnerable to certain types of stimulation of the olfactory bulbs.

The olfactory sense has not been studied by the basic researchers to the extent that the other senses discussed above have been. The direction of current research suggests that the situation may soon be remedied, although species differences will present a formidable problem of generalization of data to man. Considering the fact that the cortex evolved as an extension of the first cranial (olfactory) nerve, it might be hypothesized that there are still important connections by which the sense of smell could be used to influence sensory integration. The fact that olfaction appears to be fairly important in organizing adaptive responses in the human infant argues further in favor of study of its role. That it can be utilized to influence perception in other senses, probably through acting on the reticular activating system, was demonstrated by Fox (1965) in her study on enhancing manual perception in blind children.

Cognitive functions grew out of the neural substrate of mechanisms which enhanced the probability of individual survival as opposed to the species survival mechanisms with which the olfactory system is still largely connected, especially in lower mammals. During the evolutionary development of man, the olfactory system did not increase in absolute size while the visual and somatosensory systems did. These conditions bear consideration when attempting to use the olfactory sense to enhance sensory integration.

As increase in understanding of the limbic system enables incorporation of its mechanisms into the theory underlying treatment, the olfactory system may gain more significance in sensory integrative treatment. For example, the hippocampus is involved in elementary perception and learning, and general motivation can be attributed to the limbic system.

It is through the interrelation of the limbic and the reticular system that the relationship of sensory integrative processes and emotional behavior may be partially understood.

Vision

The human being is not only a highly visual animal, he is conscious of being visual. He is so conscious of it that the very word "perception" is usually construed to mean visual perception, although auditory perception is also a matter of concern, especially among those attempting to ameliorate learning disorders. Its role in early academic learning is self-evident and vision itself is never taken for granted, as is the sense of gravity.

Yet visual perception, especially of space, is an end product and all of the conditions that enter into producing the end product deserve study in depth. That study is contained in the chapter on form and space perception. Only a few pertinent points about the visual system are mentioned here.

Each eye sends impulses to both cerebral hemispheres, the left half of each visual field to the right hemisphere and the right half to the left hemisphere. It is assumed that integration of the two halves of the total visual field requires some type of interhemispheral communication. Furthermore, neural interaction between neighboring areas of a visual field contribute to the perception of a configuration. MacKay (1961) has presented evidence that this neural interaction process is particularly sensitive to direction of contour. While this study on human beings is not directed to the problem of integration of the two halves of the visual fields, it did show that there was interaction of widely separated areas of the visual field, that the interaction was not likely retinal, and that it was sensitive to contour direction. Disorder in the perception of directionality repeatedly has been linked with reading problems and is believed related to interhemispheral integration. The relationship is deserving of more neurological investigation than is given here.

At the cortical level, vision, just as is the case with the other senses, is influenced by nonspecific reticular or thalamic stimulation. In fact, some action of that system is essential to visual perception. Some of the early significant work in this area demonstrated that the capacity to differentiate the flashes in a flickering light was increased through reticular stimulation (Jung, 1961; Lindsley, 1961).

Postural Responses and
Related Functions

Posture is that motor response which reflects an individual's relationship to the earth's surface and gravitational force. That relationship involves position, equilibrium, and locomotion. It is primal in nature and, generally speaking, primal functions hold significance for many aspects of human behavior. Man's response to gravity, as it is expressed in his antigravity reactions to it, is one of the phyletically oldest sensorimotor responses. It serves as a substrate for much of the later sensorimotor and sensory integrative development.

While the postural substrate to certain aspects of visual perception appears to be accepted rather generally, it extends beyond vision, influencing perception in other sensory modalities. The possible extent of this influence is exemplified in a study of McFarland, Werner and Wapner (1962) which showed that postural tilts changed tactile sensitivity in the hand and the organization of tactile-kinesthetic space. Children with irregular development of postural mechanisms not infrequently also demonstrate disorders of tactile perception (Ayres, 1969a, 1972c). The possible influence of postural mechanisms on the development of sensory integrative processes requires that these mechanisms be studied, not for the sake of posture or motion itself, but because of what they contribute to the neural integration required for academic learning.

While a number of scientists have studied isolated aspects of postural mechanisms with great precision, the therapist's need is better met by understanding some of the over-all principles of these and related functions. It is the work and thinking of clinicians that have organized these principles for direct application.

The Role of Gravity

Gravity, as the source of sensory stimulation to the labyrinth and as producer of the body's weight, is central to all thinking about posture. The ability to retain the balance of one's body, to regain that balance when lost, to assume a position for locomotion, and to move about efficiently on the earth's surface are all responses to gravity. They have assumed a critical role in the evolution of vertebrates because of their survival value. Locomotion is essential both to obtain a meal and to avoid becoming the meal of another animal. Locomotion is dependent upon balance or equilibrium and upon the ability to assume a quadruped or biped position.

Most postural responses are antigravity responses, i.e., a movement or position that prevents the body or a part of it from being pulled to the earth (or floor) by the gravitational force. Examples of antigravity responses are raising the head when in the prone or supine position, coming to a sitting position from a lying one, and standing. Other than establishing the general intention of action, these responses are not planned in the praxis sense. They contain a large degree of automaticity and are gross as opposed to fine or skilled. Most prolonged or static muscle responses are antigravity postural reactions.

The methods of locomotion in the subhuman species and in the infant are dependent upon assuming a prone, including quadruped position. The prone position includes that of lying face down and the quadruped posture. Significantly, the position is defined relative to the earth's surface and gravitational force. Some of the righting reflexes which predominate early in a child's life center around the objective of placing the body in a prone position. From a phyletic standpoint, it is reasonable to assume that most of the postural mechanisms evolved when the normal non-resting position of the body was prone or quadrupedal as opposed to supine. If this assumption is correct, then it may follow that maturation of certain postural mechanisms can best occur if the child's body simulates that position. The point is important for therapeutic practice. It is, for example, one of the theoretical bases for frequent and prolonged use of a scooter board. In therapeutic practice, it is helpful to be aware of how gravity is acting upon the sensorimotor system of the child and whether that source of stimulation is making a positive contribution to the total therapeutic process.

One of the pitfalls of depending upon basic research for knowledge of postural mechanisms lies in the fact that most of the research has been conducted on quadrupeds. While most of the resultant information may hold true for man, there is a tendency to overlook possible contributions from brachiating ancestors. On the other hand, educators have tended to focus on strictly bipedal postural reactions, overlooking the developmental sequence and brain stem functions which lead to accenting the prone position.

Neural Level of Organization

A function that is as well, but perhaps not as complexly, integrated in lower vertebrates as it is in higher ones can be expected to have major organizing centers in the older parts of the brain, especially the brain stem and cerebellum and possibly basal ganglia. In man, the cerebral cortex assumes general direction or over-all planning of motor activity while the details of integration occur below. In fact, many of the postural mechanisms can operate independently of volition. Maintaining this cortical-subcortical relationship is central to effective therapy.

In gaining a perspective of the role of noncognitive functions in man, it is helpful to look at the actual brain of man and to note the proportion of total brain structure devoted to higher functions and then to observe the large amount of neural substance remaining. Postural responses have their major integrating mechanisms in that part of the brain that lies below the cortex. Man tends to be less aware of functions below the cortex. The very automaticity of postural functions leads to their being taken for granted, even in the remedial situation. This tendency toward lack of awareness is especially true if mild dysfunction does not obviously interfere with locomotion. One of the more difficult tasks of the therapist is to recognize not only the existence, but more importantly, the significance of slightly disordered postural mechanisms.

It is not so much the resultant poor coordination that is of concern but the fact that disorder, when found in conjunction with symptoms such as reading retardation, strongly suggests poor integration in some aspects of brain stem function. It is because some type of sensory integration which occurs in the brain stem appears to be critical to the reading process that postural reactions are important in treating learning disorders.

Although the postural responses, like many brain stem reactions, are largely automatic and inherent, they are definitely adaptive, i.e., the response changes behavior in a life-supporting direction. They represent some of the most elementary, primary, and essential adaptive responses.

The inherent design for maturation and maintenance of equilibrium and locomotion is so well structured that the normally developing child needs only the sensory input and opportunity for motor expression for these functions to mature. The objective of sensory integrative therapy is to replicate these conditions, but the opportunity must provide something that previous opportunities did not, for previous conditions demonstrated their inadequacy. The "something" is the difference between therapy and mere exercise or activity.

The concept of "inherent design" needs further explanation. "Design" is used to refer to one or more mechanisms, either complex or simple, or to a predisposition toward a given pattern of motor response that is not cortically or cognitively planned. The description in earlier chapters of motor responses obtained by stimulation of the brain stem of lower animals provides a good example of "inherent designs." Inherent patterns, especially at the brain stem level, do not show the natural individual differences among children as do, for example, such functions as language, which are largely dependent upon the neocortex. This homogeneity enables the therapist to employ deviations in postural responses to assess developmental problems.

In considering these "inherent designs," Roberts (1967) refers to "pattern-generating mechanisms" behind the coordinated postural response. He suggests that these mechanisms are the adaptive response to and the counterpart of sensory mechanisms for pattern recognition. Some of the cells concerned with pattern-generating mechanisms, according to Roberts, are grouped into anatomical entities such as the basal ganglia, cerebellum, and the reticular formation.

Denny-Brown (1962) attributes most of the postural responses to the midbrain. While his basic research has been conducted primarily on monkeys, his observations on man have led him to believe that the midbrain of man is organized in a manner similar to that of the research animals. Denny-Brown attributes to the midbrain mechanisms for integrating the tonic neck reflex, tonic labyrinthine reflex, eye reflexes, righting reflexes, and even sitting, standing, walking, and climbing. He finds the midbrain contribution to organization of movement and locomotion essential. "Further," to quote Denny-Brown, "though there is reason to believe that the reactions concerned are at the primitive instinctive level, our experiments indicate that they are the essential substrate for all the more highly developed behavioural reactions."

The significance of midbrain influence over postural and loco-motor integration lies less in motor functions than in the possible interrelation of those motor functions with midbrain visual and auditory functions and interhemispheral integration. Trevarthen (1968) feels that the visual functions and motor functions related to vision, including the oculomotor and locomotor responses of the midbrain, are essentially one integrated function.

The trained observer can see these ideas manifested in the child in treatment for sensory integration. A cortically directed postural response is far less smooth and effective than one which occurs automatically in response to appropriate sensory input. Something of the inherent nature of a natural response was reflected in the comment of an eight-year-old boy upon finally mastering quad-rupedal balancing on a large therapeutic ball, "It's just as though I've always known how." The design was there. His environment and his sensory integration were modified sufficiently to enable its manifestation. At the time of this evidence of enhanced neural integration, the teacher of the child reported a slight improvement in his reading ability.

It is the goal of therapy that certain types of sensory integra-tive dysfunction elicit the responses that are mediated by "pattern-generating mechanisms." Postural responses mature best if volition is used only to create the general plan of action, which, when put into effect, evokes the postural response without thought. The postural response, in turn, is dependent upon a pattern of sensory input arising out of the activity and the force of gravity. Focusing attention on the postural response can inhibit subcortical activity. It is possible to try too hard to evince a postural response. Taking the child's direct attention away from the task with conversation or substituting a task analogous to an earlier stage of development often enables the subcortical response to be more effective.

The Developmental Sequence

Within the first few weeks of postnatal life, the primitive postural reflexes, i.e., the tonic neck reflex (TNR) and the tonic labyrinthine reflex (TLR), are either obviously present or more easily elicited than they are later on in life. The stimulus which evokes the tonic labyrinthine reflex is the earth's gravitational force. It acts on the neuromuscular system in such a manner that when the head is prone, flexor muscles are facilitated and when the head is supine, extensor muscles are facilitated. The asymmetrical TNR is elicited by stimulation of receptors in the neck joints. When the head is turned to the right, so that the chin approximates the shoulder, extensor tone is increased in the right arm and flexor tone increased in the left arm. When the head is turned to the left, extensor tone is increased in the left arm and flexor tone in the right arm. Response in the lower extremities varies from child to child. The most commonly reported pattern is increased extensor tone in the leg ipsilateral to the arm with increased extensor tone and increased flexor tone in the other leg. Occasionally a child will show a crossed diagonal pattern, i.e., contralateral arms and legs will both show either increased flexor tone or extensor tone, depending upon head position. In the symmetrical TNR, flexion of the head facilitates flexor tone in all four extremities, and extension (sometimes referred to as dorsiflexion) of the head facilitates extensor tone.

As a child matures, these reflexes become integrated into the central nervous system largely through inhibition as higher centers of the brain mature. They never disappear during the life of the individual but the degree to which a person suppresses or attains mastery over them usually reflects the degree of maturation and integration of postural mechanisms. When these reflexes are present to an abnormal degree following adult brain damage, their manifestation is called a "release phenomenon." The higher centers have lost some of their inhibitory functions, thereby releasing some of the more primitive sensorimotor patterns. Their presence is significant in that they tell the therapist that the higher portions of the brain have failed to integrate some aspects of lower function. It is interesting and possibly significant that the TLR is a progravity response. The reflex pulls the body and its limbs toward the earth, whereas later, more mature responses are antigravity in nature.

Hypothesizing about the neurophysiological method by which maturation brings about the integration of the primitive postural reflexes has led to effective treatment methods for their inhibition or suppression.

As the central nervous system matures, it appears to go through developmental stages in which it is sensitive to certain sensory stimuli which are related to motor responses for which there is a drive to emit. Because it is necessary to survival for the organism to master, in a postural sense, the earth's gravitational force, there is an innate drive to master that force. Thus the infant's brain may be especially sensitive to gravity, for he soon begins to lift his head up against gravity, then adds his shoulders to the antigravity response. By three or four months of age, he spends much time arching his back into extension in the prone position so that he is pivoting on his lower abdomen with head and extremities held up against gravity. The posture is essentially the reverse of that facilitated by the TLR in the prone position. It is proposed that assuming the prone extensor posture helps the sensorimotor system to inhibit or integrate the TLR. The prone extension posture has been noted as a significant step in motor development by Rood (Ayres, 1963), who refers to it as the pivot prone position, by Gesell and associates (1940), and by K. Bobath (1966).

The prone extension posture is possibly related to the Landau reaction in which the five- or six-month-old child holds his body, especially trunk and legs, in extension when supported at the abdomen by the examiner. Bouncing the child helps elicit the response. Passively flexing the child's head interrupts the sensorimotor reflex and the child crumples into a flexor pattern. It is generally believed that the gravity receptors and the neck proprioceptors are the receiving source of sensory input for the reflex, but clinical experience strongly suggests that motion is also involved and perhaps even the touch-pressure on the abdomen contributes. In the therapeutic situation, motion when the child is resting on his abdomen is certainly the most effective stimulus in bringing about an arched back. K. Bobath (1966) has made a pertinent observation in regard to the effect of sensory input on behavior. The infant's "startle reaction" disappears at the same time as the Landau reaction and protective extension of the arms appear, which is at about six months of age.

One of the early tasks of the infant is the development of postural responses that enable him to master gravity. This maturational process begins with righting reactions. These reactions have been particularly well explored and presented by Bobath and Bobath (1955, 1964) and by Fiorentino (1963). For a thorough explanation of postural responses as tests for the very young child, the reader is referred to Millani-Compareti and Gidoni (1967).

In essence, the righting reactions are all designed to align the head and body with the earth's surface so that the organism is in a position for locomotion. The head is brought to a position so that the chin is pointing toward the earth's surface with the face raised enough to see ahead. The sagittal plane of the head strives to become perpendicular to the earth's surface. The trunk and limbs attempt reflexly to align themselves with the head, i.e., to assume a prone position. The distaste of quadrupeds for the supine position suggests some of the significance of the righting reflexes. Animals are more vulnerable when supine than when prone and the functional or survival value of the reactions is more evident in the quadrupeds. The righting reflexes provide an excellent example of mechanisms which involve receptors representing more than one sensory modality, i.e., vision, touch, and proprioception from muscles, ligaments, joints, and labyrinth.

In addition to righting reflexes, man is potentially endowed with equilibrium reactions and these have evolved to a more complex level than their counterpart in quadrupeds. Equilibrium reactions begin to develop somewhat later than the righting reactions and continue to mature for a number of years. To a certain extent they take the place of the righting reactions in man's postural behavior, inhibiting those reactions as the equilibrium reactions mature. Thus the presence of equilibrium reactions is considered a sign of maturity and normalcy to the extent that the reactions are normal. Too much residual TNR, TLR, or neck righting reflex, on the other hand, is considered abnormal. Equilibrium reactions help one maintain or regain a given posture, usually quadrupedal, kneeling, sitting, or standing. Sometimes the reactions are easily seen; often they are subtle, sometimes consisting only of muscle contraction without movement. They are elicited when the surface which is supporting the body's weight is altered or when the body has changed its center of gravity. The reactions consist of attempting to move the body's center of gravity to maintain balance, including moving the extremities to assist in that maintenance.

Postural background movements that simply place the extremities in a more appropriate position for fine work also appear to be part of the mature postural mechanisms. They or deficits in them are observed in children especially when they are seated and attempting tasks involving the arms.

The early maturation and automatic nature of some equilibrium reactions can be observed by watching the responses of a young child being held on the hip of his mother as she reaches across a counter when shopping, bends over to pick up something from the floor, or struggles to put a bag of groceries in the car. Without the child's natural inclination to adjust its body to its changing center of gravity, the mother would have to pay more attention to the child's safety and less to her own activity. Observations of the more subtle equilibrium reactions can be one of the most effective means of detecting minor disorders of them.

Muscles and Their Major Receptor

Some aspects of the status of sensory integration are reflected in the type of muscle contraction manifested by a child. Muscle contraction can be divided roughly into two types: (1) phasic, characterized by skeletal movement and short periods of contraction followed by relaxation and (2) tonic, characterized by prolonged or static contraction and skeletal stabilization. When two antagonistic muscles are statically contracting simultaneously, the result is cocontraction of muscles. Many children with learning disorders tend to show better phasic than tonic muscle contraction, and cocontraction is noticeably deficient, suggesting inefficient mechanisms for tonic muscle contraction. The probable association between muscle cocontraction and status of postural mechanisms leads to the necessity for exploring and theorizing about different types of muscle contraction, the role of the muscle receptors in these types of contraction, and the relationship of the neuromuscular response to postural responses and hence to perception and other aspects of sensory integration.

Many of the postural reactions are tonic in nature. Prolonged contraction of certain muscle groups is necessary for maintenance of a sitting, quadruped, and biped position. Proximal muscles must stabilize proximal joints over prolonged periods (a matter of minutes) so that distal joints are free to move to accomplish tasks. The sensory flow resulting from prolonged postural muscle contraction may well have a significant influence on sensory inhibition and integration. The stabilization necessary to provide proximal support for free distal movement must not be confused with the lack of postural background movement seen in children with mild disorders of postural integration. On the contrary, the lack of postural background movement is probably associated with inadequate ability to obtain or change the constellation of muscle contraction which must provide the stable base for more distal phasic skeletal movement. In short, flexible tonic muscle contraction, able to change in relation to desirable equilibrium reactions, is critical to implementation of postural reactions.

Phasic and tonic types of muscle contraction have been referred to as "mobilizing" and "stabilizing" responses by Rood (Stockmeyer, 1967), who, as a clinician, has made a particularly thorough study of the neuromuscular system. Rood proposes that muscles have both mobilizing and stabilizing components. The stabilizing function is maintained by a constant flow of sensory stimuli, such as those from the skin, muscle, and joint receptors.

According to Stockmeyer's interpretation of Rood, mobilizing or movement function occurs ontogenetically before the development of the ability to cocontract musculature. The pivot prone position is the first motor pattern which develops stabilization, for the position activates the deep tonic extensor muscles. When these muscles are contracting, antagonists are placed on stretch and thereby contract to provide stability of the body. Muscle spindles in deep extensor muscles are believed to provide the sensory feedback necessary to initiate cocontraction.

In view of what is currently known about the muscle spindle, the following conditions which are significant to the role of postural mechanisms in sensory integration are believed to prevail. The situation is presented in a simplified manner. A fuller account can be found in Roberts (1967) and Eldred (1967a, 1967b), on whose works this discussion is based.

Most muscle spindles have two types of sensory endings or receptors, each associated with different gamma efferent or intrafusal fibers innervating different fibers of the muscle spindle. The two types of sensory endings enable two types of sensory discharge back into the nervous system. Although technically afferent discharge cannot be subdivided neatly by type of spindle receptor, tonic contraction is most apt to be associated with secondary afferent endings and phasic contraction with primary afferent endings, although these endings also have static qualities. To oversimplify a complex neurophysiological arrangement so that the concept can be used in therapeutic practice, a "static" intrafusal neuron innervating the muscle spindle may bring about a tonic muscle contraction through afferent flow from secondary and certain primary afferent endings.

Similarly, a "phasic" intrafusal neuron is most apt to be associated with phasic muscle contraction. If this relationship holds, the therapist needs to give special attention to activating the tonic afferents through the "tonic" intrafusal fibers in order to increase the effectiveness of the tonic and cocontraction component of muscle contraction. To make the hypothesis even more clear, it is proposed that the abnormalities in postural mechanisms seen in learning disabled children are often reflected in poor "tonic" afferent flow from the muscle spindle and that the postural responses can be helped toward normalization by activating the "tonic" afferents. The spindle receptors associated with static and hence cocontraction of muscles have a higher threshold and are best activated by a continuous flow of stimuli. The stimuli which seem most effective in activating the secondary afferents are proprioceptive, especially vestibular, in nature. The emphasis on the vestibular contribution finds support in the work of Gernandt (1964), who has studied the vestibular system in detail. It must be remembered, however, that there are many kinds of vestibular stimulation resulting in many kinds of responses.

In addition to its role in implementing postural reactions, the muscle spindle assumes an equally important but more general role in movement. Successful direction of a motor act is dependent upon having at hand accurate information about the body and its movements. Therefore information about the degree of tension in a muscle must be known, and signalling that tension is a function of the muscle spindle. Although there is growing evidence that some muscle spindle sensory discharge does reach the cortex, material presented in previous chapters makes it fairly clear that direct cortical receipt of all sensory information is not necessary to direct motor action. Sensations received at lower levels are utilized indirectly. Execution of the cortex's broad plan is ultimately dependent upon muscle spindle information which is furnished plentifully to subcortical structures.

The function of the muscle spindle is central to maintaining muscle tone. A number of children with sensory integrative deficits have reduced muscle tone, a condition which may hold considerable significance. Low muscle tone suggests inadequate sensory flow to the intrafusal fiber. It may result in inadequate sensory flow from spindle afferents, which in turn reduces sensory integration. These children often evidence inadequate function of the vestibular system. The problem may be as follows. Inadequate integration of vestibular and other sensations reduces excitation of the intrafusal fiber, resulting in an insufficiently contracted muscle spindle, which is then less efficient in its role in the implementation of all motor output, including postural reflexes and planned, skilled acts. Furthermore, the brain of a hypotonic child is receiving less sensory input than it would if tone were normal. This reduced input may have relevance for sensory integration in general.

Postural Mechanisms and Extraocular Muscle Control

Normalizing postural mechanisms helps normalize extraocular muscle control. The extraocular muscles are skeletal muscles. They respond fully as much as other muscles to the neurophysiology of postural mechanisms. Postural mechanisms and muscle contraction offer one of the most effective and natural means by which extraocular muscle control can be influenced. Furthermore, the approach is especially acceptable to the child, who is not even aware that he is receiving "eye exercises."

One type of influence is through proprioceptive facilitation, i.e., the extraocular muscles are facilitated to respond through neural bombardment of the cranial nerve nuclei from which they receive innervation. The bombardment is by sensations arising from contraction of other postural muscles or from the vestibular apparatus. The impulses from the muscles are carried over the medial longitudinal fasciculus, a large fiber bundle receiving input directly from the nuclei of the accessory nerve, which supplies the sternocleidomastoid and trapezius muscles. It follows, then, that strong contraction of these muscles facilitates eye movements.

The vestibulo-ocular reflexes provide one of the most powerful influences on the extraocular musculature. Each time the head moves, one or more of the semicircular canals are stimulated, and each time they are stimulated, one or more pairs of the six pairs of muscles that move the eyeball are affected. The specific effect of movement in each semicircular canal on the eye muscles has been traced in basic neurophysiological research and that literature can be searched for guidance when individual muscle contraction is to be stressed.

Reflexes of the semicircular canals affect muscles other than those of the eyes, especially those of the limbs and neck, and provide an indirect route for influencing extraocular muscle function. For example, when moving rapidly while prone on a scooter, the semicircular canals facilitate those muscles that cause the head to raise, the back to arch, and the extremities to be held up away from the floor. Contraction of the trapezius and of the sternocleidomastoid muscles is necessary to hold the head up and stabilize it. This muscle contraction elicits a proprioceptive flow which adds its influence to the direct influence of semicircular canals on the eye muscles. The entire sensorimotor response becomes self-supportive through proprioceptive facilitation.

It is quite likely that other muscles than the neck musculature also have a profound effect on the eyes. It is a fairly safe hypothesis that utilizing simple prone or quadruped postures will involve the interaction of extraocular and other postural muscles in a mutually facilitatory manner, possibly through mechanisms not yet recognized or well understood.

The optical righting reflex reverses the direction of posture-eye influence. In this reflex, perception of verticality acts on the postural mechanisms to help keep the body upright. The reflex is easily observed by comparing standing balance with eyes open and closed. The question often arises about the process through which the brain learns to recognize a vertical line as vertical. It is possible that the earth's gravitational force, acting on the labyrinth, contributes to the initial perception of verticality, again demonstrating the complex intermeshing of visual and postural mechanisms. Children with problems in postural responses tend to have poorer perception of verticality (Ayres, unpublished data).

In addition to the optical righting reflex, ocular movement is believed to have an effect on some of the postural reflexes, including the righting reactions. There is some evidence that looking to the side can trigger the sequence of neck righting reactions and possibly the tonic neck reflex.

The postural reactions and extraocular muscle control have been shown to be intimately related on a reflex level, each one affecting the other. In most instances, the relationship appears to be related, directly or indirectly, to the mediation of an adaptive response of a postural nature — usually obtaining or maintaining a prone, quadrupedal, sitting or bipedal position. The majority of the reflexes evolved in vertebrates before man assumed the upright position as his major position during locomotion. Similarly, most of the postural reactions mature before the child walks. It is their maturation that enables him to walk.

This close interrelationship between eye musculature and postural reactions provides the basis for the assumption that activating and normalizing postural mechanisms, especially in the prone and quadruped positions, will provide a fundamental, natural, and optimum approach to improving extraocular muscle control. When postural mechanisms are employed to help normalize eye musculature, it is assumed that simply being meaningfully involved in a purposeful activity under therapeutically enhanced sensorimotor integration will encourage the eye musculature to perform in a normal manner. Given a chance, the brain is self-organizing.

The use of sensory integrative therapy to improve ocular control also has a built-in safeguard against inflicting the therapist's ignorance on the sensitive eye muscles of the child. Any specific exercises to the eyes as more isolated anatomical structures might well follow attempts to enhance their function in a manner that includes them as part of the musculoskeletal system and replicates normal development. The methods which are more specific to the eyes, such as the use of machines, fall into a different therapeutic system.

Extraocular Muscle Responses and the Development of Visual Space Perception

Hebb (1949) was among the first theorists to suggest that the afferent input from the extraocular muscles, as the eyes traversed the outline of a visual stimulus, aided in the development of visual form and space perception. While there is little evidence that the afferent input from these muscles travel very far within the brain, so also is it argued that impulses do not need to go far to have a profound influence. If such an influence does exist, normalizing afferent flow from the skeletal eye muscles may aid appreciably in the development of form and space perception.

Having assembled and studied the research on the role of saccadic eye movements, Abercrombie (1969) concluded that "brain injured children whose eyes cannot accurately locate and fixate a target will be seriously handicapped in mental development." To the extent that Abercrombie is correct, then to that extent the increased ability visually to locate and fixate a target will aid in the child's development.

Furthermore, there is something to be said for the process of organizing efferent discharge to the extraocular muscles. From experiments with human subjects, Walsh (1969) concluded that the efferent flow to the eye muscles was monitored and played a part in visual space perception. Apparently the directions the brain gives to the eyes for movement in some way contributed to sensorimotor integration. Increasing the precision and normalcy of the directions of efferent discharge may directly enhance visual space perception.

Chapter 7

Factors, Syndromes, and Neural Systems

Children with learning disorders have shown a variety of under-lying symptoms, many of which are assumed to be manifestations of deviations in brain function, especially sensorimotor function. The fundamental goal in building the theoretical system presented in this book has been the interpretation of those behavioral symptoms in neurophysiological constructs that can serve as guides to the development and administration of treatment procedures intended to influence the neural disorder underlying the learning problem.

The Concept of Syndromes or Neural Systems

The use of behavioral observation requires the organizing of discrete bits of interrelated observations into constellations or patterns that can be interpreted by meaningful theoretical constructs. The method employed to meet this objective was the organizing of symptoms into naturally occurring clusters through a series of factor analyses of scores on perceptual, motor, cognitive, auditory, language, and neuromuscular tests administered to several different sample populations of learning disabled children (Ayres, 1965, 1966a, 1966b, 1969a, 1972c). The consistently recurring symptom complexes have been interpreted as representing disorder in neural systems or subsystems, i.e., groups of neurons that tend to function as a unit, relatively independent from but in some way related to the processes of the rest of the nervous system. Each system is responsible for a different aspect of the total brain function. Since the neurons of each system tend to function as a unit, they are inclined to have the same level or degree of integration and hence scores on measures of behavioral parameters usually vary in the same direction. In other words, if the score on one test reflecting the status of a given system is low, the score on another test which also reflects the function of that same system is apt to be low, whereas scores on two tests identified with a different system are both more apt to be high if dysfunction in that system is less.

Constellations of symptoms that repeatedly appear together are often called syndromes and that term is employed here, although the presence of the syndrome components is less specific and invariable than in the classic concept of syndrome. The term "disorder in a neural system" encourages more accurate thinking, although it is more cumbersome. It assumes that the central nervous system is composed of a number of subsystems which can be subject to greater or lesser degrees of integration. These functional systems involve, simultaneously, several different levels of the brain and many different anatomical structures. The statistical analyses have helped to confirm that vertical functional systems exist in the brain and to delineate the nature of those systems. One characteristic of each of the syndromes or systems has been some type of learning disorders. Each also shows some type of sensory integrative dysfunction.

The idea that symptoms of brain dysfunction tend to cluster is not new. The value in conceptualizing behavioral manifestations in clusters has been recognized by a number of clinicians. Categorizing of related characteristics is an early step of development of an area of knowledge. Classificatory methods have a subjective as well as objective element, the number of subdivisions being in part a function of how many divisions of behavior are made, which, in turn, is partly a function of the stage of knowledge development; the later the stage, the greater the number of categories derived. Each classification is correct in its own way. A sample of variations is reported here to point out the subjectivity of their determination. There are as many statistical factors or categories in any analysis as the researcher chooses or is able to derive, within certain acceptable statistical procedures. The categorizing of data has heuristic value and possibly the procedure, as a method of building a body of knowledge, should be judged on that basis.

Gerstmann is recognized as an early observer of dysfunction in the adult and a classifier of perceptual-motor deficit. He described (1940) a syndrome, now named for him, consisting of finger agnosia (a symptom which he recognized and named, considering it part of body scheme disturbance), disorientation for right and left, agraphia, and acalculia (difficulty in calculating with numbers). Gerstmann ascribed the syndrome to a lesion in the parieto-occipital convexity of the brain and felt there was a functional relationship among the various components, such a relationship causing the symptoms to be termed a syndrome. Much later Kinsbourne and Warrington (1963) reported seven cases of the Gerstmann syndrome in children. All of the children had finger agnosia plus two or more other elements of the syndrome, but they also manifested other perceptual-motor deficiencies, such as apraxia or speech and reading problems. It would seem that these later investigators were applying the label of Gerstmann syndrome to what others would now call perceptual-motor dysfunction in general. Today, a more detailed method of classifying could result in the different components of the Gerstmann syndrome falling into different statistically derived factors if one chose to organize knowledge in that manner. In other words, the identification and determination of the composition of syndromes is partly a function of the construction of the brain and partly a function of how much man knows about it at any given time. This point is worthy of keeping in mind in considering the neural systems or syndromes suggested by the theory presented in this book.

Another early and creative attempt at categorization of disabilities resulting from brain injury in the mature individual was made by Halstead (1947). His four factors, rather broadly interpreted from a relatively small sample of behavior taken from fifty adult males, included (1) a central integrative field factor with highest loadings on a pencil and paper intelligence test, speech perception, and a test of categories; (2) an ability to comprehend similarities, best represented with loadings on the category test, tactual recall, and a performance intelligence test; (3) an unclear factor that appeared to represent the ability to buffer demands made on the emotions, identified by loadings on the factor by tests of flicker-fusions, tactual memory, and a test involving form and color perception: and (4) the "exteriorization of intelligence," which carried loadings on tactual performance and peripheral vision.

Halstead's work presaged recognition of the relatedness of simultaneous functions in several different sensory modalities and represents a possible attempt to think in terms of neural systems.

More recent studies of dysfunction in children (Bortner and Birch, 1962; Brenner and Gillman, 1966; Cole and Kraft, 1964; Culbertson and Gunn, 1966; Ernhart and associates, 1963; Lyle, 1969; Rutter, 1969; Silverstein, 1965; Smith and Smith, 1966) generally show a strong inclination toward correlation of scores on tests given children with neural dysfunction but not a sufficient difference to enable or even encourage meaningful categorization. Learning disorders are not a single condition but an end product of many related and interacting variables. Determining what the different variables are that contribute to disordered learning and categorizing those variables has been an early step in planning remediation of those conditions. Concomitantly, the idea that the brain operates to a certain extent on the basis of subsystems, both somewhat independent and somewhat related to other systems, is generally accepted by modern neurophysiologists (cf. Jasper, 1966). The theoretical system presented by this book has taken statistically derived factors that categorize behaviorally observed symptoms in learning disabled children and interpreted them as neural systems or syndromes in order to treat the sensory integrative problem underlying the learning problem.

The idea of different kinds of sensory integrative systems is not inconsistent with personal experience. J. J. Gibson (1966) points out that human beings are aware of patterns and transformations of simultaneous sensory input from several different sensory modalities, rather than from one sensory modality alone, all contributing to a unified perceptual end product. The experience fits neatly into the idea of neural subsystems, each system serving a common function for transmission and assimilation of related information involving several sensory modalities simultaneously. For example, when one rides a bicycle, one experiences the motion of the body through space, the pedaling of the feet, the demands made upon one's equilibrium and the adjustments made to maintain that equilibrium, the turning of the handle bars and the sight of the passing landscape all as part of one perceptual-motor act. Each of these functions is, actually, involved in the same neural subsystem.

Of the contemporary behaviorists, Luria (1966a, 1966b) has submitted some of the most lucid reasoning about functional neural systems. His ideas have evolved from the study of behavioral parameters manifested in the mature human being sustaining local lesions. Luria considers higher brain processes, such as perception, cognition, and learning to be performed by a number of dynamic functional systems or "working constellations" of neurons involving many central nervous system structures at many different levels. These systems involve the combined working of parts of the brain which may be remote, each contributing to the integrated functional system. Cerebral cortical areas are "junctions" in the systems, and operate in conjunction with lower structures.

Groups of neurons can belong simultaneously to different functional systems. These systems, according to Luria, mature independently of each other and in accordance with the individual's interaction with the environment. Interference with one link of the system affects the end product of the system. Luria considers the capacity to form functional systems during ontogenetic development one of the most important evolutionary products. The process of developing higher cortical function, he believes, is characterized by an early focus on elementary sensorimotor processes which continue to form the basis, although they diminish in importance with maturation. Luria's conceptualizations are consistent with those presented in this theory.

It appears, then, that the thinking on brain function and dysfunction in terms of functional neural systems and types of dysfunction does hold promise for understanding the neural basis of human behavior. Just how those types and systems are described is still very much dependent upon the theoretical orientation upon which data gathering is based and interpreted. The factors and hypothesized neural systems discussed in this book are presented with that limitation.

At this time treatment methods have not been differentiated on the basis of the different conditions causing the irregular neural function, although the appropriateness of eventually doing so is recognized. Etiology may be related to prognosis. Some evidence (Silver and Hagin, 1964; Ingram, Mason and Blackburn, 1970) is suggestive that there may be two major etiological categories of learning disabilities, one developmental and the other showing conventional, overt, "organic" or brain damage symptoms. The developmental groups showed more deficit in reading than in arithmetic, a difference not found in the "organic" group (Ingram and associates, 1970) and a greater tendency toward partial recovery over a period of years (Silver and Hagin, 1964). It is clear that in these studies the term "organic" symptoms is used with a connotation which differs from that of such terms as "dysfunction" or "neural disorder" as used in this book. An eight-year-old child who cannot learn to read in spite of adequate instruction is considered to have some dysfunction of the brain, although that dysfunction may not be due to brain damage.

There is need for much more clarification of etiological factors. At this time "behavioral" symptoms vs. "neurological" symptoms seem to be based on man's epistomological systems of conventional areas of knowledge, i.e., psychology and neurology. The division is arbitrary, of course, for both fields are dealing with functions of the brain. Until etiological factors are understood well enough to incorporate them into the theoretical structure, the therapeutic approach will of necessity continue to be based on neurophysiological symptoms as observed and interpreted by the neuropsychologist and therapist.

A considerable quantity of research leaves little doubt but that most of the symptoms, especially if considered in constellations, are related to learning, especially reading disorders, although some are more closely related than others. Perceptual and sensory integrative factors are most important in acquiring the ability to read, but once the perceptual demands are mastered, conceptual and other higher cognitive functions assume greater significance (cf. Birch and L. Belmont, 1965).

The Syndromes or Neural Systems Identified

From the author's statistical analyses referred to above, five factors emerged with sufficient frequency and similarity of operative parameters to be considered functionally related aspects of human behavior. It is hypothesized that they reflect neural systems in which disorder has been found in children with learning problems. Terms designating them are (1) disorder in postural, ocular, and bilateral integration; (2) apraxia; (3) disorder in form and space perception; (4) auditory-language problems; and (5) tactile defensiveness. A sixth type of disorder, unilateral disregard, has been only tentatively identified.

Each of these syndromes is discussed in a separate chapter; however, a few general remarks are pertinent here. Each of these six types of disorder has been identifiable in a clinical situation, although seldom is a child seen with disorder in one and only one system. Auditory-language dysfunction comes closest to being discrete and is most frequently seen independently of the other syndromes. Tactile defensiveness is often seen in the apraxic child. Apraxia and disorder in postural, ocular, and bilateral integration often are present in the same child, suggesting a strong relationship between the two neural systems involved. Form and space perceptual problems are usually, but not inevitably, seen in the child with apraxia or a disorder of postural and bilateral integration. Unilateral disregard, a symptom recognized for some time as occasionally occurring in the brain injured adult, has been clinically observed in a small percentage of children with learning disorders and with other related disorders manifested on the left as opposed to the right side of the body.

One possible symptom complex that has been recognized clinically among children with learning disorders but not to a sufficient extent to enable its statistical identification in completed research shows as its major characteristic an athetoid-like dyskinesia and often a muscle twitch. Children with this type of sensorimotor problem often do not show other identifiable symptom complexes or syndromes. This type of disorder may be related to the "choreiform syndrome" described by Prechtl and Stemmer (1962). These authors demonstrated the presence of the syndrome electromyographically in children presenting learning and behavior disorders. They described it observationally as a sudden, slight, jerky, "chorealike" muscle contraction occurring irregularly and arhythmically and of short duration. The contractions were more easily seen with increased muscle tone or when the child was under stress. They occur somewhat more frequently in head and trunk muscles, including extraocular muscles, than in the extremities. Poor eye fixation, poor tendon reflexes, clumsiness, hyperactivity, distractibility, and lability of mood were associated with the muscle contractions in the sample of children in whom the syndrome originally was identified. Rutter, Graham and Birch (1966) failed to find significant associations between the presence of the syndrome and reading disabilities, psychiatric disorder, or neurological abnormalities; however, Wolff and Hurwitz (1966) found the syndrome to be significantly more frequent among children with learning and behavior difficulties than among normal children.

These studies serve to show that many conditions of inadequate sensorimotor function probably exist which have not yet been identified, let alone sufficiently understood theoretically to plan appropriate treatment.

Recognition of different types of disorder in children has its major value in making possible hypotheses regarding the nature of sensory integration. From these hypotheses treatment methods have been developed which are effective in enhancing neural integration. From assessing a child's sensory integration, treatment can be made specific to the problems and hence maximally effective within current knowledge.

Chapter 8

Clinical Evaluation of Sensory Integrative Dysfunction

Planning of a therapeutic program requires a basis for the plan. In addition to reasonable mastery of a theory from which to derive a plan of action, the therapist needs to have some understanding of the status of the sensory integrative processes in the child whom he is attempting to help and, most essentially, where the dysfunction lies. Results from intervention can hardly be expected unless remedial procedures are in some way related to the condition in need of remediation.

Evaluation of sensory integration requires careful observation with a good understanding of the typical characteristics of the significant behavioral parameters. Since far from all of the important symptoms are recognized at this time, it is appropriate that the therapist be alert for additional types of symptoms that may help bring insight into some of the problems not yet solved.

Many aspects of sensory integrative dysfunction can be evaluated objectively with tests developed and standardized on children four to eight, and in some instances ten, years of age. These standardized neuropsychological tests are available as the Southern California Sensory Integration Tests (SCSIT) (Ayres, 1972b). The tests are referred to briefly in the chapters on the various neural system disorders. The SCSIT manual should be used as a reference in connection with the material in the book relative to the various syndromes. A brief description of the tests follows:

Space Visualization: Form boards are utilized to involve visual perception of form and space and mental manipulation of objects in space.

Figure-ground Perception: Stimulus figures are superimposed and imbedded to require selection of a foreground figure from a rival background.

Position in Space: Simple geometric forms are presented for recognition in different orientations and sequences.

Design Copying: The visual-motor task involves duplicating a design on a dot grid.

Motor Accuracy: The visual-motor task requires that the child draw a line over a printed line. The motor coordination component is much more demanding than the visual component.

Kinesthesia: With vision occluded, the child attempts to place his finger on a point at which his finger previously had been placed by the examiner.

Manual Form Perception: The test requires matching the visual counterpart of a geometric form held in the hand.

Finger Identification: The child points to the finger on his hand which was previously touched by the examiner without the child's watching.

Graphesthesia: The child draws a simple design on the back of his hand, attempting to copy the design previously drawn by the examiner at the same place.

Localization of Tactile Stimuli: The child is expected to place his finger on a spot on his hand or arm previously touched by the examiner.

Double Tactile Stimili Perception: Two tactile stimili are applied simultaneously to either or both the cheek and the hand of the child who then identifies where he was touched.

Imitation of Postures: The child is required to assume a series of positions or postures demonstrated by the examiner, a process that requires motor planning.

Crossing the Mid-line of the Body: The child imitates the examiner as the latter points either to one of the examiner's eyes or ears.

Bilateral Motor Coordination: Performing this test requires smoothly executed movements of and interaction between both upper extremities.

Right-left Discrimination: The child is asked to discriminate right from left on himself, on the examiner and relative to the location of an object. The only verbal responses required on the entire SCSIT are on two items of this test.

Standing Balance: Eyes Open: The test measures the ability of the child to balance himself while standing on one foot with his eyes open.

Standing Balance: Eyes Closed: Standing balance on one foot is measured with the eyes closed.

Not all symptoms of poor sensory integration are of such a nature that they can be evaluated adequately through standardized tests. In these cases, clinical observations in structured situations are necessary to assess the child's function in vital areas. Some of the more important of these structured observations are outlined below.

The Primitive Postural Reflexes

Postural mechanisms are among the more important areas of assessment of children with learning disorders. Skilled professional observation in these areas is indispensable. Foremost in this evaluation is the detection of the degree of residual or poorly integrated tonic neck and tonic labyrinthine reflexes. Abnormal presence of these reflexes is indicative, if found in conjunction with certain other signs, of poor sensory integration that is often associated with learning disorders. While normally overtly present in the very young infant, maturational processes should gradually incorporate the reflexes into the sensorimotor system so that they do not interfere with further maturation of postural mechanisms.

The tonic labyrinthine reflex (TLR), a function of the vestibular system, manifests itself as increased flexor tone in the extremities when in the prone position and increased extensor tone when in the supine position. The result of this proprioceptive facilitation is difficulty in raising the head, shoulders, and legs up against the gravitational pull. The TLR pulls the bodily segments toward the earth's gravitational force. The degree to which the child can resist the effects of the TLR and the earth's gravitational pull on the head and extremities indicates the extent to which his nervous system has integrated or is able to inhibit the effects of the reflex.

Accordingly, a test which has provided a fairly objective and quantifiable means of detecting the degree of influence of the TLR in the prone position is performed by observing how well the child can assume a position in which the extensor muscles must hold the head and extremities up in spite of the increased tone in the flexor muscles brought about by the reflex. The child is asked to assume a prone position with arms flexed at the elbows and the elbows

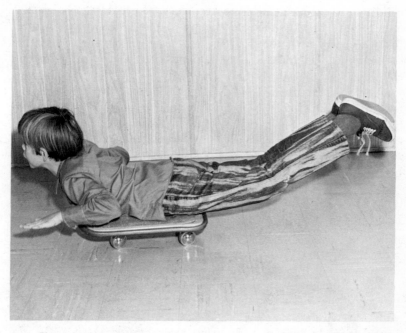

Figure 1.—Normal posture when riding a scooter board at a rapid rate.

placed about four inches from the body. The child is first helped to know what is expected of him by passively placing him in a prone extensor posture with head, shoulders, and arms raised and legs held straight and hyperextended at the hip. The posture is demonstrated with optimum quality in a young school-age child in Figure 1. A position involving somewhat less hyperextension would still be considered within normal limits. The position is sometimes referred to as the "pivot prone" position, for the infant, when assuming this posture as a natural step in the developmental sequence during the first year of postnatal life, tends to rock or pivot on his chest and abdomen. The child being prepared for the test of the TLR should be held in this position only long enough to allow him to get the idea, for the posture is fatiguing and fatigue will reduce the effectiveness of his response on the test proper.

After the child knows what is expected of him, he is asked if he can assume and hold the position for thirty seconds, while counting aloud up to thirty. The child's motivation can be increased by watching the stopwatch that is timing him and counting with the therapist, who times his counting to the number of seconds. The child's counting aloud helps to keep him from holding his breath, only to have to let it out and collapse before reaching the goal of thirty seconds. Assurance that the knees are off the surface can be determined by slipping a piece of paper back and forth under the child's knees during the testing period.

Neuromuscularly and orthopedically normal children ages six and above can usually — but not invariably — hold the position for twenty to thirty seconds, depending upon age, with moderate exertion. A lesser time should be expected of children under six years, not only because of lower endurance and motivation but also because the reflex is probably less well integrated at younger ages.

The quality of the response is as important an index as is the ability to maintain a prone extensor posture for a half minute. The well integrated child can lift both ends of the body simultaneously in a smoothly coordinated manner without an excessive amount of effort or instruction but may release it to rest before the end of the test period because there is inadequate reason, from his point of view, to maintain such a difficult posture. If a knee touches the surface during the thirty-second period he can usually lift it again with a reminder. On the other hand, some children with poor neurological organization, knowing their limitations and the importance of performance, will clumsily assume the position, often as though each limb acted independently of the rest of the body, rather than as a coordinated whole, and will hold the posture for the thirty-second period with great expenditure of effort and will power. This type of response does not deserve a grade of "normal," whereas a posture assumed with better coordination and greater ease and held less than the half minute may be indicative of normalcy in this aspect of sensorimotor integration. Orthopedic abnormalities must, of course, be taken into consideration.

Another neuromuscular condition which definitely influences the child's response to this test and must be taken into consideration is the status of the child's muscle tone in general. The muscles of many children with learning problems are hypotonic and this condition influences the degree to which the increase in muscle tone elicited by any proprioceptive reflex is experienced. If muscle tone is low to begin with, the addition of tone in the flexor muscles brought about by the reflex does not add up to a degree which is difficult for the child's extensor muscles to overcome. Hence a child with low muscle tone but with poorly integrated postural mechanisms often can assume the prone extensor posture but, because of abnormality of function of the mechanisms involved in

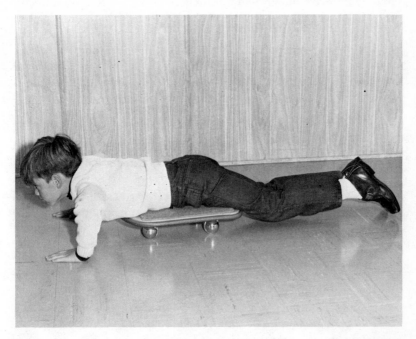

Figure 2.—Posture assumed when the tonic labyrinthine reflex is poorly integrated.

maintained, tonic, or prolonged postural response, he usually cannot hold the position for thirty seconds without a great expenditure of energy.

Using the same neurophysiological principle, the TLR in the supine position can be tested by observing how well the child can hold his head, arms, and legs flexed so that they are off the surface on which his body's weight is resting. The child is asked to "curl up" without giving himself the advantage of clasping his arms around his knees for a mechanical as opposed to muscular hold. In this position, the flexor muscles must exert extra force against the proprioceptive facilitation elicited by the TLR in the extensor muscles in the supine position.

It is always wise to confirm structured clinical procedures with observations made during therapeutic sessions. When riding a scooter board in a prone position, a child with a poorly integrated TLR will tend to flex his hips and knees and fail to hold his head up properly. Figure 1 illustrates the position of a child with normal neuromuscular integration. Figure 2 illustrates the position of a child with poor integration pushing himself on a scooter board. Since a lot of energy must be expended to hold both ends of the body up against the TLR facilitation of the flexor muscles, the child with an immature TLR will soon tire of riding a scooter board in the prone position and will want to sit on it, or even more comfortably, place a cardboard carton on it into which he places himself with a minimum of demands being made upon his postural mechanisms.

Assessment of the asymmetrical tonic neck reflex (TNR) is equally important in the learning disabled child. The essential responses of the reflex, which is elicited by stimulation of receptors in joint capsules of the neck, is facilitation of extensor tone in the muscles of the arm toward which the head is turned (facing) and a relative increase in flexor tone (or decrease in extensor tone) in the opposite arm. A similar response may be seen in the lower extremities but a contralateral response is sometimes seen. In that event, turning the face to the right would facilitate extensor tone in the right arm and left leg. In general, the effect of the TNR on the lower extremities is less than that in the upper extremities and hence does not provide a good basis for objective evaluation.

The change in muscle tone elicited by the TNR can be observed by turning the child's head while he is in the quadruped position. The turning may be performed passively by the examiner. It is appropriate for the child's eyes to be closed. The elbows should be slightly flexed before the head is turned, for a locked elbow will prevent the observation of the slight movements that indicate changes in tone. Flexion of the arm contralateral to the side toward which the jaw has been rotated is considered indicative of the TNR influence, as shown in Figure 3. Resistance to passive turning of the head is believed to be a function of the child's attempt to avoid the disorganizing influence of eliciting the TNR. Figure 4 illustrates a normal response to head turning in a well-integrated child about five years of age.

The influence of the symmetrical TNR on the musculature should also be observed, either when the child is in the quadruped position or during the clinical situation. When the head is held in mid-position (as opposed to rotated) and flexed, the TNR increases flexor tone in the arms. When the head is extended, i.e., dorsiflexed or chin raised, extensor tone is increased in the arms.

Schilder (1964) developed a test which has been widely used in various forms by many clinicians for different purposes. It has been brought to attention especially by the work of Silver and Hagin (1960) and Clements and Peters (1962). One variation of

Figure 3.—Arm position elicited by poorly integrated tonic neck reflex.

Schilder's test, called the arm extension test (AET), has been one of the best indicators of disorder in the neural system concerned with postural and ocular mechanisms. In that test, the child is asked to stand with his feet together, toes even, eyes closed, and arms stretched out before him, parallel to the floor but not touching each other. Fingers are abducted. With forewarning to the child, the therapist slowly rotates the child's head from side to side, observing (1) the freedom with which the head is rotated; (2) any marked change in arm posture, especially difference between the

Figure 4.—Normal reaction to test of degree of integration of the tonic neck reflex.

two arms; (3) any tendency toward disturbing the child's equilibrium; and (4) negative emotional response. Any one of these reactions may be suggestive of immature postural mechanisms, especially the TNR, although the influence of the neck righting reflex acting on the body cannot be overlooked. If the child with an active TNR allows his head to be turned, the tone in the arm changes and may result in a divergence or convergence of the arms or the marked raising of one and the lowering of the other arm. The tendency for both arms to lower is also considered an

Figure 5.—Spinning in a net hammock.

abnormal response due to a lack of adequate tonic or automatic holding response of the neuromuscular system.

If the TNR appreciably influences the legs of the child, and it often does, equilibrium may be upset by eliciting the TNR and the avoidance of such condition may be attempted by the child's resistance to head turning. Sometimes the child will rotate his entire body in an effort to avoid rotation at the neck. This test not infrequently brings about rather severe negative emotional reactions from a child. Age is an important factor in the AET and must be

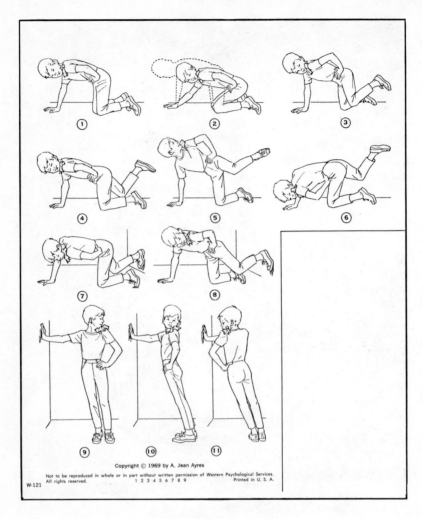

Figure 6.—Positions for inhibition of the tonic neck reflex.

taken into consideration. It must be interpreted cautiously when used with children under six years of age.

It is essential that the evaluator recognize that the TNR and TLR are present in all individuals at all times, but age and the degree and type of central nervous system integration determine the ease with which they are elicited, or stated otherwise, the degree to which they dominate the sensorimotor system. It is the degree to which these reflexes have been integrated into the nervous system that is under evaluation, not whether they are present. Under eight years of age, the younger the child the more easily they can be manifested because the postural mechanisms of the child are less mature.

The treatment situation offers an opportunity to check the results of the formal clinical evaluation. The exercises designed to inhibit the TNR and shown in Figure 6 are an even more sensitive index of the status of the TNR, for the child is asked to balance himself in a difficult position in spite of the reflex's influence. In evaluating the presence of the TNR, it is sometimes helpful to try to detect any difference between effects when the face is turned to one side as opposed to the other. Even when there is a difference, the results cannot always be easily interpreted. As a general rule, the side of the body showing the greater manifestation of the TNR is reflecting the lesser degree of integration in the contralateral part of the brain.

The TNR and TLR are not the only reflexes pertinent to evaluation of sensory integrative function. These and other clinical procedures can be viewed in a film prepared for that purpose (Ayres and Heskett, 1970b). For an extensive coverage, the work of Fiorentino (1963) provides an appropriate guide for the therapists working with cerebral palsy children. The tests described in that reference need adaptation for children with learning disabilities associated with minimal brain dysfunction.

Cocontraction of Antagonistic Muscles

A decrease in the capacity simultaneously to contract muscles antagonistic to each other so as to immobilize one or more joints frequently is evident among children with learning disorders, especially those who also show inadequate maturation of postural mechanisms, including poor standing balance. As with postural mechanisms, there is a relationship of visual space perception. It is reasoned that a similar type of neuromuscular response is involved in both postural reflexes and cocontraction of muscles, possibly through the secondary afferents of the muscle spindle. Certainly postural support in any part of the body is dependent upon the automatic capacity to stabilize a portion of the body, especially while another is involved in phasic contraction that results in movement of short duration as opposed to the prolonged tonic contraction necessary to maintain posture.

Formal test of the ability to cocontract musculature can be made by sitting before a child and asking him to grasp the thumbs of the therapist. Grasp enhances cocontraction. Holding the hands of the child, the therapist instructs him to flex (bend) his elbows slightly and then to hold them in that position, letting them neither flex nor extend as the therapist alternately pushes and pulls on the child's hands. Comments such as the following help the child to grasp the nature of the test: "Don't let me push you; don't let me pull you; make yourself stiff like a statue." It is also helpful for the child to try to push and pull the arm of the therapist while the latter cocontracts the muscles of his upper extremities and trunk to prevent movement. A child of seven or eight years should be able to stabilize his arms and trunk against considerable resistance. Below that age allowance must be made for age. If the child alternately flexes and extends his arms in response to the therapist's pulling and pushing or if the shoulder girdle or trunk "give," the response is indicative of reduced cocontraction ability.

A similar test should be made of the neck musculature, especially since those muscles assume a vital role in the total postural-ocular system, as in eliciting the neck righting reflex and in neural connections with cranial nerves III, IV, and VI, which innervate the extraocular muscles. To test cocontraction of the neck musculature, the therapist places his hand on the top of the child's head and attempts to move the child's head back and forth and from side to side while the child attempts to stabilize the head by contracting all of the neck muscles simultaneously. As with the test of cocontraction of the upper extremities, verbal commands such as "Don't let me move you" and letting the child try to move the examiner's head will help the child to grasp the meaning of the request. The task is one which normally is executed through automatic subcortical mechanisms and is not motor planned as these tests require. Less strength should be expected of the neck musculature, but strength of a phasic muscular response should not be confused with the ability to cocontract muscles. Anterior neck muscles are usually less strong, especially in tonic contraction, than the posterior or lateral musculature; accordingly, less strength should be expected of them.

During the treatment period, the ability to cocontract muscles in a more normal situational demand can be evaluated by asking the child to sit on a scooter board and grasp a plastic hoop or similar frame. As the therapist alternately pushes and pulls the frame, the child is expected to hold his body sufficiently rigid in a static posture so that the force is transferred to the scooter board which moves with the child sitting on it and in the direction in which the therapist is pushing. The child can help stabilize himself by keeping his elbows on his knees. A plastic device is preferred over a wooden frame, for a child with poor cocontraction can easily allow the frame to come up and hit his face when it is pushed by the therapist. It is appropriate to give a child several opportunities to attempt these tasks, for often the desired neuromuscular response is facilitated by the reciprocal application of force by the therapist, resulting in greater success on subsequent tries. While a later success does not necessarily indicate integration as solid as that suggested by early success, it does help the child's morale. It is also appropriate to check cocontraction capacity in the lower extremities.

Muscle Tone

Muscle tone in general reflects the amount of neural impulses reaching the small interfusal motor neurons serving the muscle spindle and which then influence the degree and kind of discharge of the primary and secondary afferents from the spindle, which in turn influences discharge of the alpha motor neurons. The amount of spindle discharge helps determine the amount of proprioceptive input being received by the central nervous system, a matter of constant concern in sensory integrative therapy. It has been hypothesized above that proprioceptive flow from the musculature contributes to organization at the brain stem level and to visual perception and other products of sensory integration.

Muscle tone also reflects certain conditions of the brain stem, especially how the brain stem is processing and directing its afferent input. Similarly, hypotonicity may indicate a paucity of sensory flow upon which normal execution of postural reflexes is dependent. For these reasons the therapist should be familiar with the muscle tone of the child, including variations in tone throughout the body. Sometimes some muscles are hypertonic, and the therapist will want to watch the influence of various activities on that tone, possibly avoiding increasing it.

For reasons explained under discussion of the TLR, hypotonicity increases the difficulty in assessing the degree of integration of primitive postural reflexes into the total sensorimotor system. It may also influence interpretation of postural reactions during the AET. Muscle tone has been found to be positively related to kinesthesia in the learning disabled child, a relationship that occasionally helps in interpreting the score on the SCSIT test of Kinesthesia.

The degree of subluxation at the elbow of the child has been found to be a fair measure for discriminating hypotonicity from normal tone when quantification of the variable on many children is required. Checking joint range at other critical points, especially at the hip and knee, are equally important and may vary significantly from that at the elbow. Analysis of tone in muscles involved in joint rotation is also advised. When marked hypertonicity is found, the principles of neuromuscular therapy must be incorporated with those for sensory integrative therapy.

Extraocular Muscle Control

The extraocular muscles are skeletal muscles, and as such their function should be understood by therapists directing remedial activity. The minimal evaluation should consist of watching the child's eyes as they follow, head stabilized, an object, such as the eraser end of a pencil, as it is moved in different directions and toward and away from the eyes. The basis for judgment of integration of function of the eye muscles is simply the degree to which the eyes follow the visual stimulus in a smooth, fluid, coordinate manner and in coordination with each other. Overshooting or losing the target, difficulty in changing direction, lagging behind, attempting to move the head instead of the eyes, making faces, blinking frequently or squinting, inattentiveness, difficulty in looking away from the visual stimulus or finding it again, inability of the eyes to work together and, especially, difficulty in crossing the mid-line are each suggestive of less than perfect integration.

Failure or difficulty in crossing the mid-line (a theoretical plane which is an extension of the mid-sagittal plane of the face or, in the case of hand function, of the body) with the eyes is of great significance, for it is one of the more reliable signs of the syndrome of disorders in postural and bilateral integration. Sometimes crossing the mid-line with the eyes can be so difficult for a child that to do so brings more discomfort than he should be expected to endure more than once or twice. Eye exercises are fatiguing. Excessive demands on the child should be avoided. All of the suggested methods of evaluating extraocular muscle control are actually designed to be indices of central nervous system integration and its neural relation to the muscle and not the actual status of the muscles themselves.

Assessment of Vestibular System Function

At the time of preparation of this book, one of the major questions centered around methods of assessing the various functions of the vestibular system, a matter made especially difficult by the lack of recognition of all of those functions. Only suggestive behavioral correlates of vestibular processes can be recommended now.

The most commonly employed methods rely on the contribution of the vestibular system to eliciting the equilibrium reactions that help maintain balance, especially on one foot and usually with eyes closed in order to eliminate the effect of the optical righting reflex. The child is either asked to stand on one foot, walk touching the heel of the forward foot to the toe of the foot in place, or to walk on a narrow board.

There is a great variation among learning disabled children as to how they process vestibular sensory input, and it is recommended that the therapist attempt to assay the manner in which each child's brain is handling those stimuli in order to plan an effective intervention program. In some children it appears that an insufficient quantity of vestibular stimuli fail to reach their natural destinations and thus do not contribute adequately to the sensory integrative process. This reduced conductance is believed to be reflected in reduced nystagmus following rapid rotation around the longitudinal axis of the body and/or a lack of a normal amount of feeling dizzy after spinning. Both amplitude and duration of nystagmus may be reduced.

On the other hand, some children seem overwhelmed by vestibular stimuli and are unable to force organization upon them well enough to make an adaptive response. They respond with fear and reluctance to activity which places them in a posturally threatening position.

Integration of Function of the Two Sides of the Body

Although some of the SCSIT tests, especially Bilateral Motor Coordination, Crossing the Mid-line of the Body, and Right-left Discrimination, help in the assessment of the degree to which the two sides of the body integrate their sensorimotor function, this dimension of neural dysfunction is so subtle that it is best evaluated by many formally structured clinical observations. This abnormal behavioral phenomenon is more often a tendency rather than an inability and, furthermore, the tendency can be volitionally overcome. Therefore astute observation without calling to the child's attention the objective of the evaluation is often essential to gaining the necessary information.

One of the procedures for evaluating this behavioral phenomenon is the degree to which a child crosses the mid-line of the body with one hand to engage in activity with the other. Asking the child to use both hands to catch a ball swinging back and forth in front of him requires alternate crossing of the body's mid-line. The child who has a tendency to want to use one hand only and that hand only on the ipsilateral side is probably showing a deficiency in crossing the mid-line of the body.

Two of the SCSIT provide an opportunity to evaluate this dimension as a by-product of the tests. In executing the Motor Accuracy test, a child with this problem often will want to use the hand corresponding to the side of the test sheet on which he is drawing a line as opposed to using one hand only for the entire test for that hand. Similarly, in performing the Space Visualization test, the child is apt to pick up a block on his right side with his right hand and the block on his left side with his left hand.

The Double Circles test of Roach and Kephart (1966) is a good clinical test of the ability to coordinate the motor use of the two upper extremities. In this test a child simultaneously draws two circles on a chalk board, one with each hand.

Choreoathetoid Movements

Some children with learning disabilities evidence a form of motor incoordination that falls more under the category of involuntary motion than clumsiness due to poor motor planning or inadequately matured postural reflexes. The involuntary aspect is not obvious unless the child is placed in a situation causing mild or greater stress in holding a given posture. The test which best elicits these movements is a version of Schilder's arm extension test in which the child is asked to hold his arms outstretched, fingers abducted, eyes closed and to count (or if he cannot, to count with the examiner) aloud up to ten. The counting directs attention away from the upper extremities and allows the involuntary motion to occur. It is most apt to occur in the fingers, but the arms may manifest it as well.

The same abnormal movement may also occur while the child is assuming the prone extensor posture, for that posture places the child under a similar posture stressful in that it is to be maintained for a considerable period of time. This type of incoordination also interferes with the use of the pencil as in the SCSIT Motor Accuracy test, where the line appears jerky as opposed to the wandering line that is characteristic of the apraxic child. Such a line is illustrated in the SCSIT manual.

Chapter 9

General Principles and
Methods of Intervention

The treatment of neuromuscular disorders through understanding the principles of sensory organization in relation to motor impairment is of relatively recent origin. In spite of its youth, its
insights have provided an appropriate stepping-stone to the development of the proposed methods of treating sensory integrative
dysfunction as seen in children with learning disorders. The advent
of neuromuscular therapy marked the beginning of an era of a
type of practical application of the growing body of knowledge in
the field of neurobiology.

Kabat and Knott (1948) were among the first clinicians to
employ proprioceptive input to facilitate motor output, especially
in groups of muscles. Temple Fay (1954, 1955) recognized that
motor patterns of man's evolutionary past still resided below man's
cortex and that these patterns could be employed therapeutically,
especially with the cerebral palsied child, by eliciting them through
sensory stimuli associated with postural responses. Rood (1954; cf.
Ayres, 1963) was the first to recognize the potential therapeutic
role of tactile stimulation in the development of maintenance of
integrated motor action. Her pioneering and creative thinking has
provided the basis for many of the theories expressed in this book.
The Bobaths were perhaps the first to recognize a relationship

between postural mechanisms and intelligence in cerebral palsied children. They developed effective neuromuscular treatment procedures stressing normalizing postural mechanisms (cf. Bobath and Bobath, 1957; Semans, 1967).

The disorders treated by these clinicians would be classified as primarily motor; the disorders to which this book is directed are considered primarily sensory integrative. Sensory and motor functions are so closely associated that an extension of knowledge of treatment of motor functions has contributed much to a theory of treating disordered sensory integration.

Influencing Sensation and Response

The central principle in sensory integrative therapy is providing planned and controlled sensory input with usually — but not invariably — the eliciting of a related adaptive response in order to enhance the organization of brain mechanisms. The plan includes utilization of neurophysiological mechanisms in a manner that reflects some aspect of the developmental sequence. The objective is progressive organization of the brain in a method as similar to the normal developmental process as is possible.

Because the developmental process in the child with learning disorders is not normal, intervention methods are employed. Insofar as it is possible, this treatment employs sensory support and innate brain mechanisms as opposed to cognitive effort or outer coercion to elicit desired behavior. Since the brain stem is the lowest level of the brain and frequently the site of disorder in children with learning disorders, it receives the greatest focus of therapeutic attention.

The intervention program is remedial and therefore is considered treatment; it is not considered exercise. Exercise and treatment differ in that the former is the latter only when it results in an actual enhancement of neural integration. Enhancement of neural integration occurs only when better organization of response occurs. Exercise may increase or optimize other body systems, such as circulatory, but it must affect the central nervous system in a planned manner designed to remediate before it can be considered treatment. The difference is not always evident to the casual observer.

Treatment focuses on sensory input and its continual interaction with motion. Sensory integrative processes have a developmental sequence which courses with the motor development and which generally is not considered in exercise. Therapy does not ask the child for a complicated motor plan or execution unless simpler and ontogenetically earlier ones have been mastered as well as possible. Treatment seeks responses that reflect better sensory integration and more normal patterns of sensory input as opposed to improved motor skill for the sake of skill itself. The motor response carries meaning in that it provokes sensory input, helps organize it, and provides an overt manifestation of neural integration.

Tactile Stimulation

Previous chapters demonstrated the significant role of tactile stimuli in neural organization of lower animals. It is proposed that tactile stimuli assume an important role in the total sensory integration of a child, although that role is probably not exactly the same as that demonstrated in lower animals. Clinical observation leads to the hypothesis that tactile stimulation can contribute to generalized neurological integration and to enhanced perception in other sensory modalities. The pervasive influence is difficult to recognize and hence easily overlooked. The tactile system also yields specific influence, such as that acting to facilitate a given muscle.

Tactile stimuli provide a primal source of input to the reticular formation, one of the oldest and most powerful central integrating systems. Through the reticular system and perhaps others, a child can be "energized" or his hyperexcitability reduced. Its descending influences act upon muscle tone and the probability of muscle contraction. Although the role of tactile stimuli in implementing the locomotor patterns of the brain stem is not clear, the totality with which the sensorimotor system tends to operate would tend to favor some relationship.

Because of the primal, pervasive, and preparatory influence of tactile input, the therapeutic session is often initiated with tactile stimulation. Stimuli may be elicited by rubbing the skin of the child with a dry washcloth or other type of cloth or by brushing the skin with any kind of brush that is preferred by the child. Silk or velvet cloths or the hand of the therapist or the child himself are often the most acceptable media to a nervous system that interprets tactile stimuli as uncomfortable. Touching oneself is less threatening than being touched by another person. Opportunity to see where the stimuli are being applied also lessens interpretation of stimuli as noxious. Rubbing before application of tactile stimulation often appears to reduce tactile defensiveness. Some sensitive nervous systems prefer the very light, rapid stimulation by a camel's-hair brush mounted on a battery-driven rotating shaft, a procedure developed by Rood (cf. Stockmeyer, 1967).

Fortunately for the therapist, who must rely on the child's response for information as to the general neurological effect of the stimulation, most children have definite ideas about what constitutes the appropriate type, duration, and frequency of tactile stimulation. The child's response is considered the best indication of how his nervous system is interpreting the stimuli. As a general rule, that which is enjoyable is considered to be integrating. Occasionally, but rarely, it seems best for a therapist to impose tactile stimuli at first to help the child get over the initial defensive stage. This course of action should be taken only when other approaches to reduce tactile defensiveness have failed. Unless the therapist has definite ideas to the contrary, it is wise to respect the child's opinion, which is generally based on what he is experiencing in his nervous system. His opinion can also be influenced by the type of stimuli his friends are receiving, the novelty of the situation, and, as the child becomes older, the attitude of others, especially adults, to the therapeutic procedure.

The skin surface to be brushed can be determined either by practical considerations such as availability (back, arms, face, legs, and hands) or by the child's choice. Usually the back of the hands and forearms provide the least defensive areas for stimulation. Those areas receive much tactile stimulation through contacts made in normal interaction with the environment and that contact helps to maintain a more normal balance of tactile functions there. The ventral surface of the body, the face, and the feet are often less accepting of stimulation, although there have been some very definite exceptions to the rule and it is entirely appropriate to check a child's response in these areas. A child can be offered the brush or cloth and asked if he would like to brush his feet, tummy, or face. Stimulation around the mouth is especially recommended because of its primal nature and its connections with language.

If a child is reluctant to accept being brushed, he may be tactually defensive. In cases of extreme tactile defensiveness, it is suggested that the child's nervous system be normalized through the proprioceptive system first or that tactile stimuli be given by contact of the body's surface against rugs and other objects during activity or by sleeping on a terry cloth beach towel at night. Tactile stimuli acceptable one day may be unacceptable another day, for interpretation of a stimulus is to a certain extent dependent upon the status of the nervous system into which the stimuli enter and that status may change from moment to moment.

The length of time a barrage of tactile stimuli will exert a major influence on the nervous system is estimated roughly at one-half hour, but the probability of some lesser but prolonged effect is very great and should be considered. Because of this prolonged effect and because of the primacy of the tactile system and its effect on other senses, it is appropriate to administer the tactile stimuli before activity or educational experience.

The brain of an underactive child can be brought closer to a normal state of central excitation through tactile stimulation, especially of the face, hands, and feet. Some children of this type seem to crave tactile stimulation as though it were needed for something analogous to "nourishment" of the brain. Being powerful stimuli, tactile stimuli can also be disorganizing. Whether the stimulation will be organizing or disorganizing should be judged by the child's reaction, which is usually fairly overt. If the child likes the stimulation, seeks it, feels comfortable following it, and is not hyperexcited by it, it probably had an organizing effect. However, if the stimuli overactivate the reticular arousal system, difficulty in sleeping and attending may result. An undesired arousal reaction should not be interpreted as an indication that the child is not in need of tactile stimulation but that he cannot organize those stimuli adequately and that alternate methods of promoting sensory integration should be utilized for a while. It is helpful to counterbalance the reticular arousal with some slow vestibular stimuli which inhibit that system.

In the course of treatment over several months, many children reach a point where they no longer want tactile stimulation, but after a few weeks without it, they ask for it again periodically. The consistency with which this response has been observed suggests that the brain's need had been filled temporarily, but without the therapeutically administered extra stimuli, the need slowly returned.

Tactile stimuli provide a type of afferent support that is needed for muscle contraction. They facilitate muscle contraction acting through the nuclei of the descending reticular activating system and possibly through other routes. In addition to providing a generalized effect on the neuromuscular system, tactile stimuli have a specialized facilitatory effect on the muscles underlying the skin stimulated, a factor which must be taken into consideration where abnormal muscle tone is present.

Some thought should be given to whether the stimuli facilitate phasic (short, temporary) or tonic (prolonged) contraction in a muscle, for some children demonstrate too much tonic or too much phasic muscle contraction and some demonstrate too little. The effect of the tactile stimuli on phasic or tonic muscle contraction is mediated through the intrafusal fiber or gamma efferent neuron acting on the muscle spindle. It is possible that light tactile sensation may facilitate phasic contraction in muscles directly under the skin stimulated. It may be necessary to counterbalance this influence by vestibular stimulation which tends to facilitate a tonic response in the muscles, if that is consistent with the demands being made on the organism during the vestibular stimulation. However, both touch pressure and slow vestibular stimuli can be inhibitory to muscle tone by reducing the general level of reticular excitation.

If a child is generally hypotonic, considerable amounts of excitatory tactile and vestibular stimuli are in order and few precautions are necessary. If a child has some hypertonic muscles, some specific techniques may be necessary to avoid muscle imbalance, such as pressure to the muscle insertion to inhibit it or tactile facilitation of the antagonistic muscle to inhibit the agonist through reciprocal innervation, in the manner developed by Rood (1954).

Tactile stimuli also can have a facilitatory effect on the pyramidal tract, which is responsible for skeletal motion of the more skilled or planned type, especially of the distal portion of the extremities. This influence, along with that exerted upon the intrafusal fiber to the muscle spindle, are some of the ways by which tactile stimulation assists the apraxic child in mastering the ability to motor plan.

Since certain types of impulses elicited by stimulation of the tactile receptors reach the cortex, it is reasonable to attempt cortical facilitation through tactile stimulation. High- speed, low-threshold neurons carry discriminative information to the contralateral cortex. Stimulation of receptors in the right hand, which has many receptors for this purpose, sends a barrage of impulses to somatic area I of the left hemisphere. Optimal function of the language center and the visual cortex of the left hemisphere are dependent upon adequate connection with the somatic area I of that hemisphere.

Activation of the smaller, higher-threshold, non-dorsal column neurons through prolonged and rapid tactile stimulation will directly activate somatic area II in both hemispheres as well as indirectly affect the brain in a more diffuse manner through the reticular activating system.

Tactile stimulation as a therapeutic process may appear to the naive observer to be a very simple procedure, unrelated to the problems at hand. When this occurs, it is helpful to recall the study (Melzack and associates, 1969) demonstrating that rubbing a cat's paw under certain conditions influenced electrical discharge in the visual, somatic, and auditory system and the research indicating that tactile stimuli exert influence upon other sensory modalities through convergent neurons. Perhaps it is most important to remember the philosophy of Herrick (1956), who stated, "The cerebral cortex never works independently of the more primitive structures from which it was derived."

Vestibular Stimulation

Vestibular stimulation is one of the most powerful tools available for therapeutic use in the remediation of sensory integrative dysfunction. It, along with tactile stimulation, is introduced early because of their subserving role to other types of sensory integration. Normalization of vestibular mechanisms mediating postural reactions should also be introduced early because of the central role of postural responses. These responses provide a background for more skilled and planned activity. Furthermore, the influence of gravity is always present. It is appropriate to recognize it early and to use it advantageously.

Passive (activated by external force instead of by voluntary muscle effort) vestibular stimulation is most effectively given by swinging or spinning a child while he is lying or seated in a net hammock, both ends of which are suspended from a common overhead point, as shown in Figure 5. The child who is particularly sensitive to vestibular stimulation or threatened by it should engage in the activity actively as opposed to passively by placing his hands on the floor and pushing to gently move himself or by pulling on a rope attached to a distant point in front of him to swing himself. The active involvement develops the adaptive responses which in turn organize the sensory stimuli.

Many children give the impression that vestibular input does not reach its final destination in either sufficient quantity or with normal processing. These children are apt to show no or diminished nystagmus and a tendency not to become dizzy easily. They usually show a very positive emotional response to and craving for spinning in the net. This need seems best fulfilled by the child's sitting in the net in an upright fetal position while the therapist winds him up and lets him unwind. The gradual appearance of nystagmus and dizziness from vestibular stimulation is assumed to be an indication that dormant pathways are beginning to be used and may then be available for other sensory integrative processes.

Rapid spinning, especially without the requisite of an adaptive response, can be excitatory and also disorganizing because of its powerful effect and hence should be used only with careful attention to the response of the child. As with all other activities, the therapist is advised to try the process himself to experience the results of the stimulation. Slow, rhythmical, and hence usually inhibitory vestibular stimulation can be achieved by letting a child lie or sit in the net hammock and swinging him passively back and forth or in an orbit, making about twenty-five or thirty revolutions a minute. Slow vestibular stimulation can also be given passively to a child lying prone on a large (thirty-six-inch diameter) therapy ball. The child lies passively on the ball while the therapist rolls him slowly back and forth. It is reasoned that the inhibition occurs in part through vestibular stimuli activating the cerebellum which, in turn, inhibits the brain stem, especially the reticular formation. It is also probable that brain stem centers governing vital functions such as respiration may be inhibited. A few undocumented instances of over-inhibition through such procedures have been reported. This type of response illustrates the necessity for careful observation of a child's response to stimuli, especially of a vestibular type.

If vestibular stimulation is found to be either too excitatory or too inhibitory, normalcy of response can be encouraged by asking the child to evince an adaptive response, such as putting his hands out to touch the floor as he is rolled back and forth on the large ball. Organizing a response tends to balance the excitatory and inhibitory components of brain function.

If a child's brain appears to have been insufficiently responsive to vestibular stimuli during his life, therapy probably should provide a bombardment of stimulation through the many different vestibular receptors. In providing stimulation through the vestibular apparatus, it is helpful to remember that rotary movement and linear acceleration or deceleration will tend to stimulate different receptors. Spinning in a net produces a different type of sensory input from swinging back and forth in it. Furthermore, spinning upside down, lying prone, supine, or on one's side will activate different portions of the canals and the otoliths to different degrees. Walsh (1960) found that human beings with loss of use of some of the vestibular apparatus were more sensitive to motion when in the supine position than when lying on the side where damage to the vestibular apparatus had occurred. Prone lying was not tested. Walsh concluded that greater sensitivity to horizontal motion was a function of the position of the otoliths. The position which most effectively stimulates the otoliths is upside down, a position not easily obtained or maintained in therapeutic practice. The horizontal position, especially prone, is easily and frequently used. This position is believed to be more effective for activating the otoliths than the upright position. It is also optimal for horizontal semicircular canal stimulation. The pertinence of these data for therapy is that many different head positions and motions are required for stimulation of all possible vestibular receptors. The horizontal position may be especially important.

During the evolutionary period when the brain stem and some of the higher brain structures were undergoing and completing their major development, the quadruped posture was predominant and determined the position of the gravity receptors and thereby the sensory flow into the brain elicited by the earth's gravitational force. It was seen above that the total brain stem sensory input related to the visual-locomotor process became so intimately connected that it functioned essentially as a unit. Sensations elicited by gravity contributed to that total sensorimotor pattern. There is significance to the pattern or constellation of multisensory input beyond that of input from individual sensory modalities. If the child's head is in a position that approximates that of the quadruped, the sensory flow from the gravity receptors more closely approaches that which would be expected to integrate optimally with other sensations at the brain stem level. The idea is purely speculative but is consistent with clinical experience and contributes to the rationale underlying frequent use of activities requiring the prone position, such as those involving the scooter board.

Children with learning disorders vary greatly in their tolerance to vestibular stimulation. Some are afraid and their fear should be highly respected. The anxiety is interpreted to mean that they experience the power of the gravitational force as being overwhelming. Furthermore, they are realistic, for they cannot integrate the sensory input and respond to it in an adaptive manner. They are at the mercy of gravity, and gravity makes no allowance for handicapped children. It is appropriate for posturally insecure children to be fearful; the fear has survival value. To crawl into a barrel lying on its side is to surrender oneself to an unstable world that knocks one about at its will. A high place *is* dangerous if there is a strong probability of falling without the ability to land on one's feet.

Children with this type of reaction need a slow, safe, non-threatening approach to the introduction and mastery of vestibular stimulation. Stimulation is introduced by the child's sitting securely in a net, hanging close to the floor and being encouraged to push the feet against the floor to begin swinging gently. The objective is to simultaneously increase the brain's capacity to integrate vestibular stimuli by developing the motor responses that aid integration and to gradually increase self-induced vestibular stimulation. As tolerance and the capacity to organize increase, the child can utilize the scooter board or the net hammock for more intense stimulation.

Children who demonstrate diminished response to vestibular stimuli generally should start treatment with as much rapid spinning as they desire and as the brain can tolerate. Responses should be watched carefully in order to interpret the probable manner in which the child's brain is processing the input. The following case report illustrates a high threshold to vestibular stimuli somewhere in its neural course and a positive response to massive bombardment of the brain by vestibular stimuli.

A nine-year-old girl with schizoid-like features, no observable nystagmus, above average verbal fluency, but reading ability at the first grade level was brought into a room in which there were three or four pieces of equipment, one of which was a toy with a rotating disk on which children were expected to sit and through bodily movement rotate themselves, a task requiring considerable coordination. The child, without direction, immediately went to the toy, lay on it prone, and asked to be spun. The therapist obliged, and even her maximal efforts did not satisfy the child, who kept calling, "Faster, faster!" When the therapist's fatigue required that she stop spinning the child, the child continued to spin herself until she had spun about twenty minutes. When she stood up she was surprised to find herself a little dizzy, but within a minute she was walking on tin can stilts. No nystagmus could be seen after the spinning. At each subsequent opportunity, the child repeated the same procedure, including the walking on stilts. Her tolerance to the stimuli gradually diminished and she became disappointed at becoming dizzy sooner, although the therapist saw this as a gradual normalizing of the brain's receptivity to the stimulation, the objective of the massive amounts of stimulation.

If the theory is correct, the vestibular input resulting from rapid spinning influences the body in the following ways. Synapses which normally are made as a result of vestibular input and are not being made in the child with dysfunction are activated. Muscle tone is enhanced and the increased facilitatory effect on the intrafusal fiber to the muscle spindle prepares the nervous system for easier activation of the alpha motor neuron supply in the skeletal muscles in subsequent activity. Muscle tone contributes directly and indirectly to the development of the body scheme. The extraocular muscles are skeletal muscles and are facilitated especially through the connections of the vestibular nuclei with cranial nerve nuclei III, IV, and VI over the medial longitudinal fasciculus. Quantities of impulses are arriving at all convergent neurons which respond to vestibular stimulation. These lie especially in the brain stem, thalamus, basal ganglia, and cortex. Of special interest is the probability that most of the visual cortex is at least potentially anatomically able to receive stimulation. The direct effect on the auditory system is less clear, but the possibility for influence should not be ignored. The reticular arousal system is in receipt of input which can be used for "energizing" the cortex as well as for acting upon convergent neurons. The influence of these vestibular messages on the limbic system is still a guess, with a hypothesis that the effect is highly significant. Perhaps most important, the vestibular input may be providing a unifying and coordinating role in relation to all other sensory input.

Other Proprioceptive Stimuli

There is less certainty about the need for increasing sensations arising from the neuromuscular and skeletal systems of children with learning disorders than there is for vestibular and tactile stimuli. It is assumed that the locomotor patterns in the brain stem in man are closely related to the visual organization that takes place there and that those locomotor patterns are in some way connected with appropriate sensory input from the locomotor system. If this is the case, proprioceptive input from the musculoskeletal system contributes through this route to the development of the environmental scheme, as explained in a later chapter.

Muscle contraction, especially against resistance, provides one of the major means by which proprioceptive input to the central nervous system is enhanced, and the major source of resistance is the force of gravity acting on a segment of the body. For example, when a child lies on a scooter board, either prone or supine, the weight of the head is considerable and necessitates strong contraction of the neck muscles. When the child is lying prone, posterior trunk, hip, and shoulder girdle muscles must contract to hold the extremities up off the floor. Motor activity which involves a prolonged contraction of extensor muscles provides a different afferent flow to the nervous system than one which requires contraction of the flexors (see R. M. Eccles and Lundberg, 1959). Extensor contraction is related phylogenetically to the maintenance of posture and ambulation, while flexor contraction provides the necessary withdrawal to a nociceptive stimulus. In the balanced bipedal position only a little prolonged contraction of extensor muscles is required to maintain the upright posture, which relies strongly on balancing the body around the center of gravity.

It is reasoned that the contraction of the muscles used in riding a scooter board prone, most of which are extensor muscles designed for prolonged contraction to support the body's weight and maintain the background posture, is particularly important in providing the pattern of sensory input that is important to brain stem integration. Scooters are designed small enough so that trunk muscle contraction is required for this purpose. Maintained or static contraction provides a different type of sensory input from quick, phasic action, the former arriving primarily over the secondary afferents from the muscle spindle and the latter over the primary afferents. Secondary afferents have higher thresholds and are best activated by prolonged muscle contraction.

There is considerable afferent flow from the muscle spindle to the cerebellum. Observation of the quieting and integrating effect of activity involving prolonged postural muscle contraction against gravity has led to speculation that the effect may lie through the cerebellum and its inhibitory influence on the reticular activating system as well as through the integration brought directly by enhancing organization through the brain stem locomotor patterns.

Kinesthesis, the conscious sense of joint movement or position, is an important source of sensory feedback arising from movement. These joint receptors have a higher threshold than some other proprioceptors and the method of increasing the probability of their discharge is still highly conjectural. It is thought that joint compression or approximation and traction may provide extra kinesthetic stimulation. Traction can be given by attaching weights to ankles and wrists. While providing a novel situation which holds the interest for a short period, it also adds resistance to muscle contraction. Joint approximation is encouraged through cocontraction of antagonistic muscles. Rapid alternating resistance to antagonistic muscles is believed to foster cocontraction. For the trunk, neck, and upper extremities, an excellent activity utilizes a strip of inner tube fastened securely at waist height (when seated) at opposite sides of an activity area. One or two children, sitting or kneeling on scooter boards, push and pull alternately on the strip, moving the scooter board back and forth. As with all activities, therapists are advised to try this one to experience its demands. It is one of the more acceptable and desirable ways of eliciting strong contraction of the neck flexors which are so frequently weak.

Rood has introduced the idea of pressure to the bony origin or insertion of a muscle to release or inhibit the muscle. While this type of input does not lend itself well to inclusion in activity, it can be employed manually prior to an activity to normalize muscle tone and thereby enable a more normal pattern of muscle response during implementation of an activity. Effective use of sensory input from bone receptors requires ability to detect hypertonic muscles and accurate knowledge of muscle origin and insertion. The effect of the sensory input seems to be quite temporary, lasting only a few minutes, as opposed to that input which has a prolonged effect through the reticular system.

Another form of sensory input, vibration, is available for inclusion in the intervention program. Its use is recommended only after the therapist is sufficiently familiar with the child's nervous system to be able to detect slight variations in response due to therapeutically introduced sensory input. Vibration is usually considered a discriminatory sense that travels in the dorsal columns, but it has been found to be transmitted also through the afferent tracts of the lateral columns of the spinal cords of the cat (Andersson, 1962). Clinical experience suggests that vibration elicits a protective or a relaxing response, depending upon the existing state of the organism. The criterion in determining its use, as well as the use of any other sensory input, is the apparent effect on the child. If he does not like it, the sensation probably is not integrating; if he finds it comfortable, it probably is integrating. Vibration is more apt to be inhibitory when applied over a muscle not contracting and excitatory to muscles under contraction. Thus it can be used to help a child contract specific muscles. It has been used effectively at the end of the treatment period to lower the central excitatory state. The child's lying down to receive the vibration on back and neck helps restore homeostasis of neural excitation.

The Adaptive Response

In the average child perceptual processes do not develop in isolation but in association with and probably because of the child's interaction with the environment, responding to it adaptively. Professional opinion throughout the world generally accepts this proposition and supports it with research (Zaporozhets, 1965; Papoušek, 1965; Riesen, 1961b; Fair, 1965).

An adaptive response is not an either/or reaction. Like most behavior, there is a continuum of degree of complexity, quality, and effectiveness of responses. The ability to evaluate the nature of an adaptive response contributes immensely to the therapist's ability for concurrent judgment of treatment effectiveness, for the degree of adaptiveness of response is the major subjective indication of degree of sensory integration. Treatment consists of making it possible for a child to evince a response which is more adaptive, i.e., more effective, than that which he has been able to demonstrate previously. Not all therapy requires an adaptive response, however. Tactile and general vestibular stimulation, such as that given in a suspended net hammock, are therapeutic because of their sensory input. No adaptive response is expected or required for their utilization.

Most adaptive responses to sensory input are movements that are related to the sensation. It is the action or reaction of the organism to the environment acting upon the organism. The adaptiveness of the system may vary in efficiency, specificity, complexity, accuracy, appropriateness, and initiative. As the phyletic scale is ascended, these qualities are seen to a more advanced degree. Similarly, the greater the sensory integrative dysfunction in a child, the poorer the quality of these dimensions.

A reflex is an adaptive response of a simple type. Standing is an adaptive response to the earth's gravitational force, but on the part of the child with learning disabilities, it hardly represents an advanced one. Simply repeating an already well-learned task, such as putting a puzzle together or riding a bicycle, would be considered an adaptive response but not therapy because the response does not represent one that cannot already be evinced fairly easily. But the same child, lying prone on the large therapy ball and holding the hands of the therapist, might demonstrate some equilibrium reactions that assist in maintaining his position on the ball (and hence are adaptive) yet represent responses which are not yet well developed in him and are therefore considered therapy.

Adaptive responses are purposeful, goal-directed actions. If the goal of the action was not reasonably well reached, the response was not adaptive, for adaptiveness implies a certain mastery over the environment, not a mastery of the environment over the person. The latter is the case when a child responds to a treatment or classroom situation by "acting up," by aimless activity, or by distractibility. Unable to "master" the environment with an adaptive response to it, the child's goal changes to either destruction of the environment or reaction to a multitude of stimuli as though compelled to do so.

An adaptive response adds functional meaning to motion. Through it the child learns what kind of motor action brings what kind of changes in the environment, and the sense of mastery is not only satisfying in itself but serves as motivation for further efforts.

Establishing of a memory trace or the transfer of a memory

trace from one hemisphere to the other is probably assisted by adaptive responses. Using spreading depression to restrict function to one hemisphere at a time, I. S. Russell and Ochs (1961) established that cats did not spontaneously transfer an engram from one hemisphere to the other just because the communicating fibers were intact. If the second hemisphere was given the opportunity to make a single response at the same time that the trained hemisphere did, transfer of the engram, which was inferred from learning a conditioning task, occurred in one trial. If learning of a simple task in children is anywhere near that dependent upon an active response, responses are central to the elementary learning process.

The effectiveness of the response is dependent upon the accuracy of the sensory feedback from the response. Precisely interpreted somatosensory and vestibular feedback enables learning the adaptive response. Watching a child with inadequate motor planning can provide the clinician with some insight into the dependency of adaptive responses upon spatially and temporally precise feedback. Apraxia, or a deficit in motor planning ability, is considered to be, in part, a function of inadequate somatosensory perception. Stated otherwise, the effectiveness of a child's action upon the environment will reflect accuracy of sensory input. So in the therapeutic situation, planning an environment that will elicit a motor response requires consideration of whether the child can interpret the stimuli from the situation sufficiently well to respond successfully. For example, a child of ten years of age with very poor proprioception was unable to sit on a stool shaped like a T because he could not interpret the impulses from his body well enough to know whether he was balanced on the stool. Before the demand for sitting on a T-stool was made upon him, more elementary activities which help develop proprioception should have been mastered.

Organizing and evincing an adaptive response which is more mature and complex than any emitted before requires effort — the kind of effort that a child gladly summons when he is emotionally involved in the task and believes he can cope with it. The child who becomes involved in purposeful activity and is willing to put forth effort to make a response of a greater complexity of adaptivity is the child who usually responds well to treatment. The importance of this type of emotional involvement is so great that often other treatment principles, such as following the developmental sequence of the therapist's carefully prepared treatment plan, should be temporarily forgotten. As long as the child is pursuing an activity and making responses that represent a level of accuracy and complexity appropriate to his degree of sensory integration, it is often best to let him guide his own activity. One cannot force a child to evince an adaptive response, one can only provide the environment which it is hoped will elicit it. The opportunity to explore may be more motivating to a child than that which the therapist had planned for the treatment period. Furthermore, observation of an exploring child helps detect areas of need and deficiency in sensory integration as well as areas in which the child may be beginning to be able to respond successfully. Occasionally a child seems to know more about the nature of his dysfunction and what to do about it than the therapist does, but the child generally cannot verbalize the problem or prepare the remedial situation. Preparation of the remedial situation so that it enables the child to explore and fulfill his needs is one of the most demanding tasks of the therapist.

The "urge to live" referred to with emphasis by Sherrington (1955) should be tapped, for it is the greatest source of the motivation that leads to adaptive responses and without it the therapist is relatively helpless. Man's brain evolved as a response structure. Promoting organization of the brain requires that the brain organize responses. It is for this reason that "exercise" that simply involves moving the arms, legs, or body according to a set routine is not therapy unless it has some particular remedial value. It may help the child's general physiological state and be of value in other ways, but it is not the most effective means of enhancement of neural integration. Organizing adaptive responses of increasing complexity is essential to the therapeutic process. For the same reason, passive movement of different segments of the body by the therapist holds a lesser place in the treatment of sensory integrative dysfunction in children with learning disabilities, although such procedures are appropriate when they prepare the child to make more effective responses.

The case against repeating already learned sensorimotor behavior must not be made too strongly, for repetition is important for the firm establishment of the neural connections which are believed to be formed during therapy. It is believed that new anatomical pathways are not developed but already existing neuronal connections which are lying more or less dormant are used with greater ease and frequency and consequently become more important in directing behavior. Therapy is believed to use potentially existing synapses and patterns of synapses or mechanisms, although the possibility of establishing new synapses, especially in the young child, is not overlooked. This explanation is consistent with pertinent research reported by Brazier and associates (1961).

Eccles (1961) has expressed the situation succinctly. Frequency of synaptic use leads to "an enduring enhancement of synaptic function" and "prolonged disuse has a deleterious effect on the potency of synapses."

It has been observed that a repeated bombardment of the nervous system by certain kinds of sensory stimuli to which some response must be made is necessary to maintain gains. A nervous system which has been organized in one manner for a number of years will have a tendency to return to that organization. While the optimum frequency of treatment is not set with certainty at this time and will undoubtedly decrease as proficiency increases, it is believed that daily treatment is far more effective than weekly if enduring changes in organization are expected. At this time at least five or six months of treatment of the school age child are required to consolidate gains made; however, that length of time will probably be reduced as increased knowledge of brain function increases efficiency of treatment.

The younger the child the more effective sensory integrative therapy can be expected to be, for the young brain is more plastic and in the process of forming neural connections. Although the brain is somewhat modifiable at all ages, its functional capacity is fairly well developed by age ten and the period of greatest sensory integrative development is completed several years earlier. Sensory integrative therapy should precede academic work ontogenetically.

Precautions

The most obvious danger in providing therapy for sensory integrative dysfunction arises from the large amount of movement engaged in by children unskilled at movement, inadequate at interpreting the environment, and lacking in judgment as to what might be dangerous to their physical welfare. The therapist copes with this situation by reducing the danger as far as possible with the following procedures: removing equipment not immediately needed so that the child will not run into it, using wood and plastic instead of metal equipment, placing mats under children where they might fall, keeping all hanging equipment as close to the floor as possible, and keeping equipment in a good state of repair. In spite of precautions, a certain amount of risk is necessary to achieve therapeutic goals, for unless a child attempts that which is difficult for him, his sensory integration will not mature. Some bumps and bruises from unsuccessful efforts are inevitable.

Somewhat less evident but just as important is the need for

precaution in increasing muscle tone in children who already have too much tone in some but not in other muscles. Handling this situation requires using neuromuscular procedures which lie beyond the scope of this book (cf. Stockmeyer, 1967). Other modifications in treatment procedures might be necessary for individuals younger or older than the young, school age child.

One of the most important hazards in employing sensory integrative therapy and one which can easily be overlooked by the unsophisticated is sensory overload. If the amount of sensory bombardment is so great that the child is unable to respond successfully his behavior may break down and the integrative effects of sensory stimuli will be attenuated, to say the least. Sensory stimuli are powerful media with potential for disorganizing as well as organizing the brain. The signs of sensory overload are hyperexcitement that is not calmed within a half hour after termination of treatment, a destructive approach to the enviroment, or a withdrawal from it.

A study by Riesen (1961a) is germane to this subject. He reported "violent emotional storms" in cats and subhuman primates when exposed to normal quantities (for a normally reared animal) of stimuli after sensory deprivation. The deprived animals sometimes responded to increased stimulation with fear and hyperexcitability. While a child with sensory integrative disorder has not usually been subjected to sensory deprivation in the usual sense of the term, his brain has not processed sensory stimuli in the same manner as most children. This may result in a type of functional deprivation, leaving the child with behavior which is not unlike that described of animals subjected to sensory deprivation.

Movement, especially the rapid acceleration that activates the vestibular system, is generally excitatory. When the excitement that comes from vestibular arousal of the ascending reticular system is added to the excitement arising from emotional reaction to the activity, a labile nervous system may become so excited that it can no longer handle the immediate situation and behavioral controls begin to break down. At that point, therapy should be redirected to reduce the central excitatory state. If behavior cannot be brought to an acceptable level within a few minutes after termination of the treatment period, the last part of the therapeutic session should be devoted to inhibitory stimulation such as, for example, slow vestibular stimulation either in an orbiting net or on a large therapy ball, through touch pressure, or through vibration to a relaxed segment of the body. The child's lying down to receive the stimuli also helps reduce his excitatory state. One method of helping a hyperexcitable child control his behavior is keeping a minimum of equipment in a limited therapeutic area. When the situation becomes overpowering to the child, most of the remaining equipment is removed, reducing the potential for maintaining sensory input. Large open spaces may serve some therapeutic purposes well, but they also invite activity, especially running in a disinhibited child. Talking in a whisper also helps calm some children.

Sensory overload, which is generally to be avoided, should not be confused with a simple increase in excitement that usually and probably should accompany a successful therapeutic experience. It is appropriate for adults who come in contact with the child excited for this reason to use a little tolerance and acceptance of his behavior following therapy, remembering that the developmental level at which the child is organizing himself is not consistent with the quiet behavior considered appropriate at a conventional school. The child who rarely becomes excited rarely makes much progress. As his nervous system becomes more integrated, his emotions will probably be less labile and his behavior more "acceptable." Often a hyperexcitable child will appear to become temporarily excited by therapy, but the cumulative effect will be a gradual inhibition as the brain's organization approaches normalcy.

The possibility of sensory overload precipitating a seizure in seizure prone children should not be overlooked, although there are only suggestive and no conclusive data at this time indicating such a probability. In the study by Riesen (1961a), animals deprived of sensory stimuli then exposed to them showed increased susceptibility to convulsive disorders. In considering the possibility of seizures, both the seizure threshold of the child and the arousal nature of the sensory input should be considered. All brains have a seizure threshold, but in the average brain it is so high that usual life experiences do not exceed it. Children with dysfunction may have lowered thresholds and the possibility of exceeding those thresholds deserves watching, particularly when there are other potential precipitating causes, such as stress in the life of the child.

Some seizures are precipitated by massive discharge toward the cortex from the reticular activating system. It would follow, then, that the therapeutic procedures directed toward activating that system might hold the greatest probability for producing a seizure. Light tactile and vestibular stimuli have highly excitatory effects on the reticular arousal system and hence, of the senses employed, are most apt to produce conditions favoring a seizure. Auditory stimuli may also contribute toward passing the seizure threshold. If a seizure should occur which is thought to be related to therapy, the degree of the child's organization after recovery from the seizure should be evaluated before the seizure is considered a negative event.

Most individuals have experienced some of the autonomic nervous system results from vestibular stimulation and can watch for them in children. If flushing, blanching of the face, unusual perspiring, nausea, or yawning occur in a child during treatment, activity should be stopped, for such symptoms may mean that vestibular stimuli have affected the autonomic nervous system to the extent that considerable discomfort may result. If the effect of sensory stimuli terminated at the end of the treatment period, long-range goals would not be met, but sometimes the effect of vestibular stimulation lasts so long that sensory overload during therapy seems probable. If children experience movement at night, especially after going to bed, or report nightmares that can be interpreted as involving reactions to vestibular stimulation, it is suggested that the amount of therapeutically induced stimulation be reduced, at least temporarily.

Perhaps the greatest potential harm arising from sensory integrative therapy is over-inhibition of the brain stem. Reports of this occurrence are rare but deserving of every clinician's awareness. In one case a child appeared to become unconscious and in another case a child became cyanotic. Both cases appear to represent depression of vital functions through inhibitory vestibular stimuli. The influence could be through the inhibitory cerebellar influence on the brain stem. If such a reaction should occur, a more normal excitatory state can be achieved through excitatory stimuli such as light touch stimuli to feet and face or ice to hands.

Some children with perceptual-motor impairment are keenly aware of and are sensitive about their limitations. For these children even activity which seems simple to the therapists may be so threatening as to elicit destructive reactions. When a child becomes destructive of therapeutic equipment or in a therapeutic situation, the therapist should consider the possibility that the task is threatening to the child regardless of whether it is within his potential capacity. In such an instance, employing equipment that is least demanding, such as swinging in a net, is recommended.

In addition to the immediate and somewhat temporary emotional response of a child to a therapeutic session, in many but not all cases there appears to be a more profound and pervasive emotional change that occurs several months after the beginning of treatment. The change seems to be overwhelming to the child and the child's behavior, if not understood, can be overwhelming to the therapist. These emotional changes do not seem due to sensory overload but appear to represent a stage in positive personality growth associated with neurological changes. As such they are not necessarily to be avoided but to be attenuated when they occur by reducing what is expected of the child.

While little is currently understood of the neurological process by which sensory integration affects the personality directly, it is known that all sensory modalities send impulses to the limbic system which has a central role in emotional development. It may be through this route that the sensory integrative therapy becomes a form of "neuropsychotherapy." As with other modes of psychotherapy, the course of change is tumultuous, with the behavior of the child often becoming more disorganized just before a more mature level of sensory integration is reached. During the disorganized period, some children show ambivalent feelings toward sensory integrative activity and are unable to enter into the program effectively at the same time that they insist on being present for it.

Other children show some euphoria and act as though all problems were solved. Later they may be dejected when they realize that that is not the prevailing situation. It appears that the psyche, but not necessarily the intellect, in some way recognizes the importance of the treatment and responds in a diffuse, highly emotional, but poorly directed manner.

Therapists should be alert to such developments, understand them, and accept them as important steps in the treatment process, providing patience and assurance to those who need it that the reaction is a positive event and, in all probability, will pass in a matter of weeks. Sometimes it is the therapist who needs the most assurance, for just as a child seems to be making progress it may appear as though he has lost all that he gained.

More flexibility in treatment planning is required at this time, allowing the child the prerogative of choosing his own activity, especially if it is a simpler one which he can do well and from which he can gain security. The child who insists on pursuing a given activity usually has a reason. It is better to honor the choice and let him "get away with something" once in a while than it is to threaten a child who is preparing himself to take what appears to be an enormous and frightening maturational step. Sometimes, of course, the therapist will be incorrect in his judgment.

Chapter 10

Disorder in Postural and
Bilateral Integration

One of the neural systems in which disorder is found frequently among children with learning, especially reading, problems is concerned with postural and ocular mechanisms and integrating sensorimotor function of the two sides of the body. At this time it appears that the deficit in bilateral integration is directly related to the learning problem and that the postural-ocular problem is related to learning in large part because it is directly connected with a neurological mechanism involved in bilateral integration. The exact nature of this relationship is not known. Since the precise neurological situation is not understood, synthesizing the behavioral traits and neurological research findings into a heuristic theory provides the tentative guidelines for understanding and amelioration of the disorder.

Description of the Syndrome

The major symptoms manifested by children with this type of dysfunction are poorly integrated primitive postural reflexes, immature equilibrium reactions, poor ocular control, and deficits in a variety of subtle parameters that are related to the fact that man is a bilateral and symmetrical being. The lack of integration of function of the two sides of the body distinguishes the syndrome. Postural and ocular problems are seen in other types of dysfunction having a different relationship to learning. In addition to the characteristics just listed, deficits in visual form and space perception often are present and occasionally the tactile system shows some disorder.

Poorly integrated postural and ocular mechanisms. Usually an abnormal degree of residual tonic neck reflex (TNR) and tonic labyrinthine reflex (TLR) are present in children with disorder in this neural system and will be manifested upon testing as described in Chapter 8. Since muscle hypotonicity often accompanies this syndrome, the degree of mastery the child has over the TLR is sometimes better observed as the child is active with a scooter board. When riding prone, he may initially arch his back but fatigue will soon result either in drooping legs or desire to change position or activity. It is possible that a child who responds in this manner is employing phasic muscle contraction as opposed to tonic contraction. Similarly, he will not want to ride the scooter board in a supine position for more than a few minutes, for great exertion is required to hold the head up against the extensor muscle facilitation by the TLR.

The residual TNR is not easily observed in most of the therapeutic activities, but its influence is seen in the use of the arm extension test and when the child attempts the postures designed to integrate the reflex as discussed later.

Immature righting and equilibrium reactions make the child clumsy in gross motor activity. When rolling over from the supine to prone positions he may push the back of his head against the floor in order to use the TLR to assist him in turning. Lifting the head up against gravity when supine and rotating the trunk may be avoided. The rolling is stiff or clumsy, as though it did not have an adequate reflex basis, which is probably the case. Children with this type of sensory integrative dysfunction tend to lack flexibility in rotation around the longitudinal axis of the body. It is hypothesized that this lack is related to an insufficient activation followed by integration of the neck righting reflex in the early developmental sequence. The tendency to not rotate the trunk is found in other activities as well as when rolling.

Shifting of the body's weight — the essence of an equilibrium reaction — is often deficient and is one of the most telling signs of the syndrome. While being pulled in a seated position on a scooter board, the child may not bend his trunk appropriately when the direction in which he is pulled is changed quickly. The result is often sliding off the scooter board. Similarly, there may be a lack of automatic shifting of the body's weight to maintain balance when in the quadruped, sitting, kneeling or biped positions. Furthermore, the child usually has no cognitive awareness that such shifts are a prerequisite for balance.

It is the lack of adequate equilibrium reactions that is under evaluation in tests of standing balance whether by standing on one foot, by walking placing the heel of one foot against the toe of the other, or walking a narrow board. Tests of standing balance should not be the sole criterion for evaluation of degree of integration of postural mechanisms. There is a fairly high natural variability in standing balance among young children and most children have a large amount of practice balancing in the biped position.

Reduced postural background movements are a more subtle expression of inadequate equilibrium reactions than that of losing one's balance. They or their diminished presence can be observed while engaged in desk activities. While engaged in paper and pencil work the child may not change his trunk position appreciably to place the hand in a more advantageous position. The same lack may be observed when administering the Kinesthesia Test of the SCSIT. The child may not shift the position of the trunk as the examiner takes the child's hand to a distant "friend's house." Such shifting is automatic in the child with normal postural mechanisms.

One of the postural responses appearing early in development is a protective extension of the arms when starting to fall. Some children have not developed this postural reaction and its lack is manifested in activity. For example, when lying on a large therapy ball and starting to fall, a child may cling to the ball or to the therapist rather than putting out his hands to protect himself as he falls.

Muscle hypotonicity and diminished cocontraction are symptoms which are apt to accompany disorder in this neural system but hypertonicity also may be seen. Ways in which they manifest themselves were covered in Chapter 8 on clinical evaluation. Hypotonicity in one muscle does not indicate that all muscles will be hypotonic, especially under the influence of certain reflexes. Sometimes hip flexors and shoulder internal rotators will be hypertonic while muscles crossing the elbow joint are hypotonic.

Signs of poorly integrated mechanisms of extraocular muscle control which are often but not invariably seen in this syndrome consist of all of those described in Chapter 8. Of those symptoms, the one which indicates disorder in this neural system as opposed to other neural systems is difficulty in the eyes crossing the mid-line, the hypothetical extension of the mid-sagittal plane of the head. To elaborate on that symptom, as the child follows an object moved by the examiner in a horizontal plane approximately parallel to the eyes, the child is apt to experience some disruption as the eyes cross the mid-line. The child's eyes may jerk slightly, he may look away briefly at that time, blink or try to follow the object by turning his head when the visual stimulus reaches the mid-point. When a child tries very hard to maintain desired control of the eyes, he may do a fair job in spite of poor mechanism integration, and distress and fatigue are the major symptoms of disorder.

The relationship of the mid-line jerk to postural mechanisms may lie in their common relationship with the vestibular system. Carpenter (1964) demonstrated that conjugate horizontal eye movements in monkeys were dependent upon the vestibular system. He cited the work of Fluur which identified stimulation of the nerve from the horizontal canal with conjugate horizontal deviation of the eyes. Neither Carpenter nor his citation referred especially to that part of horizontal eye movement which involves crossing the mid-line. Some of the pertinence of these connections between the semicircular canals and horizontal eye movement lies in the position of a child lying prone on a scooter. In that position, his horizontal semicircular canals are in maximal position for stimulation.

Bilateral integration. One of the most significant characteristics of disorder in the neural system under discussion is a tendency on the part of the child to use each hand independently of the other and on its own side of the body. Since the symptom is a behavioral tendency rather than an inability, excepting in the severe cases of dysfunction, it is easily overlooked. The structured methods of evaluating integration of function of the two sides of the body covered in Chapter 8 demonstrate the most easily observed manifestations. Some further elaboration of interpretation of those procedures is needed here.

The body's mid-line has been noted to have special significance to the body scheme in many disorders (Schilder, 1951). The head seems to be harder to cross than the trunk (Schilder, 1951) in spite of the fact that somatosensory supply is more bilateral in the face than in the rest of the body where contralateral innervation is more apt to be the rule, especially for discriminating sensation. Although children with this type of dysfunction tend not to cross the mid-line of the body with either hand, when faced with the necessity of crossing, certainly do so. In the Crossing the Mid-line of the Body Test of the SCSIT battery, the children with mild dysfunction often will cross the mid-line. The test is a little too obvious for the perceptive child, but it is revealing in some cases.

A non-standardized and unpublished test consisting of asking the child to pick up a number of buttons, one at a time, placed in a row on the test table was somewhat more sensitive to the tendency to use each hand on its own side of the body rather than to use the preferred hand most of the time (Ayres, 1965).

Because motor actions of the two hands are not well coordinated, the child's performance on the Bilateral Motor Coordination Test is apt to be jerky with motions of the two hands tending to be independent of each other as opposed to reciprocal. If the child has apraxic or athetoid-like movements, they will interfere with any motor test and must be taken into consideration when attempting to evaluate the status of coordination of the two sides of the body as opposed to coordination in general. A profile of SCSIT scores on a classical case of disorder in postural and bilateral integration is given in the SCSIT manual.

The child may fail to hold down a shifting sheet of paper while writing on it with his other hand. This lack of automatic response may be a symptom of a tendency toward unilateral disregard or it can suggest lack of integration of function of the two sides of the body.

In severe cases, a child may shift his entire body to avoid drawing a line from one side of his body to the other, or the very young child may draw with one hand on one side of his body, then want to change hands for drawing on the other side. If he does use one hand for the complete performance, the line drawn on the other side of the body may be poorer. When being pulled with a rope while riding a scooter board, the child may prefer to hold the rope with one rather than two hands. He may even have trouble jumping with two feet together, preferring to have one foot lead in the jump.

The field of optometry developed a clever eye-hand task using a small ball suspended by a long string. Holding a short wood dowel at each end, the child repetitively hits the ball with the dowel, a task requiring integrated function of the two sides of the body. If a cardboard tube is used instead of a piece of wood, the condition of the tube after use is a fair indication of how well the two hands moved together. If they tend to move independently of each other, the tube wears out quickly.

A similar well-known task involves tossing a ball attached to a string, the other end of which is attached to a cup-like device which provides both a handle and a receptacle for catching the tossed ball. The receptacle can be made by cutting off the top of a plastic bleach bottle. The top contains a handle. If a child holds one of these devices in each hand and attempts to toss both balls at the same time, the degree to which both sides of the body work together will be evident from the ball and cup activity. Children with poor bilateral integration tend to want to toss one ball at a time instead of both simultaneously.

Good bilateral motor function requires, firstly, two adequately coordinated extremities. If dysfunction of another type is present in either extremity the two sides of the body cannot very well be expected to be well coordinated. It is not easy to differentiate poorly integrated bilateral function due to deficiency in one extremity as opposed to deficiency in an interhemispheral integrating mechanism.

One of the most consistently occurring non-motor indices of disorder in this neural system is a low score on the test of Right-Left Discrimination (Ayres, 1965, 1971), a symptom frequently associated with retarded readers. Although learning to differentiate between right and left is in part a higher cognitive function, it is also a sensory integrative one. Vereeken (1961) associated inability to relate active hand and verbal concept of the right hand with crossed, vague or labile hand dominance. Silver and Hagin (1960) found poor right-left discrimination in subjects with reading disability, but Coleman and Deutsch (1964) failed to find such a difference in children about age ten. In studying retarded readers, Belmont and Birch (1965) found difficulty in right-left discrimination. The reading test most affected involved sequential reading. Subjects who made total reversal of right and left were poorer readers than those who were inconsistent. Since the scores on the tests of right-left discrimination were not related to verbal IQ or total IQ on the Wechsler Intelligence Scale for Children but were related to performance scores, the authors suggested the right-left awareness was an aspect of body scheme and praxis rather than a language skill.

As a tentative theoretical guide, it is suggested that right-left discrimination is a faculty that matures only after integration of the two sides of the body occurs. After the body can function as two integrated halves, it becomes easier for those two halves to be differentiated and to attach verbal labels to them. A similar point of view was expressed by Kephart (1960), one of the leaders in the field. He maintained that laterality must be learned by experimenting through movement with the two sides of the body and their interrelationship. Sensory impressions help to distinguish the right from left sides. He views laterality as a function of internal awareness of the two sides of the body and their difference. Kephart also considers control of the eyes important in developing the sense of directionality, a developmental step which follows the sense of laterality. Directionality refers to awareness of directions in external space.

It has been observed clinically that children with this syndrome sometimes do not establish strong hand preference. Dominance is usually right, but more left handedness has been found among these children than among children with apraxia (Ayres, 1971). It is hypothesized that the failure to integrate function of the two sides of the body reduces the tendency to establish one hand as the dominant hand because the non-dominant hand performs most of the motor duties on its side of the body. When a child is not establishing dominance at the proper age, the presence of dysfunction in the neural system mediating interhemispheral integration should be checked.

Visual perception. Some form of visual perception deficit usually accompanies dysfunction in postural and bilateral integration, but a specific type of visual perception problem has not emerged sufficiently consistently to identify only one type with the neural system involved. In one sample population it was most closely related to discrimination of right-left reversed images (Ayres, unpublished data). Space relations and visual figure-ground perception are also frequently deficient (Ayres, 1971; unpublished data). Rosenblith (1965) reported that right-left reversed image perception was associated with organic difficulty. Wechsler and Hagin (1964) found rotational errors were associated with levels of early reading achievement but that left-right rotation was not the most frequent type. Neither the Rosenblith nor the Wechsler and Hagin studies associated the right-left visual discrimination with other symptoms of this syndrome.

Research Related to the Neural System

The neuroanatomical locale of the symptoms described above is probably primarily in the brain stem, probably mid-brain. It is hypothesized that the postural mechanisms in that region are associated with an interhemispheral integrating mechanism and that a deficit in functioning of this latter mechanism is responsible for the symptoms of poor bilateral integration and learning disorders. It seems likely that the proposed interhemispheric integrating mechanism is part of Penfield's centrencephalic system. A question important to this chapter's discussion that nevertheless remains unanswered is this: In what way, if any, is interhemispheric communication via the corpus callosum related to the brain stem interhemispheric integrating mechanism? The potential importance of such a mechanism requires consideration of the significance of the fact that man has two cerebral hemispheres.

The forebrain's evolutionary development into two symmetrical halves presumably had survival value, especially in enhancing the adaptive capacity of the vertebrates. The increased ability is dependent upon the two cerebral hemispheres coordinating their activity. Since every part of the central nervous system appears to be potentially connected either directly or indirectly with every other part (and there are about ten billion neurons to make these connections), integration is essential to avoid chaos, let alone permit constructive action or the skill of reading.

Two hemispheres integrating their function are more effective than two hemispheres operating relatively independently of each other. The most obvious and primal need for interhemispheral coordination is for direction of locomotion which, without integration of function of the two sides of the body, would hardly be sufficiently effective to serve survival needs. Not incidentally, the presence of brain stem neural structures mediating locomotion was pointed out above.

The role of interhemispheral communication in higher cognitive function is less clear. Some indication of this necessity is indicated by studies such as that by Sechzer (1970) on lower animals in which it was demonstrated that lack of interhemispheric transfer through the corpus callosum (the brain stem was intact) resulted in learning time that was prolonged, sometimes at least twice as long as that when interhemispheric transfer occurs.

The need for interhemispheric integration for higher functions is dependent, to some extent, on the functions of each hemisphere. In lower animals, homologous cortical neurons within the hemispheres subserve approximately the same function. Interhemispheral connections in the monkey are such that a response conditioned by electrical stimulation to one hemisphere can be elicited when the stimulus is applied to the analogous part of the alternate hemisphere (Doty, 1965). In man, the arrangement is less exact, with greater localization, especially in the left hemisphere. Nevertheless, opinion favors the involvement of both hemispheres in most functions in man (cf. Luria, 1966a; Semmes, 1968; Teuber, 1967).

Luria (1966a) found the most severe gnostic disorders in man arose from bilateral lesions in corresponding parts of the cortex. The degree of involvement of each hemisphere varies from function to function, with speech probably being most lateralized and visual perception less so.

The importance of interhemispheric communication for coordinating the two halves of the visual field (each half of which is directed to a different cerebral hemisphere) is one of the more self-evident processes requiring interhemispheral exchange at the neocortical level. The fact that many learning disabled children have trouble with reversing letters and numbers leads to reporting a study in pigeons which have complete crossing of the optic neurons at the chiasma and as a result only a contralateral versus a mixed contra- and ipsilateral visual representation at the highest center. The pigeons were found to transfer a mirror visual image as opposed to an exact image from one hemisphere to the other (Mello, 1965).

Vision is especially dependent upon interaction of the two cortices for coordination of the two visual half fields, but the integrative process that results in perception is not that simple. In studying chiasma-sectioned monkeys, Gazzaniga (1966) found that intercommunication of visual information need not be immediate and that it was more apt to occur if the perceptual task was difficult. The investigator considered the possibility that attentional mechanisms might need to be activated in order to bring about integration of information of the two hemispheres. From these observations, it might be hypothesized that reading requires more interhemispheral integration than watching where one is walking and that brain-stem mechanisms for attending to the task are likely involved in the interhemispheral integration.

In addition to the brain stem and cortex, the temporal lobes have been demonstrated in man to contribute to the visual perception process. Bryden (1965) found that individuals with right temporal lobe impairment showed deficits in both visual fields but that those with left temporal lobe impairment had deficits in the right visual field only. The results suggest that in accord with other studies the right temporal lobe is dominant for visual perception. If the left hemisphere is dominant for language in the learning disabled child and the right hemisphere is required for visual perception, reading certainly requires interhemispheral communication and that provided across the corpus callosum is necessary but not sufficient for academic demands. Furthermore, asymmetry of function of the two cerebral hemispheres requires interhemispheric integration. If the latter is present, the hemispheres are free to differ, specialize and optimize their function because information from one hemisphere is available to the other.

Akelaitis (1943) studied twenty-four epileptics in whom the corpus callosum had been partially or completely sectioned. Language functions including writing were not disturbed on the sub-ordinate side of the body, even though, presumably, the left hand's sensorimotor activity was a function of the right hemisphere. In addition, some patients were able to perform complex synchronous bilateral activity such as piano playing, touch typing and dancing. The investigator suggested that a commissural system other than the corpus callosum was utilized for interhemispheral communication. Clearly, interaction of function of the two sides of the body has been intended and provided for in the evolution of the brain. Integration of sensory impulses entering the two sides of the brain is an obvious advantage. Interaction of the two sides of the verte-brate body in an adaptive manner appeared long before it reached the stage of proencephalization.

Actually, there are mechanisms at all levels of the central nervous system for integrating function of the two sides of the body. At the spinal cord level, motion of the trunk and extremities are coordinated through spinal interneurons. At the level of the mid-brain there are interneurons between the nuclei of cranial nerves III, IV and VI that assist in conjugate eye movement. Most cranial nerves supply both sides of the face, providing some struc-tural basis for coordination of both sides of that structure. In addi-tion, there are commissures between the superior and inferior colliculi which could be involved in coordinating visual and audi-tory information entering opposing sensory structures. The inferior commissure provides for interhemispheric transfer of olfactory and other information. The posterior and habenular commissure and those of the hippocampus and fornix are additional channels. The role of the corpus callosum in interhemispheral transfer of neo-cortical information is well established. While these communicating structures offer a neuro-anatomical means of bilateral integration, biochemical processes may also be involved (cf. Morrell, 1964).

In addition to these recognized structures, evidence from re-search using lower animals, some of which was cited previously, favors the presence of an interhemispheral integrating mechanism associated with the brain stem and diencephalon. Additional re-search consistent with the proposed mechanism has been conducted by Black and Myers (1965), Ebner and Myers (1962), Glickstein and Sperry (1960), Hamilton (1967), McCleary (1960), Trevarthen (1965), and Rutledge (1965).

Nelson and Lende (1965) found that electrical stimulation of the neocortical surface of the opposum, which has no corpus cal-losum, produced electrical responses in the homologous areas of the other hemisphere. The responses were present after section of the anterior and hippocampal commissures and midbrain suggesting interhemispheral integrating mechanisms in the lower brain stem.

Particularly interesting evidence of a brain stem integrating center is found in the work of Myers, Sperry and McCurdy (1962). Using cats and monkeys to investigate possible different neural pathways for visual control of limb movement, they found that interrupting either the conduction between cortical visual areas and cortical motor areas or the interhemispheral commissures did not block the visual direction of the upper extremities, even when occipital centers in one hemisphere and pre- and post-central motor centers in the other were destroyed to control the availability of pathways for eye-hand coordination. These authors suggest that information from the visual cortex needed for motor guidance may first be relayed through brain stem centers. An alternative explanation, they suggest, may be that the pre-central convolution may be involved in mediation of visual guidance of a motor response initiated elsewhere and visually guided through brain stem mechanisms. Either interpretation places emphasis on the probability of the existence of complex visual functions at the brain stem level.

That there is a similar brain stem interhemispheral integrating system in man is favored by the observations of Akelaitis (1944) and Bridgman and Smith (1945). The latter research supported the view that subcortical levels of the central nervous system serve a major role in binocular perception and visual fusion independently of bilateral cortical integration. Bremer (1966) hypothesized that the floor of the brain stem with the ascending reticular activating system it contains and the thalamic non-specific system "may act as a long loop commissural link and a synergy mechanism between the two cerebral cortices." He found the system less specific than the callosal one and able to maintain behavioral singleness after callosal commissurotomy. Bremer expressed the opinion that fusion of the two halves of the visual field does not necessarily involve the corpus callosum.

Some theoretical elaboration on the proposed brain stem interhemispheral integrating mechanism may help the therapist to relate treatment to its rationale. Adequate visual perception of complex stimuli is dependent upon this mechanism. Furthermore, associating language with the visual stimuli of reading requires brain stem interhemispheral interaction. Vision and postural mechanisms have evolved in an intricate inter-relationship with posture leading vision. The sensory integrative and postural-motor functions at the phyletically old brain stem level operate so much as a unit that normalization of the postural and other mechanisms enhances integration of visual perception mechanisms and the interhemispheral integrating mechanism in general, allowing more complex sensorimotor development to occur.

The Remedial Program

Neuronal connections change as a consequence of experience. For a neuron, experience consists of either receiving or emitting an impulse. Therapy consists of experience specifically planned to control sensory input and elicit output that will bring about more normal function, especially at the brain stem level. The objective, of course, is to enhance perception and learning, not to develop motor skill. The motor activity is a means of reaching the objective; it is not an end in itself. The two basic principles employed are recapitulation of the pertinent ontogenetic sequence and control of sensory input in a situation conducive to its integration and adaptive response to it.

The major steps in reaching these objectives are (1) normalizing the tactile and vestibular systems in general, (2) inhibiting the primitive postural reflexes, (3) developing equilibrium reactions, (4) normalizing ocular movements, (5) enhancing coordination of sensorimotor function of the two sides of the body and (6) developing visual form and space perception. These steps follow the natural ontogenetic sequence, although there is an overlapping of the steps. In treating the young school age child, the steps may overlap more than they naturally do ontogenetically, for the learning disabled child has gaps in his maturation rather than being equally slow in maturation in all areas.

Normalizing the tactile and vestibular systems in general. The rationale for initiating therapy with tactile and vestibular stimulation and the treatment methods were covered in Chapter 9. The second remedial step, integrating the primitive postural reflexes, is introduced at approximately the same time as initial tactile and vestibular stimulation.

Integration of primitive postural reflexes. The first step in treatment is the most critical step, perhaps because it seems to be the hurdle the child has the hardest time overcoming by himself or with the help of a therapist. As long as the primitive postural reflexes remain poorly integrated into the nervous system, the developmentally later equilibrium reactions will not mature optimally, although they may develop to a certain extent. Integration is achieved through a process of suppression which has generally been referred to by therapists as "inhibition." The term "inhibition" is not quite neurophysiologically correct for the process entailed, but because of its common usage and the idea it connotes, it is used here to indicate a special form of integration which involves discouraging the probability of a given response. The objective in inhibiting or suppressing the reflexes is to enable the later maturational steps to occur. The recommended methods for inhibiting the primitive postural reflexes are an outgrowth of and an extension of the work of the Bobaths (Bobath, K., and Bobath, B., 1964) and Rood (Huss, 1965).

The procedure for inhibiting either the TNR or the TLR involves the child's actively assuming a posture or movement requiring contraction of muscles antagonistic to those which are activated by the primitive reflex. The integrative process is hastened when the positions are assumed in spite of concurrent activation of the primitive reflex. For example, optimal integration of the TLR will be achieved by the child's assuming a prone extensor posture. In the prone position the TLR increases flexor tone. The extensor posture is assumed in spite of increased flexor tone. Assumption of these postures is facilitated through sensory input, for it is desirable to activate the opposing posture as much as possible at subcortical levels — the level at which integration is most needed. Too great an effort at the cortical level may interfere with the reflex activity essential to enhancing integration. The less conscious effort a child exerts in the execution of the posture, the less cortical the response is assumed to be.

The most effective procedure for promoting integration of TLR in the prone position is riding a scooter board prone down a ramp made from a piece of four feet by six feet plywood with one end elevated one and one-half to two feet. Ideally, the ramp is placed at one end of a fifty-foot runway. The accelerated motion resulting from going down the ramp apparently stimulates the vestibular system which in turn reflexly facilitates an arched back position as shown in Figure 1. A natural (reflex) inclination toward assuming an anti-gravity response probably contributes to the prone extension posture. The excitement of the task and its purposefulness encourage emotional involvement which seems to enhance the desired response.

It is proposed that the *pattern* of sensory input resulting from assuming the prone extension posture or any other normalizing position provides the therapy. It is not the movement *per se* that is remedial. Twitchell (1954) found that when the arms of monkeys were totally deafferented by cutting the dorsal nerve roots, the movements remaining were elaborations of the TNR. While this study does not directly indicate that the normal somatosensory input inhibited the TNR, the hypothesis that such did occur is consistent with the treatment principle of providing normalizing sensory input.

It is often helpful to precede reflex inhibiting activity with normalizing muscle tone through manual methods. The more normal muscle tone enables a more normal motor response which, in turn, provides a more natural sensory input. The objective is to decrease muscle tone in muscles receiving excess innervation because of the TLR. There are three major methods of inhibiting excess tone: through the lengthening reaction of muscles, through pressure on the origin or insertion of the muscle, and through reciprocal innervation.

When a muscle is placed in its lengthened position for several seconds, it tends to reduce its tension. At the same time, the muscle spindles in that muscle will be "re-set" or biased so that there will be less sensory flow over the primary afferent from the spindle and therefore less sensory facilitation of contraction of that muscle. A method recommended by Rood to achieve this inhibitory effect is placing the child in the prone position for a few minutes, with shoulders, hips and extended legs propped up so that he is held in the arched back position passively. The child can lie on the floor with rugs or bolsters supporting him or he can lie in a net hammock. If he swings while in the hammock, further inhibition of the flexor muscles will be achieved from vestibular facilitation.

Inhibition of muscles facilitated by the TLR through pressure of the therapist's fingers on the origin or insertion is accomplished in the following manner: pressure on the upper anterior surface of the humerus to inhibit the pectoralis major, latissimus dorsi and teres major; to the coracoid process to inhibit the short head of the biceps and the pectoralis minor; to the pelvis to inhibit the sartorius and rectus femoris; to the upper medial aspect of the femur to inhibit the ilio-psoas; and on the tendinous insertion of the biceps femoris, semimembranosus, semitendinosus and gracilis.

The use of reciprocal innervation not only inhibits the muscles receiving too much proprioceptive flow but also facilitates the antagonists which must contract to place the body in the arched back position. Rapid tactile stimulation over the muscle belly with a brush as developed by Rood (Huss, 1965) not only facilitates the muscles stimulated but will bias the muscle spindles through the gamma efferent nerves. The result of the biasing is increased afferent flow from the muscle, assisting in their contraction. Tactile stimulation to influence individual muscles must be employed cautiously with concern for whether tonic or phasic contraction is being facilitated by the stimuli. A tonic contraction is desired in the prone extension posture. If brushing facilitates too much phasic contraction, it may be offset by vestibular input to increase tonic contraction.

Proprioceptive facilitation with reciprocal innervation can be augmented by rubbing the contracted muscle belly (not the origin or insertion) in the direction of the muscle fibers. The rubbing stretches the muscle spindles, increasing sensory flow over the primary afferents. The muscles which are particularly available for this tactile and proprioceptive facilitation are the trapezius, rhomboid, posterior deltoid, erector spinae and gluteus maximus. Tactile stimuli can be applied while the child is passively placed in the arched back position, but rubbing of contracted muscles must be done while the child actively holds the position.

While the use of a ramp is the most efficient method of facilitating the prone extensor position through accelerated motion, it can be accomplished by other means. An alternate method involves pulling the child on the scooter board while he holds on to the end of a rope. The therapist stands in the center of a fairly large area wrapping the other end of the rope around his body. The child is then pulled in a circle of which the therapist is the center. The activity can become very exciting if two children, one on each end of a rope with the middle of the rope going around the therapist's body, are pulled in circles and one tries to catch the other. The "catching," of course, is dependent upon the therapist who controls the rope.

The position which the activities are designed to activate reflexly will be recognized as similar to the prone extensor posture described earlier as one of the early and critical developmental steps. The back is arched, head and shoulders raised, legs and hips extended, arms flexed at the elbow, as shown in Figure 1. With the exception of the flexion in the upper extremities, the position involves contraction in muscles, the antagonists of which are facilitated by the TLR in the prone position.

When the heads extends (raises) it facilitates extension in the arms through the symmetrical TNR. Since flexion of the arms is the position facilitated by the activity, it serves as an inhibitor or integrator of the symmetrical TNR when the head is extended (dorsiflexed).

Better integration of the TLR when in the supine position is fostered by riding the scooter board on one's back instead of stomach. Either end of a rope is attached to a stable point and the two points are a considerable distance from each other so that the rope is taut and about eighteen inches from the floor. The child pulls himself hand-over-hand on the rope, pretending to ford a river with his barge (scooter) without getting himself wet. The same activity can be attempted in the prone position. As a variation of the task, one end of the rope is attached to the scooter board, then passed through a pulley attached at a fixed point, and brought back to the child who pulls on that end to make the scooter board move. The reciprocal hand activity serves as a bilaterally integrating activity, and children with poor bilateral integration often have trouble with the hand-over-hand movement.

Children with very poorly integrated primitive postural reflexes and with normal or hypertonicity of the muscles may find the scooter board activities too difficult. Similarly, some children have such inadequately developed adaptive responses that scooter board activity is frightening to them. In these cases it is appropriate to begin reflex inhibition with the child's lying prone in the net hammock. One edge of the net is under the arms and the other is under the thigh, passively positioning the child in a prone extension posture. Lying on a piece of carpet placed in the net makes the net more comfortable. The passive position places the flexor muscles in the lengthened position for a number of minutes, thereby reducing their tension and allowing the muscle spindles to be re-set for a different length as explained previously. Swinging the child back and forth provides movement which facilitates the extensors. Additional facilitation can be obtained by the child's pushing against a wall with his feet or the therapist's pushing the child by his feet. Contraction of the hip and leg extensor muscles increases the extensor tone of muscles in the trunk and neck, and pressure on the sole of the foot activates the positive supporting reaction. Letting the child hold on to the end of the rope, the other end of which is attached to a fixed object, enables the child to swing himself. Another non-demanding action promoting prone extension is sliding down the ramp which has been elevated and temporarily carpeted. The child uses a piece of slick plastic as he would a sled.

A very large inner tube, useful for many kinds of sensory integrative activity, can be hung so that the hole of the tube is vertical and about two feet from the floor. A rope providing two handles is also hung overhead. The child hangs on to the handles and attempts to jump so that his legs go through the hole of the inner tube. As the child jumps his body tends toward the supine position and he must flex his legs against or in spite of the extensor tone produced through the TLR. A trapeze can be used to meet the same objective. While the child swings by his hands, he lifts his legs to jump over a large inflated bag, landing on his feet on the other side of the bag.

The prone extensor posture is facilitated through motion and in connection with activating equilibrium reactions when the child lies across and through the hole of the inner tube, balancing himself on his stomach which is resting on the inner tube. Turning the inner tube so that it winds up and letting it unwind provides the motion to stimulate the vestibular system.

A number of other activities involving use of the scooter board in the prone and supine positions to promote integration of the TLR can add variety to the treatment process. Lying prone on the scooter board, the child backs up as close to the wall as possible with his feet against the wall. With a sudden push against the wall he propels himself toward a goal, such as touching the other side of the room, reaching for an object or crashing into a tower of cardboard cartons. The last activity is particularly effective in enhancing cocontraction of the neck muscles. Two children on scooter boards can play games of tag, race one another to pick up a bean bag or destroy a pretend town of cardboard cartons — a good opportunity for release of feelings. A group of children can be involved in relay races. Placing a large piece of plywood on a small box or other object that can act as a pivot at the center of the board, the child rides the scooter board up one end of the board and then, as he crosses the pivot point and the board tilts in the other direction, coasts down the other end. This activity assists the posturally insecure child to become accustomed to riding down a ramp.

Lying supine on the scooter board, the child can follow a simple map or maze pushing with his feet, or he can push himself with his feet so that his head goes to a specific place, such as through a hoop. Spinning a child who is lying supine in the suspended net hammock, head and legs extending beyond the net, will reflexly activate a flexor position in neck and all extremities, the arms flexing to hold on to the net. Centrifugal force increases resistance to flexion. Holding the head up for a prolonged period of time while in the supine position requires much more effort than in the prone position and is often resisted by children although it is usually needed.

Attempts to develop pleasurable and exciting activities which assist in integrating the TNR have been less successful than comparable attempts at suppressing the TLR. The positions shown in

Figure 6* assist in integrating the TNR by providing sensations from a position requiring contraction of muscles antagonistic to those activated by the TNR. Proprioceptive facilitation of the opposing position through neural mechanisms helps the inhibitory process and reduces the disorganizing effect of maintaining a posture which feels unnatural. In the positions shown in Figure 6, the head of the child is turned to his left and held there. Holding a piece of crumpled paper with the chin against the shoulder helps the child maintain the head position. The position of the head activates the TNR which increases flexor muscle tone in the right arm and extension in the left. Contraction of muscles antagonistic to those facilitated by the TNR is obtained by placing the left hand on the hip and extending the right arm to support the body's weight. The pressure on the right hand activates the positive supporting reaction which provides reflex afferent support to extension in the right arm. Additional proprioceptive support may be given by rubbing the contracted triceps.

In this position, the TNR may facilitate flexor muscle tone in the right leg. If such is the case, the primitive reflex action can be inhibited by pressing the right foot against the wall as shown in position 7. If it facilitates flexor tone in the left leg, the left foot pushes against the wall as in position 8. Pressing with the ball of the foot activates the positive supporting reaction. Before using positions 7 and 8 the child should be checked to determine whether the effect on the legs is ipsilateral or contralateral. Reinforcing the TNR through the positive supporting reaction should be avoided. Contraction of the extensors of either leg against resistance increases the amount of sensory support to the extensors of the supporting arm, for muscles tend to act in patterns, one of those patterns being a total extensor thrust.

Activating equilibrium reactions in the quadruped position while the TNR is being inhibited is believed to enhance further sensory integration. These reactions are shown being elicited in positions 3, 4, 5, and 6. Bearing the body's weight on one knee and attempting to maintain balance while in positions 3 through 8 encourages cocontraction at the hip joint, a response frequently in need of promoting. Manually applied pressure on or rubbing of the contracting hip muscles and a gentle pushing back and forth further facilitate hip joint cocontraction.

Inhibiting the TNR in many different positions is desirable, for

---

*Copies of Figure 6, entitled "Positions for Inhibition of the Tonic Neck Reflex" may be secured from Western Psychological Services, 12031 Wilshire Blvd., Los Angeles, California 90025.

each position provides a slightly different pattern of sensory input, and it is the sensory input that is the critical factor. Positions 2, 5, 6, 9, 10, and 11 illustrate different ways of varying the sensory input pattern. In executing the last three postures, the child begins in position 9, then turns in place to assume first position 10 and lastly 11. There are, of course, many intermediate positions. The TNR is thus inhibited during movement in which the positional relationship between the arm and trunk is continuously modified. The reverse of the positions illustrated, with the head turned to the right instead of left, should also be employed.

These positions are not appealing to children. In fact, they often are initially disorganizing to a child who has adapted to a predominating TNR. Emotional upsets and resistance to assuming the positions are not unusual. In these cases it is suggested that the child not be pushed too rapidly in mastering the postures and that his reaction be considered an expression of his neurological problems and valuable clinical information.

When the postures can be assumed without much effort, it is suggested that they be attempted under greater demands for equilibrium responses, such as when balancing on an equilibrium board or on the platform swing. If an adaptive response more difficult than any before emitted is not required, therapy is not optimal.

Only a few relatively "fun" activities which integrate the TNR have come to attention. One activity employs a device similar to a short hockey stick which is attached to a head band. The child hits a puck by turning the head when in the quadruped position with the forward weight of the body on the arm in which flexor tone will be increased by the head rotation. To execute another activity, the child sits on a scooter board which is a pretend canoe and pushes himself with a dowel with a crutch tip on it or with a "plumber's helper." The child looks away from the stick which is held to the side of the canoe and in the direction toward which he is "rowing," thereby rotating the head and eliciting the TNR which is integrated through active extension in the arm in which flexion is reflexly facilitated.

Response to primitive reflex inhibiting activities is not necessarily immediate, and permanent change may take weeks to months. Furthermore, after the reflexes are apparently inhibited, they can regain supremacy if continued neurological development is not actively supported. It is advisable to occasionally re-introduce the basic inhibiting procedures for both the TLR and TNR to assure their integration.

Activation of righting and equilibrium reactions. The righting

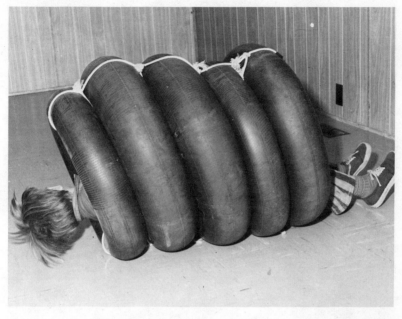

Figure 7.—Activating the neck righting reflex.

reactions begin to appear soon after birth and their activation probably helps inhibit the primitive postural reflexes. Accordingly, it is appropriate to help the integration of the primitive reflexes through those motor patterns which were initially related to the righting reflexes. The labyrinthine reflex resulting in head righting is recapitulated in the prone extensor posture while riding the scooter board. Rolling over is another important motor pattern initially related to the righting reflex. McGraw (1963) presented four stages of ability of the infant to roll from supine to prone. In the fourth stage, which McGraw calls a deliberate stage and an integral part of the righting response which carries the child into the quadruped position, the child flexes his neck, trunk, hips and knees and swings the arm over the body as he rotates to the prone position. In this action, the child must act against the increased extensor tone resulting from the TLR. Rolling with emphasis on tucking the chin down and flexing at the hip to start the roll is recommended to both integrate the TLR and to lay a better foundation for equilibrium reactions. Interest can be increased and extra stimulation added by having the child roll up an inclined board

Figure 8.—Use of a large therapy ball.

with a rug on it. Rolling up in a rug or large cloth (a parachute works well) adds incentive to rolling. Rolling inside a barrel (lining it with carpet increases comfort and tactile stimulation) activates a variety of postural reactions.

The neck righting reflex acting on the body involves the head's rotation when the body is supine. The motor response to the sensory input resulting from turning the head is rotation of the body to the prone position. The most effective activity for utilizing the reflex is rolling in a tube made of five inner tubes tied or taped together as shown in Figure 7. The freedom of the head encourages turning the head and the confined space for the body allows rotation of the body's longitudinal axis and discourages compensatory movements. An earlier chapter pointed out that rotation of the longitudinal axis was frequently deficient in children with this syndrome.

Use of the rolling tube provides excellent touch-pressure stimulation from the extensive contact of the body with the inner tubes. It also generates a great deal of vestibular stimulation in planes that are not affected as much by positions assumed in the net hammock or on the scooter board. Because of the sensory stimulation it provides along with activation of the neck righting reflex, extensive use of the rolling tubes is usually appropriate for children with this syndrome.

Since equilibrium reactions are subtle, sometimes even virtually unobservable when they involve little or no motion, eliciting them and observing their response requires special skill. It is particularly easy to overlook the importance of equilibrium reactions in the prone position. Argument for activating postural mechanisms in the prone position was presented in a previous chapter. A particularly appropriate activity which replicates an early stage of development and keeps the child in a prone position is the use of a large (about three feet in diameter) ball, a therapeutic procedure which has been in wide use with children with neurological problems. The child lies on the ball, holding the hands of the therapist as shown in Figure 8. The child with normal postural reaction need not be told what to do; he pulls and pushes against the hands of the therapist and assists his balance with movements of his trunk and legs. The child with certain types of postural mechanism dysfunction will tend to just lie on the ball or, in more severe cases, feel like an inert bag of potatoes to the hands of the therapist.

Simply maintaining balance on the ball while holding on to a therapist requires very slight but essential equilibrium reactions. Without them the ball tends to roll, especially during movement, and the child either falls off or the therapist provides the force necessary to keep him balanced.

If the child does not know how to respond to the ball, the therapist asks him to pull and push so that he simply goes forward and backward on the ball. If he starts to lose his balance and does not automatically respond, the therapist can assist either through his hands or through verbal instructions. If the child does not begin to show some equilibrium reactions within a few days' attempts, returning to normalizing postural reactions reflecting an earlier developmental stage may be in order.

The use of the therapy ball illustrates several important principles of sensory integrative therapy:

1. The activity provides the child with sensations that enable reactions not experienced before. Those sensations are largely vestibular but tactile and other proprioceptive input in the prone position also make a considerable contribution to promoting equilibrium reactions in the prone position.

2. The activity is particularly non-cognitive. Children know what is expected through innate mechanisms, although a few suggestions from the therapist help activate those mechanisms.

3. The child learns through self-directed activity. He must be the active participant, taking the initiative. Therapists cannot force organization on a brain; they can only provide the environment and encouragement to the child whose brain must organize itself.

The following account of a child with a learning disability and poorly developed postural reflexes illustrates these principles. As he lay on the ball holding the hands of the therapist he started to fall off to the side. Instead of attempting to protect himself as he fell by extending an arm and leg, he made the not infrequently seen response of clinging to the ball. To protect the child, the therapist tried to pull the child back on the ball, to which the child responded, "Quit pushing me; you're pushing me off the ball! You're making me lose my balance!" The same chain of events happened on several different occasions. Each time, after a few objections from the child as to what the therapist was doing, the therapist said, "I am going to let you down slowly." After repeated reality testing (falling) the child learned a more accurate interpretation of the sensory input and was able to stay on top of the ball. For the educational therapist, one of the hardest redirections of professional approach to sensory integrative dysfunction is to avoid "teaching" and to provide a situation in which the child can learn under his own direction. When the therapist can tap that inner direction and allow its expression, he has been of optimum help to the child.

Another piece of commonly employed equipment which elicits equilibrium reactions in the prone or supine position is a board on rockers. The child lies on the rocking board which is gently rocked by the therapist. Shifting the position of the child activates equilibrium reactions, including the protective extension of the arms.

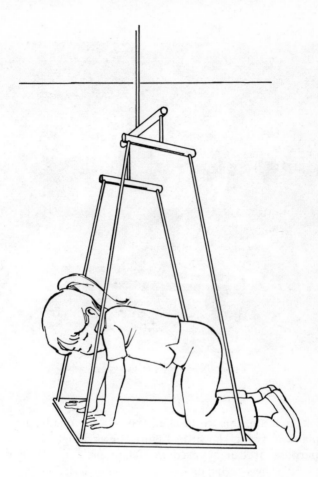

Figure 9.—One use of the platform swing. A commercial version of this and some of the other equipment illustrated is available from Developmental Design, P. O. Box 55, Carpinteria, California 93013.

The protective extension reaction of the upper extremities is also elicited through use of a smaller therapy ball (about eighteen to twenty-four inches) or by lying prone over a barrel, either length-wise or crosswise, and rocking back and forth. If the top of a one-leg stool is large and sufficiently comfortable for a child to lie on, lying on it while he places his hands on the floor makes a considerable demand on equilibrium reactions of the trunk. Rolling a ball with one hand while in this position makes further demands.

After the child emits automatic postural reactions in the prone

Figure 10.—Quadruped balancing board.

position, it is appropriate to elicit them in the quadruped position. The platform swing shown in Figure 9 was designed especially for this purpose. It can be used in the prone and sitting positions. Figure 10 shows a balancing board also designed especially to elicit equilibrium reactions in the quadruped position. Quadruped balance can also be promoted by balancing on a piece of plywood to the bottom of which is attached a piece of wood about two inches in width and four inches high. At the more advanced level, the child can — and will — try to balance on hands and knees on the large therapy ball. Almost as demanding is the riding of a scooter board in the quadruped position while the therapist pulls the scooter.

The equilibrium board illustrated in Figure 11 promotes maturation of equilibrium reactions in the seated position. By shifting his body's weight forward, then to one side, then backward and lastly to the other side, the child maneuvers the device so that a constantly changing part of the edge of the board is touching the floor. Sitting on the platform swing (Figure 9) and throwing ob-

Figure 11.—A sitting equilibrium board.

jects or sitting on a one-leg stool (Figure 12) and kicking a ball demands more refined equilibrium reactions. Since falling backward can be dangerous, the stool is placed next to a mat.

A steep carpet-covered ramp can provide a ski slope, the skiing being performed squatting with sheets of slick paper magazines as skis. An activity making only slight demands on equilibrium in the seated position is a swing with only one rope. A spring in the rope adds sensory input and increases the amount of skill required for the response. For the young child a rocking horse is an excellent promoter of postural development. A horse for older children can be made by suspending a barrel or similar object from the ceiling. A spring adds to the demand for an adaptive response.

If the postural responses have been well developed up to the sitting stage, little further emphasis need be placed on eliciting them in a kneeling or standing position. It is not inappropriate, however, and it does add variety to include a few activities that demand balancing in those positions. The therapist can assume the role of the horse, pulling reins (ropes) held in the hands of a

Figure 12.—Use of a one leg stool.

charioteer (child) riding on his knees in his chariot (scooter board). Kneeling on the platform swing or on the quadruped balancing board requires considerable skill.

A rope stretched out on the floor with the ends taped to keep it in place provides a minimal obstacle for activating equilibrium reactions in the standing position. The child can walk on top of it without stepping off, jump with both feet first to one side, then to the other, beginning at one end of the rope and ending at the other, do the same thing hopping, or walk the rope moving sideways, crossing one foot over the other either in front of or behind the other. A considerable amount of motor planning is required when the child walks the length of the rope, either forward or backward, placing the left foot on the right side and the right foot on the left side of the rope.

Playing catch while standing on the rocking board theoretically utilizes equilibrium reactions to improve eye-hand coordination. A "two by four" board has long been standard equipment for perceptual-motor training. The demands made upon a child when walking it can be varied by clamping one-leg stools upside down on the board and by balancing a pillow on the head. Old fashioned tin-can stilts are popular. They are made by putting a rope through holes in a tin can, the rope providing a means by which the child holds the cans up against the sole of the foot when taking a step.

A nervous system which has maintained one organization for many years and then is encouraged to assume a more mature organization will have a tendency to revert back to its previous organization. This tendency requires that occasionally the therapist check the status of the primitive postural reflexes and righting and equilibrium reactions, and if they have not remained well integrated re-introduce some of the more basic activities.

Developing muscle cocontraction. When the ability of antagonistic muscles to cocontract is insufficient, attempts to develop it should begin early in the remedial program, because of the important role this type of muscle contraction assumes in implementation of postural responses. The concept of cocontraction appears to have been introduced by Riddoch and Buzzard (1921). In observing reflexes in adult hemiplegic patients, Riddoch and Buzzard found much concurrent innervation resulting in cocontraction of antagonistic muscles that, in effect, was more like a "posture" than a "movement." They observed in adult quadriplegic and hemiplegic patients that concurrent innervation was a feature of all postural reactions of trunk and limbs, both at rest and secondary to strong reflex and voluntary movements. These early observations are consistent with recommended procedures for enhancing cocontraction, i.e., a strong, maintained postural reaction where coinnervation of antagonistic muscles is required to maintain a posture, as in stabilization demands.

A warning also arises from the early observations. If the neural dysfunction in a child results not in diminished cocontraction of muscles but in normal ability to cocontract with normal or heightened muscle tone with some release of primitive postural reflexes, increasing concontraction may be contraindicated. It may increase muscle tone when its increase is not desired, as in muscles already showing increased tone due to the influence of the primitive postural reflexes.

Muscle cocontraction is encouraged by providing alternating resistance to a muscle group. An appropriate initial activity is alternating pushing and pulling the child who sits on a scooter board. Both the therapist and the child grasp the hoop. The child tries to make himself stiff "like a statue" while the therapist provides the force that alternates the direction in which the child moves. Resting his elbows on his knees helps a child to grasp the idea of muscle contraction without movement. A similar activity which demands strong cocontraction, especially of trunk and neck muscles, utilizes a scooter board and a strip of rubber, such as from an inner tube, the ends of which are attached firmly to a frame or wall. The rubber strip should be about fourteen inches off the floor and slightly stretched. Seated on the scooter board, the child grasps the rubber strip and alternately pushes and pulls, making his scooter board move back and forth. Two children can work together on opposite sides of the rubber strip.

Normalizing ocular muscle control. Because the extraocular muscles are so closely associated with postural mechanisms, all of the foregoing treatment recommended in this chapter is believed to exert a positive integrating influence on the control of muscles that move the eyeballs. The means by which this influence is hypothesized to occur was described in Chapter 6. Here that influence is related to some of the activities. Spinning in the net acts reflexly on the eyes through the semi-circular canals. If nystagmus is not produced by spinning, adequate brain stem connections are probably not being made by the vestibular system. Prone and supine scooter board activity not only provides movement which produces vestibular stimulation but a considerable amount of contraction of the neck muscles that are closely associated with the medial longitudinal fasciculus and through it to the cranial nerve nuclei which control oculomotor functions. The activity also makes heavy demands on the muscles innervated at cervical levels. These muscles are influenced by vestibular input entering the medial longitudinal fasciculus (Brodal, 1964) and, in turn, proprioception from the neck muscles appears to be important in helping the brain to interpret vestibular functions. Cohen (1961) found that lower primates did not have balance problems following detaching of extraocular muscles but did have severe deficits in balance, orientation and motor coordination of the entire body when the neck proprioceptors were anesthetized. Those same muscles are also believed to influence the extraocular muscles and this influence is likely added to that derived from muscles supplied by the cranial nerves. There seems to be constant interaction and interdependence of the extraocular muscles, the vestibular system, and the neck muscles. The latter two elements of this triad offer a means of influencing the former and the neck muscles offer a means of helping interpretation of vestibular information.

The stronger and longer the muscle contraction, the greater the probability that contraction will influence other muscles through proprioceptive facilitation. All neck muscles must contract strongly to stabilize the head when the body accelerates or decelerates in motion through space. The neck muscles can be observed to stand out strongly when the child is involved in cocontraction activities. It is hypothesized that muscle cocontraction involves activation of the high threshold tonic muscle spindle receptors. The sensory input from these receptors which are believed to be especially associated with postural responses may well have a particularly important effect on the eye muscles and one that is in addition to and different from that resulting from discharge of the phasic receptors of the muscle spindle. Both postural mechanisms and mechanisms governing extraocular muscle control are largely brain stem functions. As with other sensorimotor functions, cortical direction is dependent upon adequate integration of brain stem function. By normalizing postural and ocular brain stem mechanisms cortical ocular control is believed to be enhanced.

Integrating function of the two sides of the body. If the preceding steps in normalizing the neural system have been reasonably well mastered, the sensorimotor function of the two sides of the body will automatically become better coordinated. If the child does not evidence more coordinated use of both hands, the possibility that he has not mastered the previous steps should be considered. If integration has occurred, the child can be offered activities which enable him to promote further interhemispheral integration.

All of the activities designed especially to involve postural mechanisms automatically require an adaptive interaction of the two sides of the body, although that interaction does not involve the cerebral cortex to a great extent. Requiring both upper or lower extremities to perform the same motor task at the same time provides an appropriate early emphasis on bilateral integration. Pushing a scooter board with both hands or both feet simultaneously is elementary but not always easy. Holding a rope in each hand while sitting on a scooter board and being pulled by the ropes requires somewhat greater control. Other appropriate activities are jumping like a bunny through hoops or over a series of dowels laid on the floor; jumping, both feet together, into then outside of a hoop or rope ring lying on the floor; and rolling a ball with the two hands held together loosely with a strap.

Two activities mentioned earlier in this chapter which are particularly good are hitting a suspended ball with a cardboard tube and tossing and catching balls on strings attached to cups made of plastic bleach bottles, one cup held in each hand. Using a large cup with two handles (one can be pieced together from the upper portions of two plastic bottles), the child kneels on the floor by the suspended ball. He catches and tosses the ball with the cup which he holds with both hands. Tossing the ball to one side and catching it on the other involves crossing the mid-line of the body.

Developing right-left discrimination and visual perception. If right-left discrimination and visual perception are, in part, functions of maturation in this neural system, they will develop as the integrative process occurs. However, it is not reasonable to expect therapy to accomplish what nature was unable to do, especially when the child is past the age critical to the development being enhanced. Some activities which stress directionality and right-left discrimination are appropriate when maturation in prior steps reaches a plateau. Activities involving visual perception directly are also advisedly stressed at that time, although occasional introduction earlier in the program is appropriate. Methods of promoting visual perception are discussed in Chapter 12.

Chapter 11

Developmental Apraxia

Apraxia in children is a disorder of sensory integration interfering with ability to plan and execute skilled or non-habitual
motor tasks. Usually, there is some inability to relate the sequence
of the motions to each other. The dyspraxic child can and does
learn specific motor skills through repeated attempts and execu-
tions, but as long as he has not acquired the generalized ability to
plan unfamiliar tasks, apraxia is still present.

A motor plan is the "scheme" within the brain for action. The
plan is based on the "body scheme" or sensorimotor awareness of
the different anatomical elements of the body, of the potential
movement of these elements and of how they can relate to each
other in movement. A disorder in body scheme does not result only
in a dyspraxic condition, for children with disorders in postural
and bilateral integration also are generally considered to have poorly developed body schemes. The concept as employed in this
theoretical approach does not refer to one's attitude toward one's
body but to a sensorimotor process of which one is generally only
semiconsciously aware unless attention is directed to it. The body
scheme which provides the substrate for praxis is a product of
intersensory integration. Schilder (1951), who used the concept in
a broad sense, stated: "The postural model of the body is not the
sum of optic, kinesthetic and tactile sensations. It is an integration." He also made the important point that the body scheme is

not static. If it is to be used for the generalized ability to motor plan, it must be fluid, ever-changing and ready to serve as a model from which any plan can be executed. It is the lack of a well-defined but flexible model of the body that is found in the apraxic child.

Behavioral research data consistently indicate that the aspect of the tactile system that is concerned with discriminative tactile sensations is particularly concerned with the ability to "program" a skilled motor act. Not all disorders of the tactile system result in a dyspraxic state. Diminished kinesthesis is not infrequently associated with poor motor planning but the relationship is not sufficiently consistent to think of it as a major contributant to apraxia. The fact that apraxic children often show symptoms of some disorder of postural and bilateral integration suggest that dysfunction in vestibular and other proprioceptive mechanisms may also contribute to a dyspraxic state. The data on the vestibular system presented earlier also argue in favor of that system's contribution to most sensory integrative processes, including the substrate for praxis.

The Development and Nature of Praxis

Effectiveness in treating apraxia, as with treating any condition, is dependent upon the therapist's grasp of the nature of the disorder. Some insight into the possible nature of the developmental and neural processes may be gained from discussion of some aspects of human evolution, growth and function.

During the evolution of the vertebrates, the central nervous system developed out of the ectoderm. Could this evolutionary genesis be related to the fact that the tactile system of a man is a sensitive indicator of the degree of certain kinds of integration of the central nervous system? In the lower animals, some of the nerve fibers carry impulses from both skin and muscle so that a given nerve impulse carries messages from both sources simultaneously. In higher vertebrates the nerve fibers are separate (Coghill, 1929). This phyletic heritage reflects a close connection between the tactile and muscle systems.

At birth, the tactile system is among the more mature structures of the brain. The infant responds to tactile stimuli in many ways. Sensorimotor reflexes are easily elicited over many skin areas. The rooting reflex causes a child to move his head in the direction of a tactile stimulus in the hope that it is a source of food. Being held closely with touch-pressure stimulation surrounding the child elicits a behavioral response suggesting comfort. Apparently the touch-pressure stimuli elicited from being held act through some integrative mechanisms and result in a lowering of the central excitatory state. The infant is more dependent upon his "near" receptors, such as touch, than upon his "distance" receptors, such as vision (cf. Schopler, 1965).

Much of the young child's early information about the world and about himself comes from contact between his skin or mucous membranes and the environment. The area within the mouth, richly endowed with receptors, is an important source of sensory stimulation of mechanoreceptors and, if the stimuli are interpreted temporally and spatially, a source of information about small objects and small segments of anatomy. While it is easy to recognize these cognitive functions of the tactile system, of equal or perhaps even of greater importance is the highly significant role the tactile system assumes in the stimulation of the arousal system of the reticular formation and that structure's general integrative functions. While it is difficult to find specific data that support the hypothesis, it is believed that this function of tactile stimulation early in life makes a considerable contribution to the development of praxis. Casler's study (1965) on eight pairs of matched institutionalized babies under one year of age demonstrated that light touch-pressure stimulation enhanced the Gesell Developmental Quotients of the experimental group in comparison with the control group. Statistically significant differences appeared on all subtests except the motor. The motor subtest appears to be related primarily to postural responses at that age while the adaptive subtest is more closely related to praxis. These results suggest that tactile stimulation made a difference in the maturational rates of the children and that it quite possibly did so through the reticular system.

Early in life, tactile stimuli are apt to be interpreted in a diffuse and imprecise manner. Not only is the child not sure of the nature of what touched him, but he is not sure of what part of his body touched the object. Perhaps the infant's early proclivity for putting every object into his mouth derives not only from an oral orientation to life but also from a need for tactile stimulation and knowledge. His mouth may be giving him one of the most precise sources of information of the environment.

Although the infant may be in doubt about the spatial qualities of tactile stimuli, he has no doubt about the emotional nature of the stimuli. Pain is felt as pain and responded to accordingly, but the source of the stimulus is not well localized. Certain types of stimuli, such as those arising from having the face washed are experienced in such a manner as to elicit an avoidance reaction. In the theoretical framework presented in this book, the reaction would be classified as "tactile defensiveness."

Early in life, it is supposed but not known for sure, kinesthesia is particularly poorly developed. An infant probably has only a vague idea about the position and movement of the different parts of his body. It is reasonable to hypothesize that, with maturation, messages from joint receptors give more and more accurate information about joint position and movement. Kinesthesia is not to be confused with information from impulses from the muscle receptors which respond especially to stretch, although the latter is also important. Stretching a muscle of an infant has been found to elicit simultaneous distinct responses in the electroencephalogram which are more mature than visual responses (Hrbek and associates, 1968).

Sensory input from the skin and joints, but especially from the skin, helps develop in the brain the model or internal scheme of the body's design as a motor instrument. Two processes are required for the development of increased differentiation of somatosensory perception: sufficient quantity of stimulation and the capacity of the brain to integrate it at both the brain stem and higher levels. The latter process includes being receptive to it. Data supporting the importance of quantity were presented by Casler (1961) who studied research on the physical, intellectual and emotional deficits observed in children and animals deprived of mothering during early infancy and concluded that an essential factor in development was the total quantity of sensory interaction with the environment.

Observation of children with sensory integrative disorders suggests the problem is less frequently of "apparent" quantity than of the capacity of the brain for normal processing. If part of the problem is diminished receptivity of the brain to sensory input, then quantity becomes a factor, particularly when considering therapeutic approaches. Of equal importance is the degree to which the type of brain processing results in impressions which coincide with reality. After making a considerable study of afferent sensation in children with different kinds of neurological disorder, Abercrombie (1968) suggested that in cerebral palsy children, the sensory feed-back and central recording of the efferent message associated with active movement makes it likely that the motor disorders of cerebral palsy affect perceptual skills. It is suggested that it is the degree of veridicality of the sensory feedback that is the critical aspect. It is possible that an athetoid child, while having a disorder of motion, may be receiving accurate and precise information regarding that motion. On the other hand, an apraxic child with better coordination may be receiving only vague sensory feedback from his action, and this vagueness certainly contributes little to the development of a precise body scheme.

Some factual basis for the assumption that maturation brings greater discrimination of spatial and temporal qualities of somato-sensory perception, as well as integration between touch, kines-thesis and vision is found in normative data for tests of that type of sensory integration and in studies involving these sensory modalities (cf. Birch and Lefford, 1967). Maturation of tactile and kinesthetic perception and their association with perception in other sensory modalities is nearly complete by the time the child reaches his eighth or ninth birthday. Optimum intersensory integration, of course, is dependent upon discriminatory perception in each mo-dality, but intersensory integration can also promote perception in a specific modality.

That there is a great deal more yet to be learned about the development of tactile functions is demonstrated by a study by Ghent (1961) in which she found changes in tactile sensitivity in girls at about age five and in boys at about age 11. The change was from greater sensitivity of the dominant hand at the younger age to greater sensitivity of the non-dominant hand at the older age. Sensitivity does not necessarily indicate spatially discriminate per-ception, but all aspects of sensation contribute to the total sensory integrative picture. A sex difference was also found in a series of studies by Fisher (1964) who concluded that females probably have a more definite, clear and stable concept of the relationship of boundaries of their bodies to the perceptual field than do males.

The ontogenetic trend in tactile perception from the diffuse to the more specific and localized is also seen in phylogenesis. The amphibian cortex, for example, has little if any of the type of localization of function that man has and the reptilian has only the beginning. These animals tend to manifest total rather than discrete sensorimotor performance. The apraxic child tends to manifest total rather than discrete motor acts that reflect a limited repertoire of behavior and lack of the kind of flexibility that is dependent upon discrete as opposed to diffuse sensory input.

One of the important developmental processes which help the maturational trend from the diffuse to the specific arises from the movement that is associated with the sensory input. The somato-motor system is constantly in a state of change of pattern, with the somatic changes arising from movement, leaving in the brain some memory by which to guide a similar or more complicated move-ment the next time it is needed. The use of the body determines the concept or scheme of the body through the result of action and the stimuli resulting from the action. As movement assumes meaning, the child learns to motor plan or how to cortically direct his movements, especially in a serial and discrete manner, to accomplish a task which, for him, has not become automatic. If the information which the body receives from its somatosensory receptors is not precise, the brain has a poor basis on which to build its scheme of the body; consequently, the capacity to motor plan cannot develop normally. This conceptualization is undoubtedly oversimplified, but it provides a coherency to the current concept of apraxia and its treatment.

The need to develop the potential capacity of the body to perform in skilled motor acts can be seen in the interest and drive of children. The pre-school child is usually on the move, exploring the various ways in which his body will perform, manipulating objects, learning about things through touch and movement, and finding satisfaction in scribbling or drawing. These scribbles are the beginning of what will later be one of the acts which require the greatest skill in motor planning — writing. The school age child structures his continued maturation of the praxic ability with use of playground equipment, with complicated games of the "peas porridge hot" type, and through such passingly popular activities as hula-hoop, chinese jump rope, jacks and yo-yos. When a motor pattern, such as walking or even tying a knot, becomes habitual, it no longer requires motor planning nor does it reflect skill in praxis. When the limits of the ability to motor plan are reached and the maturation of the body scheme is essentially complete, most individuals settle down to a less active life. It is worthy of note that the slowing-down period begins rather early in the second decade of life while the cognitive processes are still maturing at a very rapid rate.

The drive for manipulation of the hands has been studied in rhesus monkeys by Mason, Harlow and Rueping (1959). They observed the manipulatory drive as early as the first day of life. Its early appearance and its consistent and persistent maturation suggested to the authors that the activity was innate and was probably augmented with self-reinforcement through the results of the manipulation. Here, again, is seen an innate drive, which, accompanied by sensory input, results in the development of a fundamental sensorimotor function.

Praxis, then, is not just movement, but a *learned* ability to plan and direct a temporal series of coordinated movements toward achieving a result — usually a skilled and non-habitual act. It is the end product of a developmental process involving afferent synthesis of the entire past ontogenetic experience related to a given motor pattern. Each previous as well as each current sensory input channel has contributed to the present act, but of all systems, the tactile seems to be the most critical contributant, or it may be that the same neurological organization that results in apraxia also seriously affects tactile perception. If the afferent information has not been synthesized, the end product will not be well integrated. Like the neural subsystem which subserves postural and bilateral integration, maturation of the neural system subserving praxis is dependent upon integrating sensory input and following a drive programmed into the brain. The system differs from the postural and bilateral integration "system" in its less direct dependence upon brain stem reflexes. It is a process acquired during the first decade of development after birth. Postural and bilateral integration mature earlier. While postural and bilateral integration appear to be especially and directly dependent upon vestibular input, praxis is especially and directly dependent upon discriminative tactile functions with the vestibular system providing more of a substrate. Both systems are dependent upon proprioceptors, with posture more related to the muscle spindle and praxis to joint receptors.

Praxis is more cortically directed, more specifically human, while postural and bilateral integration are shared with the lower animals. In some instances, lower animals excel human beings in postural and ambulation feats, but none exceeds man in planning fine, skilled motions, especially of the hand and tongue. These differences are consistent with the difference in what are considered to be the major sites of integration of the two neural subsystems. The major substrate of praxis is believed to be diencephalic and cortical while the brain stem is the major integrating site for postural and bilateral integration. These differences help determine differential treatment of the two syndromes, treatment of the postural disorders preceding, generally, focus on the treatment of praxis.

Description of the Syndrome

The fact that apraxia has been considered (and not incorrectly) an output disorder is due to the fact that the motor component is more observable than the sensory component, especially without specific diagnostic tests. The problem lies not so much in sensory input or motor output but in that in-between process of sensory integration and planning and motion. The Russian term "acceptor of action" (Anokhin, 1961) conveys the idea of the essential integration of the sensory and motor factors of apraxia, although the term's meaning extends far beyond skilled motor planning. The "acceptor" is concerned with the intention, aim or idea of action.

Because of its motor component, developmental apraxia is easily observable as the child's lack of knowing how to go about executing an unusual motor task. It is this behavioral parameter that is under evaluation in the test of Imitation of Postures of the SCSIT, and a score on that test is one of the best single indicators of a child's praxis ability. Occasionally a child, usually a particularly intelligent one, can approach a perceptual-motor problem through higher cognitive processes such as reasoning and will do acceptably well on that test. For this reason, and because reliance should never be placed on a single test of sensory integration, additional observations are advisable. The apraxic child usually has difficulty with the demands of the Motor Accuracy test and with the test of Bilateral Motor Coordination. Compensation through intellectual means is not possible on either of those tests.

Observing a child in free or playground activities, especially if he has not learned them as splinter skills, can help confirm the degree of motor planning skill. The dyspraxic child is slow in learning to dress himself but usually, with time, he does so. Having learned to do so does not eliminate the praxic problem, however. He has trouble with constructive manipulative play and may resort to destruction of the objects. Difficulty in drawing, cutting, pasting and assembling will usually be seen in the pre-school child and learning to write is an extremely and usually overly demanding task for an apraxic child just entering school.

The apraxic child's motor problem differs from the athetoid child's problem in that the latter has no difficulty in giving his body directions for motor execution. The muscles lack the control to follow them without extraneous motion. On the other hand, the apraxic child is not troubled by involuntary motion but does not know how to give his body precise directions.

As a disorder in integration of somatosensory stimuli, differential diagnosis of the syndrome is greatly assisted by inspection of the scores on the somatosensory tests of the SCSIT. Performance on most but usually not all of the tactile tests is usually poor and in severe cases the score on the test of kinesthesis is low. Difficulty in knowing just where one was touched on the arm or hand or in recognizing or duplicating a simple design drawn on the dorsum of the hand suggests poor perception of the spatial qualities of the tactile stimuli.

The ability to identify which finger was touched without having seen the contact is often but not invariably difficult for the apraxic child. If a child cannot tell which finger is receiving a tactile stimulus, he cannot be expected to know well how to move that finger in a skilled manner in manipulation of objects or use of tools including a pencil. Finger localization is more than a test of tactile perception. Halnan and Wright (1960) studied the ability to localize fingers and toes and concluded that proprioceptive and visual stimuli contributed to the ability. Similarly, McKinney (1964) found that sighted children with eyes closed used a visual scheme to indicate which finger had been touched in a finger identification test. His conclusion was based on the fact that children made many errors if fingers had been touched when the hand was supine and the response given in the prone position. Blind children did not make comparable errors, but many of them made errors if the hand was turned over and back between stimulus and response. The movement apparently interfered with the tactile impression. These data are consistent with factor analyses of Ayres (1966b; 1972c; and unpublished data) in which the SCSIT test of Finger Identification tended to share variance with tests of visual perception. A profile of SCSIT scores of a classical case of apraxia is shown in the manual for those tests.

Apraxia is not adequately detected by skill in assembling a puzzle of the human form or by drawing a picture of it (cf. Abercrombie and Tyson, 1966; Bergès and Lézine, 1965; Ayres and Reid, 1966; Kraft, 1968). Statistical tests suggest that these tasks are more related to visual than to somatic perception.

Extraocular muscle control, just as control of other skeletal muscles, is often affected by apraxia (Ayres, 1965; Sandifer, 1963; Abercrombie, 1963). Considering the precision of control demanded of extraocular muscles, the involvement is logical. It is observed as difficulty in following an object steadily with the eyes. Motions at the far end of the muscle range may be especially irregular. Eyes that will not follow a volitional command make desk work most demanding.

Motor impersistence or the inability to sustain certain voluntary acts such as keeping the tongue protruded, fixing the eyes on an object lateral to the subject, or holding the fingers in a specified position may be part of the syndrome of apraxia (Garfield, 1964; Joynt, Benton and Fogel, 1962; Ayres, unpublished data).

In considering somatosensory perception, the oral region should not be overlooked. McDonald and Aungst (1966) found evidence to support the view that the quality of oral motor proficiency is related to oral sensory capacity and that experimental disruption of oral sensation seems to produce a deterioration of articulatory proficiency.

It is the clinical impression — and it is consistent with what is known from animal experimentation — that a child with poor somatosensory integration is apt to be emotionally labile and to have a greater than average tendency toward behavior problems.

Neurological Considerations

As often is the case with most attempts to coordinate basic research data into a composite picture to subserve therapeutic practice, the goal is not reached in an entirely satisfactory manner in studying the neurobiological substrate of praxis. Instead of confidence-inspiring clarity, one must be content with pieces of the whole and hope that greater cohesion will come with time.

Exploration requires looking especially at sensory integration at the cortical and diencephalic levels, remembering that there is a constant neural flow between the diencephalon and cortex. Furthermore, the tendency of the brain to function as a whole with some interdependency among structures must always be under consideration. Luria (1966b) considers praxis to be the function of the entire brain, with each segment of the brain assuming its own part in organizing skilled movement. The motor cortex is the "analyzer for movement," and is functionally an afferent apparatus, for it is there that afferent synthesis must occur before movements can be planned. A characteristic direction of evolution has been an increase in the proportion of cortex devoted to controlling afferent input and a relative decrease in the cortical cells from which muscular contraction is elicited. According to Luria (1966a), the highest association areas of the central nervous system, the cortical motor areas, are the phylogenetically youngest regions of the neocortex. In Luria's words, "The frontal portion of the cortex, in which external and internal information is integrated and transferred into definite motor acts that determine the behavior of the organism as a whole, may be considered to have become of cardinal importance in man."

Review of the work of many people in addition to considering his own led Teuber (1966) to an opinion consonant with that of Luria; namely, that visual-motor coordination takes place at some level higher than the primary visual pathways. This opinion allows the candidacy of the frontal motor areas for the highest level and provides support for the use of skilled motor action as an integrator of cortically received sensory flow, including visual input. The probable role of the brain stem integrating center in this coordination process needs recognition. It is adequately explained in the manner in which Myers, Sperry and McCurdy (1962) present Penfield's centrencephalic system: "Patterns of visual stimuli destined to regulate motor response . . . are channeled first inwards from occipital cortex to a central integrating mechanism, subsequently to be redirected outwards to the precentral cortex where final pattern of volitional activity is elicited."

If sensory input from tactile receptors contributes a large part of the sensation to be integrated at cortical and subcortical levels, they and the routes of their discharge deserve some discussion. The anatomical and physiological aspects of tactile functions are far from clear and growing increasingly complex as neurological research continues.

In order to provide some basis for tentative conceptualization of the receptors in the skin, the work of Siminoff (1965) is cited. He identified two specific mechanoreceptors in hairy skin, one in the hair and one in the skin between hair shafts. The receptors to the hairs respond to movement of the hairs and may have either high or low sensitivity. These receptors are rapidly adapting. The receptors to the skin are more slowly adapting. Activity in the receptors may be either specific or non-specific, the former contributing to tactile discrimination and the latter to pain and temperature. Pain and temperature (served by the small C fibers) are not basic modalities but the result of patterning of sensory impulses over the neurons. Different types of tactile function share fibers, allowing temporal patterns as well as receptors, fibers and tracts to determine the message sent to the brain.

The C fibers are the oldest somatosensory neurons. They are small in size, slow in conduction rate, and high in threshold. They carry messages of diffuse touch as well as pain and temperature, all of which are messages more fundamental to survival than spatial tactile information. Many of the fibers end in the brain stem to meet a quite low level of adaptive sensorimotor function. In view of their high threshold, it seems likely that their activation might require rapid and prolonged stimulation of the receptors. The proposition by Bishop (1959) that the more discriminative system is superimposed on the primitive and pervasive one would indicate that activation of the smaller tactile neurons is important to the development of discriminative touch, possibly enhancing the probability of activating the large fibers carrying spatial tactile information.

Specificity of information may be present in the afferent nerve ending and its fiber, but the specificity may not lie necessarily in the type of receptor (Mountcastle, 1957). Specificity, i.e., projection of a single stimulated point resulting in a discharge in cortical cells, would cause a lesser discharge in a larger surrounding area. Some neurophysiologists suggest that it is more appropriate to think of pools of neurons than individual ones. In addition, there is the possibility that the thalamocortical systems project multisensory components as an integrated message (Jung, 1961). Some of the brain's capacity for specific localization of a tactile stimulus derives from an inhibitory process (Mountcastle and Powell, 1959), the inhibition of cortical cells surrounding those which will yield the conscious experience of a specific spot on the skin being touched.

From this brief and simplified review of the anatomical state of affairs, there are two major concepts which emerge and should be considered in sensory integrative therapy for the apraxic child: specificity versus non-specificity of sensory process and excitation versus inhibition of sensation. Integration very likely involves a balance of all four conditions.

Occasionally an apraxic child is hypotonic, suggesting some failure of receptivity or processing on the part of the central nervous system or an overactivation of the inhibitory functions. More frequently, muscle tone is normal and the child tends toward greater than average activity. It is suggested that, in these cases, part of the difficulty lies in inadequate inhibition of the barrage of diffuse tactile stimuli which almost always bombard the brain. Such normal inhibition, when present, usually arises from tactile and proprioceptive stimulation, especially that elicited by touch-pressure or in receptors concerned with postural responses. The inhibition may allow greater specificity of sensory analysis.

Apparently, the neural disorder resulting in apraxia arises from a neurodevelopmental deviation that prevents the maturation of the inhibitory mechanisms and the development of the integrative mechanisms. Or it may be that the brain's receptivity to the inhibiting stimuli has been reduced. Both tactile receptors and proprioceptors contribute to the inhibitory mechanisms of the brain.

These facts do not point clearly to therapeutic methods, but the direction is certainly toward the need for intersensory integration with emphasis on the tactile and kinesthetic systems, or sensations arising from planned motion and for sensory inhibition from proprioceptive sources. The discussion of neurobiology in the chapter on tactile defensiveness is also appropriate to this chapter and will add to an understanding of the physiology of the tactile sense and thus to a theoretical base for the treatment of apraxia.

Treatment Plan and Principles

Consistent with the theses that the cortex will not function optimally unless the lower centers of the brain are well organized and that the discriminative system is superimposed upon the diffuse system, the amelioration of the disordered sensory integration begins with focusing on the enhancement of sensory integration at the brain stem level. The approach is that described in Chapter 9, General Principles and Methods of Intervention, which recommends initiating treatment with generalized vestibular and tactile stimulation. The intermodality influence may result in the vestibular stimuli enhancing the organization of the tactile, as well as other sensory stimuli in the reticular formation. Rationale supporting the integrating properties of tactile stimulation in general is discussed rather extensively in earlier chapters and in the chapter on tactile defensiveness.

Theoretically, rapid light brushing with a battery-driven device may be most apt to activate the smaller tactile neurons with a high threshold because of the opportunity for temporal summation. The strong inclination and frequent preference of children for light rapid brushing of the skin suggests the appropriateness of that form of tactile stimulation for the apraxic child. The use of a common paint brush, such as that used for painting furniture may serve a similar purpose. A guide to type and quantity of stimuli recommended earlier is the reaction of the child. In general, that which is most comfortable to a child will be most integrating. The assumption, of course, is that comfort reflects integration and, given an opportunity, the brain will attempt to organize itself.

Only when a therapist is fairly certain about his approach should he impose tactile stimulation on a child. One condition in which forcing stimulation might be acceptable is when a child becomes emotionally distraught and the therapist knows from previous experience that certain types of tactile stimulation have been acceptable to the child's nervous system. The influence of tactile stimulation given at the beginning of the treatment period will last for about a half hour, thus interacting with subsequent activity. Other stimuli entering into the nervous system will interact with the previous input, of course.

Tactile stimulation can be provided as an inherent part of an activity, such as through the lining of a barrel in which the child rolls or through contact with a strip of carpet on the bottom of a tunnel through which the child moves himself in various fashions. A rug attached to a slanted board on which the child rolls gives tactile stimulation, especially if the slant of the board is so great the child has a tendency to slip down the board from the force of gravity. There is likely special neurophysiological value in combining the tactile stimulation with the purposeful motor act, for that is the manner in which each child's tactile-motor planning domain matures. Furthermore, skin surface and underlying muscle are closely related functionally.

A further advantage to combining the tactile stimulation with the activity lies in the child's initiating the stimulus himself. A self-initiated stimulus is often more acceptable, especially to those who are tactually defensive. Similarly, if a child has difficulty tolerating tactile stimulation administered by a therapist, he may be able to accept direct stimulation that he gives to himself. Touching oneself is not the same neurological process as being touched. Apparently, the act of touching oneself, even passively as in walking on a carpet, automatically activates an inhibitory process which makes the stimuli acceptable to and usable by the nervous system. It is probably this very inhibitory process that is in particular need of activation in order to allow the discriminatory tactile process to predominate over the more diffuse, emotionally loaded, non-spatially specific response.

In giving tactile stimulation, the therapist must consider that the response of any child's body to a sensory stimulus will be strongly determined by all of the previous neural experience and the current state of the brain (cf. Brazier, Killam and Hance, 1961). Since the therapist can only guess at previous neural experience and the current state of the brain, the child's response to tactile stimulation provides the clearest guide and the indirect evidence for the previous and current neural state. Since some reactions to tactile stimuli occur immediately and some of the more cumulative ones not for ten or fifteen minutes, observation should last for that period. The therapist, of course, should take into consideration the sensory stimuli entering the nervous system after the tactile stimulation. The advantage of using the child's reaction to the therapeutic effort in this and all other cases lies in the fact that the child's brain operates on the basis of all of those aspects of the nervous system of which the therapist is still ignorant, and even at best, could not know all. Additional considerations in giving direct tactile stimulation is found in the chapter on tactile defensiveness.

Studies supporting the use of tactile stimulation to enhance tactile perception and praxis are not plentiful. Most small studies require an isolated and discrete use of tactile stimulation without its incorporation into a more natural comprehensive intervention program. Nevertheless, studies do demonstrate a considerable influence of tactile stimulation. Adams (1965) found that it could increase kinesthesia in children with neurological disorders. Fox (1964) demonstrated enhanced finger identification and manual perception of two-dimensional forms in hemiplegic adults following five minutes of touch-pressure stimulation such as that received from rubbing with a cloth. In a study with children, Griffin (1964) found that touch-pressure tended to enhance recognition of designs drawn on the skin and to decrease two-point discrimination. Neither difference reached statistical significance; however, two-point discrimination was enhanced significantly following light touch stimulation administered with a battery-driven brush compared to following touch-pressure stimuli. A possible explanation for these results is that light touch stimuli enhance sensitivity through the ascending reticular activating system while touch-pressure may inhibit that system. The interpretation is consistent with the findings of Armstrong (1968). She demonstrated with statistical significance that tactile stimulation with the battery-driven brush increased tactile discrimination as measured by the Semmes-Weinstein Pressure Aesthesiometer. The subjects of the study were considered neurologically normal. Of particular significance is the previously cited study by Casler (1965) in which institutionalized babies under one year of age responded to impersonally administered light touch-pressure stimulation with enhanced Gesell Developmental Quotients. The outcome of experiments of the effect of motor activity on praxis is likely to be dependent upon the type of interpretation the researcher gives it. Painter (1966) found that rhythmic and sensory-motor activity with kindergarten children with low Goodenough mental age scores made significant changes over a control group on tests purported to test body image and perceptual-motor integration.

Since the sense of kinesthesis contributes to praxis, procedures which are believed to activate the joint receptors are appropriately included in the remedial program. Both joint traction and approximation may increase discharge from joint receptors. Traction is accomplished by placing weighted cuffs on wrists and ankles during activity. Joint approximation is accomplished through cocontraction of muscles surrounding a joint or through manually pushing on the heel or hand with the extremity extended or pushing on head or shoulders of the seated child. Activities described earlier which promote cocontraction are recommended for apraxia. Jumping on a jumping board, hop scotch and jumping rope stimulate the joint receptors. Whenever the weight of the body is borne on the hand, comparable joint compression is exerted on the upper extremities, especially if the arms are extended. Bouncing in the seated position on an inner tube, a large rubber ball or mattress will activate co-innervation of trunk muscles, presumably through joint approximation, as well as the activation of equilibrium responses.

The possible contribution of stimuli from the muscle receptors to praxis can only be inferred, and one route to that inference is their probable role in contributing to and organizing of the sensorimotor patterns of the brain stem. Developmentalists generally assert that complex motor patterns develop out of previous, more simple patterns, and the brain stem harbors the integrating centers for some of the simplest total-body motor patterns. Activating these motor patterns may bring about integration of stimuli entering the brain stem.

For a similar reason, any disorder of postural mechanisms in the apraxic child should be treated according to recommendations previously given. Even when disorders which can be attributed to brain stem dysfunction appear not to be present, some emphasis on activities especially involving brain stem integrating mechanisms is appropriate for the apraxic child. The rationale supporting this recommendation lies in the possible strengthening of the foundation for more cortically directed motion and also in the possibility that mild deviations in brain stem directed motor functions might be overlooked. Even the most skilled motion has a reflex basis.

Several important principles guide the selection of the activities. Initially, the entire body should be involved in the motor execution, even though the plan emphasizes movement in only one segment of the body. Scooter board activities exemplify use of the principle. The more of the body that is used the greater the sensory input and usually the more generalized the learning. Furthermore, a child's development proceeds from the gross to the fine and the apraxic child's sensorimotor system can be construed as behind in development.

That aspect of the intervention program for the apraxic child which most distinguishes it from remediation of other syndromes is the inclusion of an endless variety of activities requiring motor planning. Since learning to motor plan or guiding a body scheme requires attempting an unfamiliar or as yet not mastered task, the availability of a diverse assortment of activity is recommended. The need for a large repertoire of activities taxes even the most creative therapist. The therapist must never forget that activities are *means* to an end; they are not ends in themselves. It is not the knowing of specific motor skills that is therapeutic — it is the increase in sensory integration that increases a child's capacity to learn and otherwise cope with life. The process of learning adds to sensorimotor integration as a whole. Once a skill has been learned, its main contribution is emotional satisfaction or, as in the case of tasks like tying shoes, the end result of the motor action. The obvious nature of motion can distract the therapist's attention from the more important focus of sensory integration.

Since apraxia is seen as a disorder of sensory integration, activities are planned, especially initially, to elicit a considerable quantity of related sensory input. The adaptive motor response of the activity forces organization of the sensory input. The purpose of the movement gives meaning to the sensory input, including that from somatosensory, vestibular and visual receptors, and meaning implies integration. In fact, sensations are given functional meaning only in terms of the result of the associated motion. Without some recognized result from action, the capacity to interpret sensation would never develop. At the same time that movement provides functional meaning for sensation, it also elicits many sensations. The greater the quantity of sensory input and the more sensory modalities involved, the more generalized the sensory integration.

The learning disabled child for whom motor planning activities are appropriate is usually able to employ some self-direction, and that self-direction should be encouraged. Only the child can integrate his nervous system; the therapist provides the nurturing environment. The inner-directed child reaches the goal of sensory integration more quickly than one that requires considerable direction from the therapist.

It is the responsibility of the therapist to provide a task involving that developmental level which enables the child to direct himself. Initially the child with a very poorly developed body scheme may be unable to follow verbal directions in order to execute a task. In this case, instruction is accomplished by either demonstrating the motion for the child or passively taking him through the required motion. Greater involvement on the part of the child is encouraged if he is asked if he *can* perform a given task rather than requiring him to do so. When the child is able to do so, his verbalizing what he is going to do before he attempts a task reinforces the organization of the motor plan. The involvement of two or more children in the same activity increases the complexity of the plan.

Suggested Activities to Develop Praxis

The recent focus on perceptual-motor dysfunction has given

rise to a number of books that direct most of their contents to the description of remedial activity. The availability of those suggestions reduces the need for extensive activity listing here. Since the theoretical system presented places more emphasis on replicating developmentally early sensorimotor experiences and on somatosensory and vestibular input and integration than do most remedial workers, some typical activities are described. Many of these activities are demonstrated in a film (Ayres and Heskett (1970a).

Scooter board activities. These activities are designed to take place in an area about ten by forty feet in size with a ramp four by six feet in size elevated at one end to about one and one-half to two feet. A platform at the raised end allows the child to get on the scooter and prepare for descent of the ramp. Many activities are designed concurrently to integrate the primitive postural reflexes while planning a motor act.

1. Lying prone on scooter board, ride between two cardboard cartons without touching cartons. Try the same task by pushing off from wall with feet and coasting through tunnel of cartons. Try either approach with eyes closed after first noting position of cartons and thinking about how to push. Attempt same activities lying supine. Try them while coasting after riding down the ramp.

2. Push off from wall with feet and "crash" into a tower of cartons. Use helmet to protect head and be sure neck muscles can cocontract enough to stabilize head. Push off from wall with hands and hit tower with feet. Try either task with eyes closed.

3. Lie prone on scooter board and back up, pushing with hands, so that legs go through a suspended hoop. Catch hoop with feet and pull hoop forward. Repeat with eyes closed after noting spatial orientation of body to hoop. Repeat using one leg, then the other. Try to catch hoop with just toe or toes and pull on hoop. Repeat all tasks lying supine on scooter board. In this position and with hoop at the head instead of feet, push so that head goes through hoop. Try putting both arms through the hoop, then the right, then left. Then try all variations with eyes closed, catching hoop and pulling slightly with arm or head. Try all of the above with eyes closed, starting out with hoop at head, then turning around while moving on the scooter board so that approach to hoop is feet first. Then try starting out with feet toward hoop and turning so that head and arms go through hoop. Try moving toward hoop so that right arm and leg go through

hoop, then left arm and leg. Can child think of any other possibilities? Therapist holds hoop for individual work and to assist child in reaching goal. Hoops are suspended for group work. A satisfactory and durable hoop can be made from a piece of old garden hose into which a wire has been inserted and both ends of which are nailed to a small piece of inserted dowel.

4. Push off from wall with feet and touch overhanging hoop with one or both hands and one or both feet. Try in both prone and supine positions. Try touching hoop while eyes are closed after first noting position of hoop. Use hanging ball instead of hoop. Approach hoop or ball feet first, either pushing off wall with hands or simply pushing against the floor with the hands.

5. Lie supine on scooter board and push self through forest of cardboard cartons without using hands or touching boxes. Try task with paper sack over head to occlude vision and feeling location of boxes with hands, but avoiding touching boxes with scooter board. Try similar procedure scattering small objects about the floor and lying prone on the scooter board. Pretend objects are rocks in river which must not be hit with canoe. Require backward as well as forward movement.

6. Sit on scooter board and turn scooter and self around longitudinal axis of body, using feet to propel self. First go in one direction, then in the other. Keep scooter over a given spot marked on the floor. Try pushing with one hand, then with the other. Then put one hand on the spot on the floor and pivot around that hand pushing with both feet. Pivot around other hand. Go forward as well as backward.

7. Sit on scooter board and push self past barrel or box and throw ball into it. Try approaching barrel back first, going as fast as possible. Lie prone on scooter, push with feet against wall and coast, throwing ball into box. Try again lying supine on scooter board. After trying all of these approaches with eyes open, try closing eyes after appraising the spatial situation and planning the action.

8. Stretch a rope between two points about one foot off the floor. Lie prone on scooter board and "ferry" self from one end of rope to the other, pulling hand over hand. Try it lying supine and later with eyes closed. Attach rope to higher points and sit on scooter board, pulling self hand over hand,

first forward, then backward. Try each again with eyes closed.

9. Lie prone or supine on scooter. Move toward empty cardboard carton feet first. Lift carton with one or both feet and carry it to designated place. Push with hands or one foot. Try same procedure using head or hands. Try it with eyes closed after position of carton is noted.

10. Place cardboard carton on floor. Lie on scooter board about five feet away. Push self around carton without touching it and return to original spot, being aware of how it feels to make the trip. Then close eyes and repeat act trying to follow same path. If it is too hard to keep the eyes closed, put a paper sack over the head.

11. Lying prone on scooter board, push self between two walls, hands touching one wall, feet the other wall. Go back and forth several times without touching floor. Repeat the procedure, touching right wall with right hand and foot only and left wall with left hand and foot.

12. Two children lie prone on scooters and push off with feet from opposite walls and pass each other touching hands. Try it again clasping hands and pivoting around them, returning to original station.

13. Place rope through pulley at distant point and attach one end of rope to scooter board. Sit on scooter and pull on free end of rope to move scooter. Try moving feet first, head first or sideways by sitting in different positions on scooter board. Try attaching rope to different parts of the body, such as the feet.

14. Sit on scooter board and hold on to the end of a suspended rope. Pull on rope and let go of it so that scooter coasts to a given point. Try coasting into a cardboard carton. Try closing eyes after position of carton has been noted. Attach end of rope to a spring suspended from ceiling and pull on other end of rope so that scooter board moves in one direction, then pull the rope again so that scooter board goes in opposite direction. Do not let go of rope.

15. Restrain one or both hands or put in hip pocket. Lie prone on scooter board or sit on it and try simple movement such as pushing or getting off scooter. Then try some of the more difficult games described above. Restrain right hand to increase awareness of left side of body.

16. Ride a scooter board prone down a ramp and hit a hanging ball with one hand. On next trip, hit it with the other hand.

Then try hitting it with both hands simultaneously. Is it possible to hit it with a foot? With a head?

17. Ride the scooter board down the ramp carrying a ball, pillow or bean bag and toss it through a hoop or into a box. Is it possible to catch the ball after it has gone through the hoop? Try to toss the bean bag into a box moving in the opposite direction. The box can be pulled on another scooter board.

18. Ride a scooter prone down the ramp and with the right hand pick up a pillow on the floor to the right side. Next trip use the left hand to pick up the pillow placed to the left side. Then try using the right hand to pick up a pillow on the left and the left hand to pick up a pillow on the right side. After mastering these, try picking up the pillow in various ways and tossing it into a box or through a hoop. Try to pick up a ball rolling along the floor, using the various combinations of hands and sides.

19. Ride down ramp on scooter board and grab leg of therapist standing about twenty feet from ramp. Pivot around therapist. First use one hand and go one direction and then use the other hand and go the other direction. Then ride scooter board down ramp and place right hand on floor about where therapist was standing and pivot around the hand. Try again using left hand. Using hands to get started, try to turn scooter board around once or twice after it reaches the floor and continues rolling.

20. Ride scooter board down ramp and knock down a tower of cartons with right hand, later with left hand, then try to hit it with the feet. Try going down ramp feet first and hitting the tower.

21. Ride down ramp and grab a sturdy ball suspended with a rope and spring. Try to hang on to ball without falling off the scooter. Try to catch the ball while it is moving. A ball can be suspended by placing it in a basketball net and tying a rope to the net. A piece of inner tube can take the place of a spring.

22. Ride down ramp in prone position and turn sideways as mat is approached. As scooter is stopped by mat, roll off of it and continue rolling across mat.

23. Prepare a strip of rubber by cutting an automobile tire inner tube in a spiral manner. Attach each of the two ends to two opposite stationary points about 20 to 30 feet from a ramp or wall. Ride down the ramp or push off from the wall

and go underneath the rubber strip without touching it. If it is safe to do so, try it with eyes closed.

24. Ride the scooter board prone down the ramp and go under the inner tube strip, catching it with both legs flexed at the knee. Try again flexing only one leg to catch the strip, then use the other leg. Try to catch the strip with the heels, then with one heel. Try going down the ramp prone, feet first and catching the strip with the shins, but be very careful and go slowly at first.

25. Ride the scooter board prone down the ramp and go under the inner tube strip, catching it with one arm raised and slightly flexed at the elbow. Next trip catch it with the other arm. Is it possible to catch the strip with both arms simultaneously? Try putting the head under the strip and the arms over the strip. Go down ramp feet first and catch strip with arms held up above head.

26. Ride down the ramp supine, feet first, and catch rubber strip with thighs. Hips and knees are flexed. Try catching strip with shins. Approach this procedure carefully and slowly to see the demands it makes on the body.

27. Sit on scooter board and ride down ramp hitting strip with trunk. Try again and grab strip with hands and with help of the elasticity of the strip and pushing with the hands push self back toward ramp. Then suspend a ball and try to hit ball with body while returning toward ramp.

28. Sit on scooter and hold on to the middle of rubber strip with hands. Push, then pull self back and forth. Try it with a partner, one going one direction and the other the other direction.

29. Sit on scooter board and push self with wood dowel with crutch tip on end or with a plunger (plumber's helper). To inhibit the TNR sit on scooter board and look to left. Place left hand on hip. Push self with right arm either to goal toward which one is looking or pivot around in a circle. Try looking to the right and pushing self with left arm.

30. Alter any of these activities by placing a weighted cuff on either or both ankles or wrists or placing a sand bag on shoulders or head. Make a game of keeping the sand bag from falling off.

General activities to develop praxis.

1. Roll up in a rug or large cloth. Roll on a rug or carpet from one given place to another, being sure head and feet arrive

at the designated place. Place rug on slight incline and roll up and down it.

2. Roll up rug. Child walks or jumps length of rug keeping left foot on left side of rug and right foot on right side of rug without letting legs touch rug.

3. Pull a tube of stretch nylon cloth over one's head and then down the body and step out of it. Step into the tube and pull it up and off over the head. Tube should be tight enough to provide considerable touch-pressure and require some effort or squirming to get through it.

4. Squirm through a tube of cotton cloth or nylon net about three yards long and two yards in circumference. Nylon net allows seeing and is recommended for the child who is threatened in a situation where he cannot rely on sight.

5. Crawl through obstacle course of cardboard cartons, assortment of odd items and sticks and ropes across the path at different heights without touching objects. Go over some sticks and under others.

6. Place a number of cardboard cartons in various positions. Step from one into the next without moving carton.

7. Place strips of masking tape on floor to indicate place where child is to start a jump and where his feet are to land. Add red and green color to tape to indicate start or stop. Strips can vary in distance from each other. Length of strip indicates position in which foot is to land. A square indicates child is to land on heels and a triangle indicates child is to land on toes. Having to meet the requirements of the specific place to land places the motor planning element in what otherwise might be mere automatic movement. Pieces of rubber backed carpet can be used in place of tape if carpet does not slip on floor.

8. Place a rope on the floor in a winding, twisted pattern. Child walks with one foot one one side and the other foot on the other side using heels only (or toes) without touching rope.

9. Place a rope on the floor in a straight line. Walk with right foot on left side of rope and left leg on right side of rope, always taking a step by bringing the leg that is behind to a position in front of the other. Try the same procedure walking backward.

10. Place a long rope on the floor in a pattern in which the rope crosses itself often. Walk along the rope, jumping over each crossing rope.

11. While therapist is slowly "snaking" a rope by moving one end of it back and forth, child jumps over rope.

12. Tie ends of a rope together so that it makes a loop of about one yard circumference. Child clasps fingers together so that they cannot be used to grasp the rope but can be used in the same way that a foot is used. Child sits on rug with rope beside him, then tries to maneuver himself through the rope ring. The task can be made more difficult by placing child on a slanted rug-covered board. The more he slips and slides on the rug the more tactile stimulation he receives.

13. Tap out a simple rhythm on tin cans or drums.

14. Using wood dowels as stick horses, pretend to be a horse walking (same as child's walk), trotting (a deliberate placing of all the body's weight first on one foot, then the other, as though jumping from one foot to the other), or galloping (the same foot always leads).

15. Hoops about two to two and one-half feet in diameter offer a wide variety of opportunity for motor planning of an advanced level. With hoop on floor child jumps into it forward, backward, bilaterally, or first one leg, then the other. He is given various instructions such as put your head and one hand inside the hoop and keep everything else outside. With the hoop held upright he leaps through it without touching it. Lying on his back, he holds the loop with both hands and braces his feet against the inside of the hoop, then rotates the hoop in a horizontal position by moving hands and feet appropriately. While the hands go in one direction the feet go in the other. The child rotates the hoop in a vertical position by having the feet "walk" against the inside of the hoop while the hands hold the hoop. The position of the hands must be changed as the hoop rotates.

16. A large inflated inner tube offers a multitude of possibilities, all with considerable sensory input. The child walks forward, sideways, or backwards, having to plan the placement of his feet so that he does not walk off the tube. He repeats the ambulation in quadruped instead of biped position. Holding the therapist's hands, he jumps on the inner tube first with his feet, then lands on his knees, then on the next bounce sits on the tube. He runs and jumps first on one side of the tube, then the other, then off onto the floor. He is asked to specify how many times he is going to jump in one spot, then how many times in another spot, then does so.

17. Child kicks suspended ball hanging behind him, then to his side.
18. The plastic rings that are used as "white walls" on tires are placed on the floor in various patterns. Child then jumps or leaps from one to the other.
19. Go through tunnel with a strip of carpet laid through it using a specified position such as both elbows and one knee only touching the carpet.
20. Roll in a barrel by putting hands on floor and turning body from quadruped to a supine position, then back to quadruped, etc.
21. Punch a plastic balloon attached to helmet with a long piece of rubber.
22. Ambulate using the knee of one leg and the foot of the other; with hand and leg on opposite sides of the body or on same side; with knees slightly flexed; without taking feet off the floor; to the side or backward; combination of these.
23. Make an elastic loop of about 16 to 20 inches circumference from an automobile tire inner tube. Child places loop around ankles and keep it from falling off by the spacing of the legs and walks. He can also place the right foot ahead of the left, then jump reversing position of the feet, trying to obtain a rhythmic motion without letting the loop fall off the feet.
24. Child sits on one one-legged stool facing therapist who tells a story with many manual gestures which the child duplicates.
25. Pretend to be a cat about to pounce on a mouse, a crocodile crossing a river, a cow eating grass, a rabbit hopping, an elephant cooling itself by squirting a trunkful of water over itself, a turtle crossing a road, a lamb frolicking in spring sunshine.

Chapter 12

Form and Space Perception

"Space *is an idea,* a product of the mind" (Gooddy and Reinhold, 1952). It, like all perception, is a quality which an individual
attributes to sensations. The method by which man organizes and
develops that capacity holds the key to treatment of disorders of
space perception.

Upon recognition that some learning disorders could be traced
to perceptual deficits, visual perception came under immediate
exploration, for the visual perception demands of reading are
fairly obvious. An exemplary study of those early years (Goins,
1958) demonstrated that among a group of 120 first-grade children,
substantial correlations existed between reading test scores and
copying patterns or designs (r = .52) and between reading and
recognizing the reversed image of a stimulus figure (r = .49).
Reading was less related to visual matching of figures. More recent
studies (for example Punwar, 1970) revealed a similar relationship
between space visualization and reading as well as other academic
work of young school age children.

Noting that visual perception problems were the most frequent
symptoms of learning difficulties, Frostig, one of the foremost
pioneers in the field, developed with others a battery of tests
tapping what she considered the major types of perceptual disorder. They included eye-hand coordination, form constancy, figure-
ground perception, position in space, and spatial relations (Maslow,

Frostig, Lefever and Whittlesey, 1964). Of the subtests covering these areas, that testing spatial relations has shown the most consistent correlation with sensory integrative dysfunction in general.

Description of Disorder in Form and Space Perception

Irregularity in development of form and space perception is seldom seen independently of other sensory integrative problems among children with learning disabilities. Usually it appears in conjunction with postural, ocular, and somatosensory disabilities. Nevertheless, statistical analyses have repeatedly indicated that a number of behavioral dimensions related to form and space perception show sufficiently strong associative bonds to appear as a meaningful functional unit which can be postulated to be a neural subsystem. It involves several levels of simultaneous brain function. As with other aspects of sensory integrative dysfunction, the lower levels are usually the seat of much of the problem, and, judging by therapeutic results, are usually the first place to focus remedial work.

The neural subsystem identified as subserving form and space perception is characterized by its cross-modality function, a condition that holds significance for the approach in therapeutic procedures. The behavioral dimensions as demonstrated by factor analyses and other statistical research consist especially of visual form and space perception, kinesthesia, manual form perception, and, to a lesser extent, visual figure-ground perception and perception in other sensory modalities that involve some kind of form perception, such as perception of geometric designs drawn on the skin with vision occluded (Ayres, 1965, 1969a, 1972c). These associations are consistent with findings by Semmes (1965), who found a non-tactual spatial factor in astereognosis, and with studies by Birch and Lefford (1967) and Semmes, Weinstein, Ghent and Teuber (1955).

It seems possible that the strong tendency for visual test scores to load together on factors independent of postural mechanisms is due in part to the fact that the tests employed tap primarily, but not exclusively, cortically mediated visual perception as opposed to that occurring in the brain stem. The cortical visual process may have responded especially to specific training. The cortical contribution to the neural subsystem may account for a greater statistical differentiation between visual perception and other neural subsystems than is generally observed clinically. While the statistical analyses support the hypothesis that space perception and postural mechanisms serve different neural subsystems, other analyses indicate a close relationship between the systems.

Visual perception problems sometimes are related to brain stem disorders, but in some children they seem to be associated with right cerebral hemisphere involvement. In any sample of children with brain dysfunction, there are probably some with fairly discrete right hemisphere dysfunction. This condition, along with the fact that cortically directed visual perception is highly subject to learning and is often "taught" in school, may contribute to the fact that visual perception tends to appear as a separate factor from that termed "postural and bilateral integration." Although disordered visual perception which can be attributed primarily to the right cerebral cortex may be considered a disorder different from that which seems to be associated with the brain stem, at no time does one system operate independently of all others. The brain stem, the thalamus, the "old" cortex, and the neocortex all contribute to the end product.

Some Aspects of Neuroanatomy Subserving Visual Perception

The occipital (visual) cortex of man's cerebral hemispheres has received the major research emphasis and credit for visual perception, but what is known of the development and function of man's brain is limited by natural restrictions in experimentation. What is not known is as important as what is known. For that reason reliance must be placed on analogies drawn from knowledge of function in lower animals.

It is appropriate to recall at this point a principle of brain function stated earlier. As the brain evolved, it added, not substituted, function. Man's highly developed visual form and space discrimination remains somewhat dependent upon his lower brain function (as well as other levels in between). An interdependence and interaction of the different levels of function may be a more accurate description than dependence alone. This neuroanatomical dependence upon lower brain function along with clinical observations that frequently link disordered visual perception and brain stem postural mechanisms draws attention to basic research at the brain stem, especially midbrain level.

Experimentally induced damage in the midbrain and nearby areas of lower animals has resulted in a variety of interferences in visual processes. Thompson, Lukaszewska, Schweigert and McNew (1967) found disturbances in visual and kinesthetic functions of rats following lesions in the midbrain-thalamic area even though the primary sensory tracts for vision and kinesthesis were not damaged. Unilateral neglect of stimuli in contralateral visual fields has been found to follow a unilateral lesion in a superior colliculus of the midbrain tectum (Sprague and Meikle, 1965) and in the subthalamus (Adey, 1964). Bilateral destruction of the superior colliculi were found to result in transitory visual disturbance (Myers, 1964), and in difficulty in visual following, localization of stationary objects, and localization of tactile stimuli (Sprague and Meikle, 1965). Superior colliculi have also been found to be concerned with movements of the head, body, and eyes (Sprague and Meikle, 1965). These investigators concluded that the superior colliculi serve visual attention and perception as well as control of movements of head and eye (Sprague and Meikle, 1965).

Craddock (1971) interpreted loss of visual discrimination in rats with tegmental damage to be due to dysfunction of the red nucleus. Thompson and Myers (1971) found that damage to the pretectal nucleus-posterior region of the brain stem of monkeys interfered with visual discrimination tasks involving retention. They suggested that pretectal area may have visual associative functions. The study supports the idea of the existence of a corticofugal system from cortex to midbrain via the thalamus mediating visual discrimination performance.

In the lower animal, there is accurate topographic representation of the visual fields or environmental space in the superior colliculi. After careful study of basic research results of his work and that of others, Trevarthen (1968) concluded that precise visual representation in the midbrain is present in the primates. However, it is noteworthy that the number of optic fibers that go to the superior colliculi is greatly reduced in man (Crosby, et al., 1962).

The brain stem provides the important lower level of brain function in this neural system which taps several levels of brain function at one time. Trevarthen (1968) has pointed out that studies "have emphasized the importance of the colliculi as midbrain sensory-motor integrating mechanisms providing a visuospatial frame for action centered on the body as a whole." He feels visual and related motor function, especially oculomotor and simple postural and locomotor responses, are essentially one integrated function at the midbrain level.

It is clear that the midbrain is assuming an increasingly important role in the thinking of investigators of the neurophysiological bases of several aspects of behavior. Basing his opinion on many sources of research, including his own, Denny-Brown (1962) has commented, "It is extraordinary that the removal of a relatively small area of the neuraxis, the tectum of the midbrain, should inactivate the elaborate hemispheric organization for reaction to events in the external world." While the tectum is vital to organization of movement, it is also important to perception, according to Denny-Brown. Trevarthen (1968) and Held (1968) are of the same opinion. From his extensive work on the brain of lower primates, Doty (1966) concluded that the mesencephalic reticular formation not only exerts considerable control over synaptic transmission in the visual system of primates but also is the source of control.

These observations and the fact that many postural mechanisms are integrated in the midbrain are consistent with the statistical analyses made of disordered sensorimotor functions in children. A definite association was found between disorders of postural mechanisms and visual perception. The postural mechanisms were closely associated with ocular muscle control. It is proposed that some of the symptoms seen in some children with learning disorders reflect a failure on the part of the brain stem visual integrating centers to contribute their part to the cortical visual process, thus interfering with the visual aspect of reading.

While the brain stem deserves particular attention in studying visual perception and its functions can be understood reasonably well at this time, portions of the forebrain other than the visual cortex are deserving of attention for they, too, make contributions to visual perception. In one of the classic descriptions of the effects on behavior of removal of both temporal lobes — including the uncus and the greater part of the hippocampus — of monkeys, Klüver and Bucy (1939) found considerable disorder in visual discriminatory reactions. This appears to be an example of another older, simpler structure being involved in the visual perception process.

The Development of Visual Perception in Man

Phylogenetic considerations — It is not implied that man's brain functions in the same manner as that of lower animals, but the assumption that there is some resemblance has led to apparently effective treatment of children with sensory integrative disorders. The research on lower animals was cited to illustrate the potential significance to visual perception of the different levels of the brain. Reviewing some of the principles of the brain's evolution helps place the basic research results in further context.

As the vertebrates evolved, there was a time when the highest vertebrates on earth — and presumably one in the line that eventually evolved into *Homo sapiens* — had very little cerebral cortex. Yet these animals ambulated successfully, and not incidentally quadrupedally, relating their bodies to their spatial or environmental world and the world to their bodies in the most fundamental type of space perception. The evolution of the environmental scheme and visual perception of it was closely linked to the primitive motor actions that were critical to survival at that time. This era long preceded the need to distinguish a "p" from a "q" or to determine into which hole to insert a peg, and the neural structure necessary to do so did not exist.

Although behavior was not complex in comparison to that seen in man today, integration of behavior was complete. A structure in the brain stem accurately recorded the visual image of the environmental scheme and other structures automatically regulated eye movements so that the visual field was coordinated with the motions that enabled the organism to act upon that environment. That action was largely locomotion, and additional brain stem and lower neural structures organized those locomotor actions. Simultaneously, the vestibular system was providing the animal with information about his relationship to the earth's gravitational force and about the speed of his body through space.

It is important to note these four closely interrelated functions essential to survival: (1) perception of gravity and motion through space, (2) extraocular muscle control, (3) locomotion and postural responses and proprioception relative to them, and (4) visual perception of space. These four functions became closely associated through brain stem integrating mechanisms. These mechanisms continue to function in somewhat the same way in man today, although cortical visual activity has vastly extended man's capacity for visual perception. It is proposed that the higher levels of brain function subserving visual perception in man do not operate optimally without adequate function at the brain stem level, especially the midbrain.

It was this principle of brain function that Denny-Brown (1962) was expressing when he wrote that the reactions organized at the midbrain level were the "essential substrate for all the more highly developed behavioural reactions."

Ontogenetic considerations — Just as the evolution of visual form and, especially, space perception was largely dependent upon the associations made between sensation and motion, so also is each individual child's visual perception development to a certain extent dependent upon a similar process. Of particular interest is the role of the vestibular system and motion in relation to information supplied by it.

The most fundamental form of space perception lies in the organism's recognition and accurate interpretation of the direction of pull of the earth's gravitational force. Derived from this interpretation is the simple but basic recognition of what is "up" and what is "down." It is the beginning of establishing an "environmental scheme," a model or map of the environment to which the body relates. The environmental scheme is analogous to the body scheme, the latter referring to the model or plan of how the body functions as a mechanical structure. The nature of each scheme is dependent in part upon the nature of the other, for the body is the center of the environmental scheme and the environmental plan exists only in relation to the body holding that map.

The body of the organism is located within the environmental scheme and acts within it according to the scheme. The environmental scheme changes each time the head or body changes position, for this scheme is a spatial relationship between the body and the earth and objects in the environment. Lord Brain (1963) has expressed the relationship thus: "All action in the external world requires and implies information as to the existing orientation of the body in relation to it, and of the parts of the body to one another."

While the most elementary perception of the environment is perception of the direction of the earth's gravitational pull, almost inseparable from it is the perception of movement, its direction and speed. These functions of the vestibular system — perception of movement and gravity — are central to the origins of space perception. As the individual moves about within his environmental space, further information about its spatial qualities are gained from other sources of proprioception and tactile stimulation. These somatosensory and vestibular bits of information give meaning to each other, and both of them, through the process of intersensory integration, provide the brain with the information that allows visual stimuli reflecting the environment to come to have accurate meaning. Thus the environmental scheme becomes primarily visual — a constantly changing visual map for the purpose of planning and executing motor acts within the environmental space. The visual interpretation adapts to the proprioceptive information, not vice versa.

One of the typical experiments within this theoretical framework (Held and Rekosh, 1963) involved active and passive locomotion during vision with prisms. Adaptation to the visual distortions induced by the prisms was made through active movement and its resultant sensory feedback. Comparable results were obtained by Held and Hein (1963) with kittens. Those kittens receiving the same visual input as control kittens but denied the somatosensory stimulation from self-produced locomotion were inferior to control kittens in performance on visual-locomotor tasks, including paw placing, avoidance of a visual cliff, and blink to an approaching object. The results suggest that normally cats associate visual and proprioceptive information for use in motor performance.

Gernandt's view of space perception (1964) also stresses a multisensory source. He sees the ocular system, the vestibular system, and sensations from muscles, joints, viscera, and skin as interdependent and acting as an "equilibration triad" with the duty of keeping the body regulated and positioned in space. He points out that the influence from these sensory sources all converge on a final common path. For the therapist concerned with learning disorders, the centripetal influence is as important as the centrifugal output. Just as attaching meaning to printed letters does not come from the visual stimulus but from some learned process (E. J. Gibson, 1963), so also is the ability to attribute meaning to the sight of the body-space environment a learned process. It is primarily the end product of adjustive motor responses.

Postural responses in general were treated in greater detail in an earlier chapter. Here a few points are made that have obviously very direct relationships to visual functions. Proprioception from the head, neck, and eye musculature is essential to balance. This combination of musculature is integrated at several levels of the brain. It has been pointed out that coordination occurs especially at the brain stem; apparently it also occurs in the frontal lobes. From a review of the literature and his own observations, Luria (1966b) concluded that frontal lobe lesions that interfered with function of the systems regulating the head, neck, and eyes will inevitably lead to disturbance of visual perception. Therapeutic procedures rely heavily on the relationship between certain musculature and the visual perception process. The neck muscles are among those receiving emphasis.

In addition to dependence upon integration of sensation from several sensory sources within the brain stem, visual perception is dependent upon adequate somatosensory information coursing through the specific sensory tracts. Cats deprived of cortical receipt of somesthesis through surgical intervention at the midbrain have shown visual as well as somatosensory deficits, even though, as far as the investigators could tell, there was virtually no in-

volvement of the afferent visual pathways known at that time
(Sprague, Chambers and Stellar, 1961). The visual deficit was
primarily inability to recognize the significance of the visual stimuli.
The cats could not utilize the visual information to make an adaptive response. When the lesion was unilateral, the visual problem
was in the contralateral visual fields. When the animals had lesions
in the area under the superior colliculi as well as in both sides of
specific sensory tracts, both visual fields were involved. The sub-
collicular area receives direct projections from the association cortex. Sprague and associates concluded that "The visual symptoms
of our animals . . . strongly suggest that normal visual functions
may depend upon the integrity of a midbrain mechanism receiving
projections from the lemnisci [specific somatosensory tracts],
ascending reticular activating pathways, and cortical as well as
subcortical areas."

After cutting the optic chiasma and corpus callosum and removing most of the cerebral cortex excepting the visual cortex, researchers found that the cat had lost nearly all previously trained
visual discriminations with the eye on the affected side. Comparable results in somatosensory perception did not follow isolation
of the somatosensory cortex (Sperry, 1958). Apparently the rest of
the cortical areas — which could include other sensory sources,
association and motor areas — are necessary for mediation of visual
perception in the cat, and quite possibly in man. After a review of
research, especially of that on rats running mazes, Gleitman (1963)
concluded that it was likely that in order to form spatial concepts,
rats must have some prior experience in exploring space by perceptual and motor means and that "complex learning does require
a considerable background of sensory experience and other forms
of stimulation." These studies may help to explain why apraxic
children very often — but not always — have a deficit in form
and space perception. Not only does the somatosensory deficit
interfere with visual perception, but the apraxic child is limited in
the amount of manipulative toy play in which he can successfully
engage, thus restricting the opportunity to learn cortically directed
visual perception.

Chapter 3 described the role of multisensory neurons and
pointed out the frequency with which receptors responded to visual
stimuli as well as stimuli from other sensory modalities. In discussing multisensory convergence on single neurons, J. C. Eccles
(1966) hypothesized that visual perception is "an interpretation
of retinal data that has been learned through association with
sensory information provided by receptors in muscles, joints, skin

and in the vestibular apparatus." The fact that some of the multi-sensory neurons in the cat are in the motor cortex (Buser and Imbert, 1961) suggests motion is an integrator of visual perception and somatic stimuli related to motion.

That visual perception can be improved through certain types of motor activity is supported by the work at the University of California at Berkeley cited above (Bennett et al., 1964; Rosenzweig, 1962). In that work with rats, emphasis was placed on climbing and moving in relation to objects, especially in a situation that offered variety and challenge. Vision was only a guide, but the greatest structural brain change was in the visual area and the least was in the somesthetic region.

Although proprioception is fundamental to the development of visual space perception, there is a concomitant need for patterned visual stimulation to facilitate the ontogenetic process. Riesen (1961b) has hypothesized that with the phyletic trend of encephalization of the visual sensory system, there has been increased reliance upon patterned visual stimuli as critical to the ontogeny of visual perception. As was pointed out in Chapter 2, mild deprivation of patterned visual stimuli during early maturation of dogs resulted in later greater difficulty in perceptual discrimination and in utilizing that discrimination (Melzak, 1962).

While the ontogeny of visual form and space perception may have been dependent, in part, upon the interaction of emitted postural and locomotor responses with simultaneous visual and proprioceptive feedback, it should not be overlooked that some aspects of visual form and space perception are innate. There is some evidence that depth perception may be innate in all vertebrates (Gibson, 1963). Perception of parallax and texture are involved as well as the muscular effort of accommodation and convergence of eye muscles (Schiffman and Walk, 1963). Simple form perception may be present at birth in man (Hershenson, 1964) as well as in lower primates (Ganz and Wilson, 1967).

Hypothesized Dual Modes of Vision

If the brain has utilized the consequences of motion to assist in the development of form and space perception, it is essential that the means be explored in a manner that will help the therapist to grasp the central concepts and apply them.

A particularly pertinent theory, hypothesizing dual modes of vision in vertebrates, has been advanced by Trevarthen (1968). E. J. Gibson (1970) has found the theory in accord with the results of her many years of perceptual research, and Held (1968), also known for his contributions to the development of perception, is in similar agreement. The theory is consistent with brain research cited above and with the behavioral research on which recommended treatment procedures are founded. Trevarthen has based his ideas on basic brain research, including his own with lower animals, but he believes that there is evidence that the ideas are also applicable to man. The two parallel visual processes are "ambient," or perceiving space to which the body is relating, and "focal," or perceiving a small area or form in great detail. Ambient space is analogous to that which has been referred to as the environmental scheme. It is related to the orientation of the head, postural adjustment, locomotor displacements, and changes of relationships of the body to space, surfaces, events, and objects in that space. The vision that occurs in the cerebral cortex is related to praxic action or assisting the organism to act on a discrete aspect of the environment, especially objects, in a manipulative manner. E. J. Gibson (1970) believes there is a difference in the phylogenetic and ontogenetic development of the two types of perception. Body-space or the environmental scheme develops earliest and is neurologically more primitive than the cortical perception, which develops over a longer period of time, is more dependent upon learning, and has evolved to a much more complex level in man than in other vertebrates.

Trevarthen points out that studies in vertebrates show that body-centered visual space is represented precisely on the surface of the superior colliculi of the midbrain tectum, providing a kind of map of behavioral space. The cortical visual map is believed interconnected to the midbrain visual system, allowing the two systems to interact, and each mode of vision is integrated with the motor system appropriate for actions related to the visual system. Monkeys whose cerebral hemispheres have been surgically separated show interference in bilaterality of visual form perception and hand action, yet the animals have adequate integration of function of the two sides of the body for climbing and locomotion. Comparable results are seen in man.

The ontogenetic development of the body-space orienting system in cats is in part dependent upon patterned visual stimulation as well as on the opportunity to move within that environment (Held, 1968). The movement must be active, i.e., acting upon the environment, as opposed to passive (Held and Hein, 1963). Both Held (1968) and Trevarthen (1968) are convinced that visual feedback from actions is essential to the integration of visual and motor processes attributed to the brain stem. There seems to be general agreement that the two visual systems, while relatively independent, do interact in close association.

All of these data, hypotheses, and clinical observations, when studied in relation to each other, result in the following postulates: Man does not develop visual perception through his eyes alone, nor does he see by his visual cortex alone. Meaningful vision is produced only by integrated action among many parts of the brain, involving — in addition to visual stimuli — other sensory stimuli, especially somatosensory and vestibular, and related motor behavior. Many children with learning disabilities have visual perception problems with inadequate ocular and postural reactions and deficits in other somatosensory functions which can be attributed, at least in part, to inadequate integrative processes in the brain stem. One of the results of failure of optimum brain stem integration is academic problems, especially in the early years when perception assumes an important role in formal learning. It is proposed that many but not all visual perception problems associated with reading problems in young children are related to lack of normal maturation of brain stem mechanisms.

Treatment to Develop Form and Space Perception

The intervention program for children who show inadequately integrated vestibular or tactile systems begins with generalized stimulation through those sensory modalities, using the suspended net and brushing as described in Chapter 9. Massive bombardment of the brain by vestibular stimuli is especially important for those children who demonstrate the symptoms of diminished nystagmus or reduced tendency toward dizziness following spinning. These symptoms suggest that the neural impulses generated by the vestibular receptors are not reaching the destinations intended by man's neural design. If the impulses do not make the necessary synaptic connections, simply going through the procedures of producing sensory input that supposedly goes to various centers of the brain will not be very effective. It is important first to do what can be done to assure an optimum amount of conductance of that sensory input.

For children whose neural circuits appear to be conducting vestibular impulses reasonably well, a lesser quantity of nonspecific vestibular stimulation serves to facilitate action in the neural system subserving form and space perception. Similarly, tactile stimuli facilitate neural response through their effect on congruent neurons and on the reticular formation and its ascending and descending paths. Basic brain research suggests that tactile stimuli also contribute to adequate visual perception in a more general manner at both the cortical, brain stem, and other subcortical areas.

Since some types of inadequate form and space perception in children with learning disabilities are believed to reflect poorly organized brain stem mechanisms, enhancing integration in that structure is an appropriate second step in the intervention program. It can overlap the initial procedures of tactile and vestibular stimulation. The brain stem mechanisms involved are those concerned with responses to motion and gravity, to neck and body righting reflexes, to locomotion (especially quadrupedal), to head and eye control, and to visual perception of environmental space.

The recommended procedures for normalizing these brain stem mechanisms were covered in detail in Chapter 10. They are only briefly reviewed here with emphasis on eye function. The primitive postural reflexes are integrated into the nervous system and maturation of the righting and equilibrium reactions promoted. Of particular importance is the activation of the neck righting reflex because of its role in the sequence of development of postural mechanisms and the close association of the neck muscles with eye muscles. It has been observed that this developmental step has not been experienced to an optimum degree by some children with neurodevelopmental disorders. A purely cortically directed rolling will not, of course, have the same integrating effect. The neck righting reflex is elicited at the brain stem level through activation of receptors in the neck. The motor response is an automatic following of the body. The reflex has particular survival value in that it assists an animal to assume a prone position from a supine position. The most effective means of eliciting the neck righting reflex is through having a child roll in the rolling tube shown in Figure 7. The child should be encouraged to "lead" with his head and to look at the goal toward which he is rolling as he turns his head toward it. The motor sequence is: (1) the eyes look to the side, (2) the head follows, rotating on the trunk, (3) the trunk follows the head. Automaticity of response is encouraged by the therapist's standing at the point toward which the child is rolling and clapping his hands at the appropriate time to attract the child's attention. At the clap of the hands the child looks at the therapist and begins the sequence of the neck righting reflex.

As described earlier, both the prone and supine positions and activities involving rapid change in direction of motion while sitting require strong contraction of neck muscles which proprioceptively facilitate the extraocular muscles. It is believed that strong contraction of neck muscles results in better neural integration in the brain stem oculomotor mechanisms. Since movement of the eyes as well as of the body as a whole is closely associated with sensation and perception at the brain stem level, improved ocular mechanism function may help the brain stem visual perception function. This hypothesis is consistent with the considerable amount of basic research cited earlier in the chapter. The postulate seems reasonable even though no significant relationships have been found between ocular control and academic achievement.

Basic research has emphasized the importance of the opportunity for associating proprioceptive stimuli from the body with visual input. The tactile and vestibular stimulation provided for its generalized effect on the nervous system is believed to promote greater proprioceptive flow from the muscles and a greater probability of discharge of some motor neurons. The motor activity, in turn, produces further sensory flow which is then available for association with visual sensations. Fredrickson, Figge, Scheid and Kornhuber (1966) studied the vestibular nerve projection to the cerebral cortex of the monkey and found an overlap of the vestibular and joint receptor representation. Kinesthesis, which is the perception of joint position and movement, has consistently been associated with visual perception in statistical analyses. Theoretically, improving kinesthetic perception could improve visual perception. Vestibular stimulation might enhance kinesthesia.

Adams (1965) improved scores on a test of kinesthesia in a group of children with neural dysfunction. Tactile stimulation was followed by assumption of the prone extensor posture against resistance for one minute and then by ambulation on hands and knees with resistance at the shoulder for two minutes. Adams found that the facilitatory effect was greatest immediately following the therapeutic procedure. Joint approximation, such as that resulting from the resistance employed by Adams, is believed to activate the joint receptors responsible for kinesthesis.

Activities which simultaneously involve assuming the quadruped position and evincing equilibrium responses provide a large quantity of the proprioceptive stimuli, which basic research has indicated are critical to the visual space perception process. At the same time, the activities require the motor output which promotes function in the visual cortex and helps translate those visual impulses into percepts.

Simply rocking back and forth on a rocking board or on a large therapy ball provides considerable vestibular and other proprioceptive input, including that from the neck musculature. Balancing on hands and knees on the large therapy ball or on the quadruped balancing board as shown in Figure 10 is more demanding and hence more organizing, provided the child succeeds. During all of these activities, of course, the space to which the body relates itself is registering on the visual cortex and, it is hoped, being more accurately perceived because of the greater normalcy of function resulting from the sensory input.

Scooter board activities provide the movement through space that especially requires the visual space perception that supervises the direction of motor action. What is seen acquires meaning in terms of the relationship between the perceiver and the perceived. That relationship is dependent upon the perceiver directing action toward that which was sensed. Perception is an active process and the overt activity helps the child check on the accuracy of the perception. It is appropriate to keep in mind Sperry's opinion that perception is preparation for an adaptive response (1952).

A more advanced level of training in visual perception involves throwing objects to a specified place. Incorporating movement of the body within the environmental scheme while throwing increases the complexity of the adaptive response acquired. Appropriate activities of this type include tossing bean bags through hoops or into boxes while riding a scooter board and throwing and catching a yarn ball while sitting and turning on the platform swing. In both instances, throwing across the mid-line of the body can be required to help unite both sides of the body-space scheme.

A complex task requiring visual direction within the environmental space scheme involves holding a map showing lines drawn between dots representing dots on the floor. Following the map lines, the child walks from dot to dot on the floor. The ability to visualize is encouraged by placing a sack over the head of a child who is riding a scooter board and feeling his way through a simple obstacle course which he previously saw. Playing catch while balancing on a rocking board or other piece of equipment, and kicking a ball while sitting on a one-leg stool (Figure 12) employ execution of a visual-motor task while responding to demands being made on the equilibrium.

The next step in developing form and space perception reduces the amount of somatosensory input and increases the demands made on the perceptual process. For this step puzzles and manipulatory toys, of which many are commercially available, are especially appropriate. Their use should be guided by the therapist relative to gradation of difficulty and problem-solving approach. Many puzzles can be quickly and easily developed by the therapist. For example, colored cubes can be used in the following ways. A paper on which is drawn a short series of colored squares is shown the child briefly; he is then asked to place colored cubes in the same sequence. In another task two or more colored cubes are placed in a cardboard tube while the child is watching. While they are out of sight, the child is asked to tell their order of appearance out of a specified end of the tube. At a simple level a transparent tube is used and the child inserts the cubes himself. At an advanced level the tube is rotated before allowing the cubes to emerge. Another sequencing game involves cutting two pieces of cardboard into several smaller pieces. Therapist and child each hold similar pieces. The therapist places a series of pieces before the child for his view, then covers them while the child duplicates the series.

For the young school age child it is appropriate to close a therapeutic session which emphasized somatosensory and vestibular stimulation with tasks that focus on visual form and space perception. It is anticipated that the earlier treatment enhances the capacity for visual perception and that sitting still while engaged in a visual perception task helps quiet the child before he leaves the therapy area.

If the visual perception problem appears to be primarily associated with unilateral cerebral hemisphere dysfunction, it is appropriate that the remedial program be initiated with manipulatory visual spatial tasks. Even in the case of cortical and not brain stem dysfunction, brain stem mechanisms are deliberately activated, for they are believed to give additional support to the cortical visual perception process.

Similarly, somatosensory and vestibular stimuli may be of help to the cortical visual perception processes. Sensory integration occurs through convergence of sensory input from several different sensory modalities upon a single neuron or in a restricted area in several areas of the brain, including the thalamus and cortex. It was noted earlier that in lower animals the vestibular system, especially, sent impulses to most areas of the cortex, including the visual cortex, and that the visual cortex is dependent upon the cortical receipt of sensations from the body for adequate interpretation of visual stimuli. It is reasonable to assume that cortical visual perception could be enhanced by providing stimuli from modalities known to send information to areas also responding to visual stimuli. Stimulation of the vestibular system directly, as in passive spinning, or of tactile stimulation directly, as in brushing the skin, could add somewhat to the cortical visual process. Similarly, the proprioceptive stimuli elicited from the body during activity, especially that designed to create a barrage of proprioception, may facilitate vision at the cortical level. Sensations from these sensory sources could also operate through the reticular activating system, in which case they could precede the visual task and still be effective in influencing it.

Contraindications to employing any of the above therapeutic activities lies, of course, in application of those very stimuli which can be the most effective. The precautions discussed in Chapter 9 are applicable. Responses to vestibular stimuli need to be watched especially. In addition to the usual precautions, special attention should be directed to any abnormal extraocular muscle function, such as consistent deviation of one eye. Activity that promotes contraction of the extraocular muscles in a positive direction can also promote it in a negative direction if the child already has a tendency toward abnormal muscle response. The best criterion of what is helpful and what is not is the child's response. It must be watched and careful professional judgments made relative to its meaning.

Chapter 13
Tactile Defensiveness and
Related Behavioral Responses

Many children with sensory integrative disorders show adversive responses to certain types of tactile stimuli. The phenomenon is referred to as "tactile defensiveness." Its behavioral correlates of hyperactivity and distractibility often are more evident to the classroom teacher than the tactile dysfunction. Tactile stimuli, of course, can be felt only by the individual with the problem. Not only is tactile defensiveness a subjective experience but the subject often is not fully conscious of the exact nature of that experience.

Factor analyses of a number of behavioral parameters related to sensory integrative dysfunction (Ayres, 1965, 1966a, 1966b, 1969a, 1972c) have consistently linked hyperactivity and distractibility, tactile defensiveness and diminished tactile discrimination. The syndrome is also frequently, but not consistently, associated with apraxia, perhaps because they share a disorder of the tactile system. Not all cases of hyperactivity and distractibility are associated with tactile defensiveness.

Tactually defensive behavior and the subjective emotional experience of an individual during tactile stimulation to which he is responding defensively are most easily and objectively observed when administering tests of discriminative tactile perception, such as those in the SCSIT, although these tests were designed to detect the precision of interpretation of the spatial and temporal qualities of tactile perception.

207

Analyzing those test conditions under which the child shows a negative emotional response or demonstrates some form of discomfort helps clarify the nature of the syndrome and how the child experiences it in relation to many aspects of life.

During the administration of the Manual Form Perception Test the child receives some tactile stimulation of the hands from the form placed in it by the examiner, but there follows a larger number of tactile stimuli which he elicits himself through manipulation of the forms. Touching oneself, either directly or indirectly, and being touched are two different neurological processes and must be considered as such. The Manual Form Perception Test does not usually elicit negative emotional responses, but in administration of the battery it is followed by the test of Finger Identification, where the child anticipates that he is going to be touched by the examiner's finger although he cannot see the event nor does he know exactly where he is going to be touched. A tactually defensive child may show signs of unrest or discomfort during this test. These may be simple signs, such as putting the hands under the table or a look of distress on the face. The test of Tactile Localization is more apt to elicit a defensive response than the tests administered prior to Tactile Localization. Three conducive conditions prevail: (1) the test is preceded by another threatening test, allowing a cumulative effect; (2) the child cannot see where he is going to be touched, but he knows that he is going to be touched; (3) the tactile stimulus is a quick, light, single stimulus. All three situations contribute toward building up a defensive or aversive reaction.

The test of Double Tactile Stimuli Perception can also threaten the child. A stimulus coming from behind his back does not allow him to prepare to defend himself. In the nonexamining situation, a tactually defensive child may react negatively to a casual touch from another person, especially if it comes from outside his visual field or is otherwise unexpected.

It is important to realize that the tactually defensive child actually experiences the stimuli in a manner which is different from that in which the neurologically better integrated children encounter them. A defensive response to tactile stimuli is easily overlooked. The therapist must be alert to the possibility of its presence in order to identify it. The response of a tactually defensive child to tactile stimuli is often expressed in socially acceptable terms that suggest he is not fully conscious of his discomfort. "It tickles," is an overt, common, and suggestive response, as is scratching oneself. "I need to go to the bathroom," "Mother, are you there?," "When will we be done?," "It's time for recess," "I mustn't miss lunch," "I need a drink," are a little more covert, and facial expressions and bodily movements are even more so. Some more obvious signs are the interpretation of the touch of a ball point pen as feeling like an injection from a needle, a mosquito bite, or an electric shock. Children who were particularly aware of their emotions have commented: "I hate this game," "I don't like this one bit," "I'm going to sit over here where you can't touch me," "It gets me scared a little bit." A few children respond with giggles or a simple motor withdrawal. One child left the testing table and went over to his father, seated nearby, and started hitting the astounded man. The more overt responses reflect anxiety, discomfort, a need to withdraw, and a kind of hostility.

Examiners testing children with behavior problems are advised to watch carefully and to compare a child's behavior during the tactile tests with behavior during the tests of visual perception and motor action. The behavior resulting from defensive arousal during the tactile tests may be interpreted as influenced by fatigue unless that behavior is compared with test behavior under equally or more fatiguing conditions in which no threatening tactile stimuli are given. Tactile defensiveness is a cumulative phenomenon and is therefore more apt to be evident as testing proceeds, and its influence will carry over into the tests following the tactile tests.

The presence of the syndrome has its major implication in behavior rather than in academic learning. Tactile defensiveness in itself apparently does not hinder learning, but some of the conditions which appear to be contributing causes of the syndrome may be related to adjustment problems of some of the children, which, in turn, interfere with learning. It has been noted (Stewart and associates, 1966) that the symptoms of hyperactive children usually start in infancy. Those children with a severe form of the syndrome were apt to have marked antisocial behavior later. It seems likely that some of these children were tactually defensive.

Although there are no objective data known to support the idea, it is proposed that tactile defensiveness is part of a more generalized "set" of the nervous system toward interpreting stimuli in terms of "danger, attend to these stimuli, and prepare for flight or fight," or at least, "I can't stand these stimuli." Over-responsiveness to auditory and olfactory and even some visual stimuli is seen occasionally in the tactually defensive child. Touch, audition, and olfaction are basic and phyletically old means of detecting environmental danger. Tactile functions, or their primitive analogous forms, were among the first means by which the organism received information about the environment so that it could adapt appropriately.

The tactually defensive reaction seems typical of the kind of primitive response one might expect to be consistent with stimulation of the small, phyletically old afferent C fibers which terminate in the lower part of the brain stem, an area which would likely mediate a primitive nondiscriminating response. Neurodevelopmental disorders often result in what appear to be less evolved and discriminatory behavior in general. In this context, this syndrome may be defined as a poorly or irregularly developed and integrated mechanism for interpretation of certain types of sensory information, especially those that are associated with primitive responses with basic survival value. All human beings need the capacity for a defensive reaction. The syndrome reflects an abnormal degree of a defensive type of responsiveness.

Hyperactivity and aversive reactions have been associated with tactile disorders in animal research. One of the results of section of the lemniscal pathways at the midbrain in cats was stereotyped hyperexploratory behavior (Sprague and associates, 1963; Sprague, Stellar and Chambers, 1960; Sprague, Chambers and Stellar, 1961). Sokolov (1963) cited Orbeli and Popov to the effect that after one of its tactile sensory paths was cut, an animal was incapable of fine specialized analysis and responded to stimulation by a "stormy defense reaction." The defensive reaction was increased after section of the posterior columns.

If a child's nervous system is biased in the direction of interpreting some stimuli as potentially dangerous, his responses hold some logic. He fails to inhibit response to many stimuli which the teacher or therapist considers irrelevant to the immediate situation but which hold relevance for the nervous system set for more basic survival issues than knowing the answer to two plus two. The child responds to the irrelevant-to-the-teacher stimuli and is hence considered distractible. He responds with movement and is hence considered hyperactive. He is apt to be an anxious child and emotionally labile. He is an often-threatened child. He is a child less well prepared to cope with this advanced civilization than the child whose nervous system is integrated in a more normal manner, but all of his reactions are consistent with the organization of his nervous system.

Neuroanatomical and Physiological Considerations

The degree of effectiveness in modifying the nervous system of the child with a tendency toward an aversive response will be directly dependent upon the depth of understanding of the condition. For that reason, the possible underlying neurobiology must be carefully studied.

The concept of tactile defensiveness has its seeds in the earlier observations of Henry Head (1920), whose insight into the function of the nervous system formed a precursor to these postulates. It is not reasonable to expect the technical aspects of his work — now over a half century old — to be completely congruent with current neurophysiological data, but many of his concepts have proved useful insights into the understanding of human function.

Central to Head's theory of tactile functions were the dual functional afferent systems, the protopathic and epicritic. The protopathic system — so named because of its primitive characteristics — was designed to protect, warn, or defend the organism against potential harm. The "epicritic" system, which was superimposed on the phylogenetically older protopathic system, was concerned with higher discriminatory function which enabled localization of tactile stimuli and recognition of two- or three-dimensional objects.

The protopathic system was particularly concerned with itching, tingling, and unpleasant sensation. The stimuli affecting this system were felt as diffuse and radiated, sometimes even referred to a distant part of the body. Both systems could carry messages of pain, but the protopathic was particularly concerned with them. This latter system was capable of eliciting affective response — either painful or pleasurable — and thus resulted in actions of repulsion or attraction. It was apt to produce motor activity.

Of particular theoretical interest was the manner in which Head conceptualized the interaction of the two systems. The epicritic system was believed to exert a checking and controlling function over the protopathic. As the higher and more specific system, it was more apt to be deficient than the lower in pathological cases.

In addition to his theory of dual cutaneous systems (which was based largely on observation of peripheral nerve injury), Head described sensory disorders on the basis of brain injury. The disorders also fall into two categories not unlike the dual afferent systems. With lesions of the optic thalamus, the individual characteristically showed excessive affective reaction with over-reaction to pain, heat, cold, certain types of tactile stimuli, and occasionally vibration. Tickling was experienced as unpleasant and sometimes music or loud sounds produced distress. Response to pleasant stimuli could also be accentuated. Head noted irregular movements in patients which increased as testing continued.

In cortical lesions Head found a lack of constancy and uniformity of response to tactile stimuli. Sometimes localization of a tactile stimulus was deficient. More frequently there was difficulty in distinguishing two points on the skin, discriminating between weights, and recognizing objects through manipulation alone. Head referred to the contrasting elements of sensation as "affective and discriminative." The excessive response to affective stimuli, he reasoned, was not due to irritation of the brain structure but to removal of cortical control, resulting in thalamic dysfunction. The situation was analogous to the lack of control manifested when the protopathic system predominated over the epicritic. The more primitive activities were modified by the advent of new centers which, in turn, could not fulfill their duty without the existence of the lower centers which the new centers dominated.

Head emphasized the protopathic process as being primitive and the epicritic as more advanced. His attribution of these processes to phylogenesis met with objections, especially by Walshe (1942), who pointed out that every animal at every phyletic level is an instrument of precision. More recent research conducted on lower animals by Mountcastle and associates (Poggio and Mountcastle, 1960; Mountcastle and Powell, 1959; Rose and Mountcastle, 1959) is particularly pertinent. These investigators found it convenient to refer to dual tracts and projections of somatic sensation, viz., the spinothalamic and lemniscal systems. Neurons of the spinothalamic system responded especially to stimuli of a potentially harmful nature but also to light touch and hair displacement. The receptive fields were large, occasionally encompassing the entire body surface. Stimulation of the system elicited escape-like behavior and produced strong emotional reactions. Inhibition sometimes occurred from a stimulus applied to any part of the entire contralateral side, much of the ipsilateral side, and the face. Thalamic nuclei of the system were found to be dependent upon the cortex.

The lemniscal system, responding only to highly specific types of stimuli, was found to serve a discriminative function in interpretation of the spatial and temporal aspects of touch-pressure and kinesthetic stimuli. Each thalamic nucleus was related to a specific restricted contralateral receptive field. Inhibition of the system, in contrast to the spinothalamic system, occurred through depression of activity in neurons surrounding the neuron which had been excited by cutaneous stimulation. These researchers have suggested that the lemniscal system could mediate Head's epicritic system, while the spinothalamic system might represent the proto-pathic system, provided the latter exists.

Part of the trigeminal spinal nucleus contains some cells which show characteristics similar to the spinothalamic tract, namely, response to tactile, noxious, or intense thermal stimuli with long latency and prolonged discharge. The receptive fields are large and lacking in somatotopic arrangement. These fibers are dis-tributed to the brain stem reticular activating system and could serve in the alerting and arousal seen in tactile defensiveness.

King, Meagher and Barnett (1956) observed the contrasting effects of putting alumina gel in the main sensory and spinal nuclei of the trigeminal nerve of cats. From the spinal nucleus (which is analogous to the spinothalamic tract) unpleasant responses were consistently observed and contrasted with lack of unpleasant feel-ing generated from the main sensory nucleus. In addition to the unpleasant responses, gel in the spinal nuclei resulted in over-reaction to facial stimulation.

One of the thalamic nuclei, the centrum medianum, is espe-cially concerned with the non-specific reticular system. Its afferent contribution is mainly from the spinothalamic or indirect spino-reticular connections, but it also receives some lemniscal input. The input from the two systems carries theoretical importance for treatment of the syndrome, for it is subject to excitation as well as inhibitory influences from the cerebral cortex.

Albe-Fessard and Fessard (1963) acknowledge a dual som-esthetic projection and have suggested the terms "discriminative" and "convergent" for the two afferent systems which Head re-ferred to as epicritic and protopathic and which Mountcastle and associates identified primarily as spinothalamic and lemniscal. The extra-lemniscal (consisting primarily of the spinothalamic tract) pathway fibers project to the convergent nuclei of the thalamus, i.e., nuclei with neurons responding to many different sense modali-ties. The convergent system was most easily activated by noxious stimuli. They state that there are also two distinct afferent systems in the face. A neospinothalamic system, developed most highly in man, provides ipsilateral somatotopic information.

Semmes (1969) has objected to identifying protopathic sensa-tion with the extra-lemniscal system and epicritic or discriminative sensation with the lemniscal. She quite appropriately points out how the phylogenetically newer and highly specific lemniscal sys-tem grew out of the older extra lemniscal system which originally ended in the brain stem or thalamus but which developed links to the cortex as the cortex evolved. The new system developed against the background of "a parent system capable of handling the entire range of somesthetic functions for all parts of the body." The lemniscal system probably evolved to facilitate carrying precise information from the mechano-receptors, especially for the distal ends of the limbs. In accord with the principle of interdependence of higher or later evolved functions with lower or earlier evolved functions, the lemniscal and extra-lemniscal afferent tracts function in relation to each other and do not mediate qualitatively different forms of sensation. The older system carries some discriminatory capacity and the new system can elicit an experience of pain.

The dualism of these response systems may be more of a continuum or an intermingling of the two than a strict dichotomy. Sprague and associates (1963) pointed out that "there is probably a continuous gradient of the functional organization of ascending systems between the most highly localized lemniscal path and the most diffuse of the reticular paths."

The concept of a number of somesthetic systems interacting to provide a continuum of information and response with a need-for-defense, interpretation, and reaction at one end of the continuum and a discriminative interpretation and discrete response at the other end is consistent with a theory of pain advanced by Melzack and Wall (1965). While the tactile or other sensory stimulus that elicits a defensive response should not necessarily be equated with a painful stimulus, the analogy does not lead one astray.

Melzack and Wall (1965) employ the concepts of central summation, input control mechanisms, and centrifugal influence along with physiological specialization in a theoretical process they refer to as "gate control" or the ability of the central nervous system to allow or prevent sensory impulses to ascend to the brain.

As the afferent impulses enter the dorsal horn, a group of cells there modulates the impulses (operates the gate) before they make connection with the neurons that start the message up the spinal cord. The neural activity which precedes the stimulus, the nature of the stimulus, and the relative balance of small versus large neuron activity all influence the opening and closing of the gate. Small, constantly active, and slow-adapting neurons tend to hold the gate open. An added stimulus such as gentle pressure or scratching will activate large fibers which not only carry a message to the brain but also partially close the gate. As large fibers adapt with the continuation of the stimulation, the gate opens again. When activity which has already been modulated by the gate system exceeds a critical level, the process which is interpreted as pain is triggered. Through descending neurons, neural activity such as attention and emotion influence the opening and closing of the gate. Some brain processes that act as gate controls are mediated over the dorsal column-medial lemniscal system and dorsal-lateral path. The gate may be set and reset a number of times as a result of these factors. These authors propose that the presence or absence of pain is determined by the balance between the sensory and the central nervous system influence on the gate control system.*

The theory of Melzack and Wall seems to unify some of the most important concepts of Head, Mountcastle and associates, and Semmes. It may be, then, that the tactile defensive response and other aversive responses to nociceptive qualities in sensory stimuli represent an insufficient amount of the inhibitory component in a functional system designed to monitor a certain type of impulse flow. Thus the behavioral response system designed for protection and survival predominates over a system designed to allow the organism to respond to the spatial and temporal qualities of the tactile stimuli.

This view is consonant with observations of tactile defensiveness and its treatment. Defensiveness varies with the emotional and other manifestations of the neural state of the child. It is influenced by tactile stimulation which the child experiences as comfortable. What is comfortable may vary from child to child and from day to day. Other sensory input, such as proprioception activating the posterior column-medial lemniscal system, also appears to "close the gate," reducing hyperactivity and distractibility. Thus a child, when asked how he felt when he returned to the classroom after treatment, replied: "The noise of the other kids doesn't bother me so much."

Developmental Considerations

What has gone awry in the developmental process when tactile defensiveness is present? If the rationale presented above is at least partially correct, the normally developing infant brain processes a large quantity of somatosensory stimuli through some innate mechanisms. The end result is a gradual but increasing tendency to inhibit an affective interpretation and response and to enhance the interpretation of the spatial and temporal characteris-

---

*Copyright 1965 by the American Association for the Advancement of Science. Cited with permission.

tics of tactile stimuli and hence tactile discrimination. Concurrently, the emotional lability, characteristic of the young child, decreases and stability increases.

Since the syndrome of tactile defensiveness has only recently been defined (Ayres, 1964), much of the relevant developmental research pertains to sensation and affective development. The considerable quantity of research on the influence of sensory deprivation on human emotional stability rather decisively links deprivation and instability. That affectional responses in monkeys is related to contact, especially tactile, has been well documented by the now classical studies of Harlow (1958).

One of Casler's (1961) conclusions from study of human and animal infants lacking normal mothering was that the ability to handle stress was related to tactile stimulation in early infancy. In rats the critical period for that tactile stimulation which contributed toward the development of the ability to cope with stress was before or at weaning. These results were supported by Eells (1961) on rats, where lack of handling was more harmful to emotional development than being handled in a manner considered "mistreatment." Gently handled rats fared best of all.

It is fairly safe to conclude that tactile stimulation of the human infant contributes to the integration of the neural substrate of emotional development. Provision of the average quantity of stimulation alone is apparently not enough, for most children with neurodevelopmental disorder have experienced what appears to have been normal sensory stimulation in infancy. The problem more likely lies in a disorder of integration of the sensory stimuli.

Using a scattering of scores on the Gesell Schedules both between subtests and within a subtest, such as "motor," as an index of the capacity for integration of neurological function, Fish (1963) found that poor integration in infancy was correlated with diminished capacity of the individuals to maintain psychological integrity in times of stress.

It is postulated that part of the disorder of integration lies in inadequacy of some of the inhibitory-like process of the system under discussion. The "processing" or "balancing" system seems to be in a state of disorder. Inhibition may not be dependent solely upon integration of tactile impulses. Proprioceptive impulses could be involved. The Moro reflex, seen normally during a certain stage of early infancy, is usually elicited through auditory or vestibular (as in sudden lowering of the child) stimuli, but pinching of the skin and subcutaneous tissue of the epigastrium can also elicit it (Lesný, 1967). All of these stimuli offer potential threats, suggesting that the reaction is part of a defensive system. Could the fact that the Landau reaction manifests itself at the time that the Moro reflex is inhibited indicate that the maturation of the posture assumed in the Landau and the mechanism relating to it has an inhibitory action on the defensive response system? If this should be the case, it would support the hypothesis which has arisen from clinical observations that certain postural responses can inhibit the defensive system.

The Therapeutic Program

The postulate on which treatment is based is that certain types of somatosensory input will inhibit or normalize that neural process which elicits a protective response and brings about a better balance between the protective and discriminative aspects of the total subsystem. The stimuli are referred to as inhibitory because this term comes closest to conveying the essential nature of a highly complex neurophysiological process which involves far more than inhibition in its regulatory or modulating role. The concepts of "input control mechanisms" and "centrifugal influence" which were employed by Melzack and Wall in their theoretical formulations hold a central role in treatment application.

The sensory input which appears especially effective in influencing the modulating mechanisms operates through the tactile system with the proprioceptive system also serving an important role. The theories of Mountcastle and associates and of Melzack and Wall favor activating the larger tactile neurons through touch-pressure. This form of stimulation has been found to be quite effective in depressing the aversive response in some individuals. Touch pressure is usually applied with cloths of various textures ranging from soft velvet to coarse terry cloth. Standard paint brushes are also effective. With the very defensive child, the therapist's or the child's hand with lotion on it may be all that can be tolerated. Each person who has experienced relief through scratching a mosquito bite has activated the process believed to be involved in the treatment process.

Regardless of deductions made from the brain research, touch-pressure stimuli are not always the choice of tactually defensive children. Many children prefer the light, rapidly applied stimuli of a battery-driven camel's-hair brush. The organization of tactile systems varies among children and the variety of central nervous system biases and responses to tactile stimulation exceeds rationale for the differences. Many children give the impression that their tactile receptor threshold is exceedingly low and a stimulus which might be interpreted by the therapist as a light touch is actually, from a neurophysiological standpoint, touch-pressure. Furthermore, the light brushing undoubtedly does activate the discriminative side of the system's continuum.

The speed of brushing or rubbing is determined by the child but is usually fairly rapid. Some children prefer pressure with brushing; others prefer a lighter touch. The length of time of brushing is determined by the child's choice or is a function of convenience. Ideally, the child is given as much as he finds comfortable and as frequently as every hour, as long as he is not employing brushing to avoid other important activity. The effect of the brushing may not become apparent for as long as ten minutes, or it may be immediately apparent. Response is dependent upon the state of the nervous system into which the stimuli flow. The excitatory state of the nervous system may be so great that the influence of the inhibitory stimuli is not apparent to the observer.

The skin area to which the stimuli are applied is often a matter of convenience. Hands, face, legs, and back are most readily available. The ventral surface of the trunk should be avoided unless the child elects to rub it himself. It is advisable to begin brushing at the least defensive skin area, which is usually the arms or dorsum of the hands, before proceeding to other areas. Beginning with the more acceptable skin areas appears to increase the inhibitory effect of stimuli applied to other areas. This effect may be an example of centrifugal influence. The diminished sensitivity of the hands and arms may be due to their frequent contact with objects, the contact having served a modulating effect. The back is usually accepting of stimuli, especially if the sides of the back are not touched. The face, especially around the mouth, is apt to be more defensive than other skin areas. It may be that because of its critical role in survival, the face has been especially well supplied by the defensive response system.

If a child is defensive, tactile stimulation should not be directed against the hairs, as the hair cell receptors are associated with the defensive system. It is also advisable to avoid crossing the midline of the body in a brush stroke unless it has been determined that a child is not adversely affected by it.

One of the more baffling questions confronting a therapist is how much and when to force tactile stimulation on a tactually defensive child who is uncomfortable with any imposed tactile stimulus. An important point to remember in these cases is that tactile stimuli therapeutically applied to a nervous system that accepts them as a normal course of events will be more apt to serve an inhibitory or modulatory role than a defensive one. The difference may be through centrifugal processes. Ordinary motor activity involves some tactile stimulation that is usually acceptable. This natural course can be exploited through use of rugs, carpeting, and sand in an activity situation. A similar effect is achieved if the child touches himself, as opposed to being touched. If he cannot give the stimulation himself, the therapist can try taking the child's hand and rubbing the child with it. Another approach is directing the child's attention elsewhere, a process which helps inhibit the defensive response system and makes the tactile stimuli more acceptable. A method which can be employed concomitantly with the above approaches is the employing of proprioceptive input that has a regulatory role on the tactile system. The threshold of the receptors subserving the defensive system is heightened by cold. A cold skin is sometimes more accepting of tactile stimulation.

Occasionally a therapist may be justified in applying stimuli in spite of discomfort for a few days in an effort to bring about a sufficient shift in balance between the protective and discriminative response systems to enable development of tolerance to some stimuli. If discomfort is still critical after a few weeks, the therapist is advised to reconsider the situation and remember that there is still much to be learned about the tactile system.

There are some contraindications to the application of tactile stimuli. If the child's activity is increased beyond desirable levels rather than decreased, the stimuli are probably having too great an effect on the reticular arousal system. For some children, the extra excitation is not desirable, although it can be counteracted with certain types of vestibular stimulation. Since tactile stimuli will definitely affect muscle tone and possibly involuntary motion, they should be used with careful judgment when hypertonicity or athetosis are present.

There is no direct experimental evidence that these procedures are effective, but the clinical impression is favorable. Some related studies add support. Blitz, Dinnerstein and Lowenthal (1964) demonstrated that mild pain induced by electric shock could be attenuated by vibration resulting from stretching the skin with rubber tabs mounted on a rotating motor shaft. Weidenbacker, Sandry and Moed (1963) studied the pain from pressure threshold of the feet of both cerebral palsied and normal children. Although they found no difference in pain threshold between the normal and cerebral palsied subjects, there was a significant difference between those children who walked and those who did not walk, with the latter having a lower threshold or being more apt to interpret the stimulus on the foot as painful. These results can be interpreted to mean that frequent touch-pressure stimuli to the feet helped to lower the threshold to painful stimuli, probably through the central control mechanism discussed earlier.

Modulation of the system under discussion through proprioceptive input over afferent pathways to the brain has an acceptable basis in the neurobiological research. Adequate opportunity for this input to modulate the defense response system occurs at cortical as well as many lower levels of the nervous system. Andersson (1962) found that the ventral spinothalamic afferent pathway of the cat produced, under certain conditions, widespread cortical effects, well beyond the somatic sensory cortex. He hypothesized that these cortical effects could have been due to removal of tonic inhibition at the cortical level or to the ascending ventral pathways, thus allowing those pathways to be more easily activated by stimuli at the periphery. He further postulated that the widespread cortical effect could be due to release of inhibition from the specific projection or lemniscal pathways on a pacemaker mechanism activated by the ventral or extra-lemniscal afferent pathways.

It then follows that most, if not all, of the activities recommended for normalization of the system subserving postural and bilateral integration may contribute to the normalization of the system involved in tactile defensiveness. Clinical impression is that they do so. Because so many of the scooter board activities require strong contraction of postural muscles, they can contribute to the sensory stimuli that help integrate the tactile system that is involved in defensiveness.

Chapter 14

Unilateral Disregard and Functions of the Right Cerebral Hemisphere

Understanding of sensory integrative dysfunction in children with learning disabilities is far from complete. Some symptoms have not shown the kinds of associations that have enabled them to be identified as syndromes. Other patterns of dysfunction have been recognized as appearing with sufficient frequency to warrant attention, but appropriate intervention programs have not been developed and tested. The task of deriving a treatment rationale involves, first, theorizing regarding the nature of the function of the neural subsystem and then painstakingly deriving the procedures. The final step is formal or informal testing of those procedures.

One syndrome, tentatively termed unilateral disregard, has been identified with both clinical observations and statistical analyses. The goal of developing a treatment rationale has not yet been attained. The material in this chapter is, accordingly, presented in a somewhat "piecemeal" manner, for that is the status of knowledge of the syndrome and its treatment. These "pieces," it is hoped, will promote continued exploration of the problem and will eventually fit into a more unified whole.

Definition of the Syndrome

In a study designed to detect as yet unrecognized types of sensory integrative dysfunction in children with learning problems, the following symptoms clustered in a Q-technique factor analysis: low Motor Accuracy (on the SCSIT) standard score of the left hand, especially in contrast to the standard score of the right hand, some irregularity in postural and ocular mechanisms, and a tendency toward adiadokokinesia. The children with these symptoms performed relatively better on cognitive and auditory-language tests (Ayres, 1969a). Later analyses of scores gathered from a different but comparable sample of children yielded only suggestive evidence that the syndrome did exist. Of the symptoms which were quantitatively measured, those that identified the type of disorder were a marked difference in left hand compared to right hand Motor Accuracy test scores and low Space Visualization scores. These deficiencies were in contrast to relatively higher scores on auditory-language tests (Ayres, 1971).

Informal clinical observations of learning disabled children with this particular problem further define the parameters of the disorder. The left upper extremity is not employed as frequently as a helping hand to the dominant extremity as is the case either with children with other forms of perceptual-motor difficulty or with children without learning problems. Upon careful observation, it is seen that the child tends to avoid moving into the left side of extracorporeal space, or stated otherwise, incorporating the left side of the body space into the environmental scheme. For example, when a child with this syndrome was asked to ride a scooter board down a ramp and then to put his right hand down on the floor and pivot around it, he did so successfully. When asked to repeat the performance placing the left hand on the floor and pivoting around it, he could put his left hand on the floor, but even after repeated tries and demonstrations, he could turn only to his right.

The subtle nature of this tendency to avoid interacting with the left side of body space is noted in the following incident. After several months of remedial work, the same child could pivot around his left hand and wanted to demonstrate his achievement to his parents. Alas, during the demonstration he extended his right hand, placed it on the floor, and pivoted around it! Incidents of this type help demonstrate to the therapist that "teaching" the child cognitively directed actions is insufficient for remediation of the underlying problem. The dysfunction must be tackled at the neurological level where the problem lies, which is probably not at the neo-cortical level.

Other manifestations of a tendency to disregard or resist inter-action with one side of the environmental scheme were evinced in this child's use of the scooter board in a confined area. When riding the scooter in a direction that would take him to a point where he would have to turn left to avoid running into the wall, he chose to stop instead. When playing a game in which he was in a quadruped position and had to rotate or laterally flex his head in order to hit an object and direct it into the left side of his environmental scheme, he consistently maneuvered his body so that he could direct the object to the same goal but into space to his right instead of his left. Possibly part of the problem the child encountered in this task was the elicitation of the TNR when the head was rotated, a response which most children attempt to avoid if the reflex is poorly integrated. It has been thought the avoidance could be attributed to fear of upsetting the equilibrium, but the possibility that there may be other reasons for avoidance should not be overlooked.

When riding a scooter board under a strip of rubber which he was to catch with one leg flexed at the knee, this same child repeatedly raised the right foot in spite of intentions to raise the left. Sometimes, even after lifting the right foot to catch the rubber strip, he would insist that he had raised the left foot.

One of the frequently employed scooter board activities involves riding the scooter prone toward a mat. As the mat is approached, the child turns so that he is approaching the mat with the side of the body. When the scooter board reaches the mat the child rolls off the scooter and keeps rolling on the mat. Children with unilateral disregard to the left have little difficulty in approaching and rolling to the right but do have difficulty rolling to the left.

Interacting with space to the left of the body during bipedal sensorimotor activity seems to pose fewer difficulties than when the child is in the prone or quadruped positions. How much of this difference is due to a wider experience in acting upon the environment while in the biped than in other positions is not known. Some of the difference may depend on the extent to which the child can guide his movements with vision. It is relatively easy to look to the left when standing and to use sight deliberately to help orient oneself in turning to the left, but rolling to the left on a mat involves considerable dependence upon the body scheme and visualization of, as opposed to observation of, the environmental scheme.

Attempts to evaluate the tendency to overlook visual stimuli to the left of the body's mid-line have brought inconclusive results. It was the clinical impression that most of the children tended to make more errors on the left, as in completing puzzles, or to interact with the stimuli on the left side only after reacting to those on the right side. For example, when a number of variously colored beads are placed before a child with a tendency toward unilateral disregard and he is asked to pick up beads of a given color, he is apt to pick up the beads to his right first and then those to his left. Inspection of drawings made by one child during his early school years consistently showed a lesser quantity of the pictorial representation on the side of disregard. In a picture he painted of a boy, one side of the face and one arm were much smaller than the other side of the face and the other arm. The hand was omitted on the side of disregard. The picture looked as though it could be a mirror image of the child's body scheme.

Since disregard is a tendency only, its evaluation is often most accurate in an informal situation when the child is unaware of being assessed. Cognitive awareness of the nature of a presented task seems to help a child realize that he must make an effort to attend to stimuli that he might overlook were his attention less strongly focused. For this reason, a child's performance in picking up beads of a given color is a less adequate test of unilateral disregard than the inspection of drawings freely made in a relatively unstructured situation.

Often it is the automaticity of response that is diminished in this syndrome. The child whose left hand lies in his lap during most of the administration of the test of Space Visualization of the SCSIT may readily use that hand when requested to do a task requiring the use of both hands.

This ability cognitively to overcome the tendency toward unilateral disregard makes evaluation of the syndrome through typical structured psychological tests very difficult. The test for Crossing the Mid-line of the Body of the SCSIT is an example of an effort to evaluate with a structured device a parameter of behavior which reflects a tendency which can be overcome by attention. Some children with unilateral disregard score lower on one hand than the other on this test, but the older and more test-sophisticated child generally will score within normal limits, possibly because of his cognitive mastery of the task.

Clinical material gathered from observations of brain damaged adults with unilateral disregard would suggest that there might be differences in somatosensory perception of the two sides of the body in the children with a similar syndrome. Attempts to detect such differences have not yielded conclusive evidence and the hypothesis of somatosensory differences needs more careful and thorough study. Similarly, the manner in which a child with this syndrome processes vestibular input bears further analysis. Some of the children have shown a low tolerance to vestibular stimulation, especially during rolling activities. The implications of this type of response are not understood but may very well be significant.

Most of the children who have presented the symptoms described have also shown behavioral problems. There is no objective evidence that conclusively relates these emotional symptoms associated with the left side of the body directly with concomitant dysfunction in a related neural structure, though such a possibility cannot be discarded. It is possible, of course, that most states of neural dysfunction, including the one resulting in unilateral disregard, reduce the capacity of the individual to cope with the difficult demands of his environment, leaving him more vulnerable to the vicissitudes of life and with increased probability of the development of problems that provide additional interference with learning. It is felt that there are a considerable number of symptoms related to this syndrome which have not been identified or explored. Some of these symptoms may lie in cognitive dysfunction that directly interferes with learning of a more advanced nature than the initial learning which is so largely perceptual-motor in nature.

Although the symptoms of most of the children with this syndrome have been related to the left side of the body and extra-corporeal space, the presence of this syndrome on the right side of the body has been observed in children whose disorder apparently was present at birth. With the exception of academic difficulties, no difference has been found in the major symptomatology of children with disregard to the right compared with disregard to the left, but the sample of children observed has been too small on which to base a firm conclusion. The symptoms, of course, are reversed as to the side of the body on which they occur. The few children with disregard to the right were left-handed even though there was probably a genetic tendency toward right-handedness and the right hand was more skilled on motor tests. More detailed information on how children with this syndrome score on the SCSIT may be found in the test manual.

Theoretical Discussion

The syndrome which involves unilateral disregard is certainly not uncommon among individuals whose brains suffer unilateral trauma after reaching maturity or even in preadolescence. It is not unreasonable to postulate that the syndrome as seen in children with no known history of brain damage is in some respects neurologically similar to that seen in adults. The lesser specificity of the symptoms may be due in part to the fact that the plasticity of the very young brain gives it an opportunity to compensate for some of the dysfunction. Furthermore, the mature brain is more specialized in its function, with the result that specific injury is manifested by more discrete symptoms. Generally, the etiology of dysfunction in the learning disabled child is so obscure as to yield little evidence upon which to base a hypothesis of specific brain trauma, but the symptoms observed in these children with unilateral disregard to the left are all consistent with the hypothesis of dysfunction on the right side of the brain. The presence of this syndrome in children is not frequently observed and the symptoms are so obscure that they are easily overlooked. Failure to see the problem, however, does not indicate that it is not there. Its frequency and its import may be greater than recognized at this time. For those reasons, some discussion of the possible neurophysiological processes involved deserve attention. Perhaps better understanding of them may help to clarify the nature and increase the ease of recognition of the disorder and its implications.

Schilder (1951) felt that the organic lesion which resulted in left personal and spatial disregard in adults produced something very similar to that which psychoanalytically would be called a "repression." In this instance, repression would be considered an "organic" way of excluding the part of the body that did not give satisfaction. It has been observed that children with unilateral disregard often have a marked negative response to any pressure to use the extremity beyond that to which they are accustomed. Perhaps "satisfaction" should be interpreted as information which is sufficient for determination of adaptive responses. The question arises as to whether the individual with unilateral disregard is receiving the information which makes it easy for him to plan a response involving one side of himself and space.

If the information is unsatisfactory, the next logical query is: Relative to what behavioral parameters is the information unsatisfactory? Most evidence from children points to some aspect of space perception as the major sensory integrative lack along with disorder in some attentional mechanism. This type of sensory integrative dysfunction may assume a larger role in the disabled learner's life than is generally recognized. Most sensory integrative evaluations involve using only the space immediate to the child's body and his dominant hand only. The ability of the child to relate his body to the "environmental scheme" is seldom assessed. This testing bias may lead to overlooking an aspect of potential dysfunction in sensory integration. Its role may be more easily assessed by watching the child in the academic or play situation.

A rationale as to why unilateral neglect of self and disregard of extracorporeal space has been observed more frequently on the left side of the body than on the right side has been proposed by Geschwind (1965). He attributes the discrepancy to a neural disadvantage of the right hemisphere in relation to the left because the pathways from the right hemisphere to the association areas of the left hemisphere are at least one neuron longer than corresponding parts of the left hemisphere. The longer the route, the more degradation of stimulus. Geschwind's argument may be pertinent to relating space and language, but the capacity for association in the right hemisphere should not be overlooked.

Unilateral disregard involves a *tendency* to avoid perceiving stimuli on one side of the body as opposed to the *inability* to do so. The failure is in registering or assimilating, as in simply overlooking. This aspect of the syndrome leads one to suspect an involvement of an attentional mechanism, especially one that might be responsive to stimuli occurring to one side of the body, such as the orienting reflex, a mechanism organized at a relatively high neuroanatomical level that registers information and assesses its biological significance. This reflex is an unlearned, vital response to detect external stimuli of survival value. It is in part dependent upon the reticular arousal system, as are all mechanisms of perception, but other structures are involved. It includes a focusing of attention on either a specific stimulus or preparation for an orientation toward what is expected to be a specific stimulus. Fangel and Kaada (1960) have referred to it as a "What is that? Let's find out" reflex. It involves both cortical as well as subcortical neural structures, the cortically induced component being dependent upon the subcortical component. These authors feel that sensations, emotions, and higher mental processes are also implicated in the orienting reflex.

As with other neurological mechanisms, the information leading to understanding of the orienting reflex comes largely from study of lower animals. In the lower animals the orienting reflex is outwardly manifested by head turning, eye and trunk deviation that would help orient animal to the originating stimulus, and a general motor stillness. Kaada (1951) demonstrated these responses in cats and dogs upon stimulation of their limbic systems. Later Fangel and Kaada (1960), upon eliciting the orienting reflex in cats, observed glancing and searching movements, autonomic responses, and, under strong stimuli, anxiety, fear, and finally flight.

When Gabor and Peele (1964) stimulated certain masses of gray matter below the neocortex of awake cats, the result was increased responsiveness to external stimuli and a turning of the head and eyes. If the stimulation continued, the trunk turned in the direction away from the stimulated hemisphere. Upon further stimulation, the contralateral foreleg was extended, causing the animal's body to lean to the side of hemisphere stimulation. The results of this study are particularly interesting in that a position similar to that elicited by the TNR was assumed. The similarity leads to speculation about the existence of a neurological linkage between the TNR and the orienting reflex. The TNR sometimes is started by the eye movement that trigger the neck turning, which in turn elicits the reflex. Ellinwood (1968) associated the unilateral attention mechanisms with the visuovestibular mechanisms. The relating of postural reactions to the orienting responses are consistent with clinical observations.

In reviewing neurological literature, there is always a danger of biasing one's thinking through selective attention to the literature. To avoid such a possibility, some attention must be directed toward the possibility of the release of reflexes that operate in a manner which is opposite to the orienting reflex. Denny-Brown and Chambers (1958) have presented the results of an extensive study of the "avoidance response" as seen in experimental animals and brain damaged adults. The response, associated with injury in the parietal lobe, was one of withdrawal of the hand and turning away of the face when somatic or visual stimulation occurred on the side opposite the lesion. The reaction is explained as a "release" of the visual avoiding reaction and a consequent suppression of a prehensile reaction. Symptoms of this severity certainly have not been observed in the learning disabled child with unilateral disregard, but the possibility of such mechanisms existing and operating in even a mild manner can hold significance.

If Denny-Brown and Chambers are correct in their assertion that the parietal lobes are critical for exploratory behavior and orientation in space, any suppression of exploration and orientation to one-half of space with accompanying avoidance of visual and somatic stimuli in that same space would impair the normal perceptual-motor developmental sequence.

It is possible that in learning disabled children either or both — or perhaps neither — of these two mechanisms, the orienting reflex and the avoidance reaction, could be involved along with a more specific unilateral spatial problem. The orienting reflex which normally should be participating in tasks requiring attention may be underactive while the avoidance reaction might be overactive.

Other Functions of the Right Cerebral Hemisphere

Since unilateral disregard is more apt to be present in right than left cerebral hemisphere dysfunction, it is appropriate to discuss some of the other means by which the right hemisphere contributes to perception and other sensory integrative function. Its role in visual perception, especially of a spatial or complex nature and regardless of visual field, is quite well established. An example of the more recent studies that help confirm this fact is that of Bogen (1969a, 1969b). The subjects were eight right-handed, mature human beings who had had their right and left cerebral hemispheres separated through a commissurotomy. Under this split-brain condition the left hand copied designs or figures better than did the right hand, but it wrote (a language function) poorly. The right hemisphere also assumes a role in auditory perception. From studies of human beings with speech centers in the left hemisphere, Milner (1962) found that the right temporal lobe assumed a major role in nonverbal auditory tasks and that the left temporal lobe carried an ancillary role in those functions. Over the years there have been a number of studies supporting the right hemisphere as the seat of musical ability, especially for discrimination for tonal pattern and quality (cf. Bogen, 1969b). Deficits of an auditory nature in the left temporal lobe were found by Milner (1962) to be of a verbal nature and more strongly lateralized than those in the right hemisphere.

Information regarding laterality differences based on observation of brain injured adults must be interpreted cautiously. Teuber (1962) has found that unilateral lesions may have contralateral consequences or bilateral consequences or there may be paradoxical effects which fail "to represent a summation of those effects which would be expected after either of the component unilateral lesions." In other words, what remains active in brain function after disorder determines the picture of the behavior. Laterality differences are further complicated when neural dysfunction occurs early in life, allowing the plastic brain to reorganize in a manner which would differ from that of the brain undergoing a normal ontogeny.

Some of the most recent research (Semmes, 1968; Bogen, 1969b; cf. McFie, 1970) strongly suggests that while the right cerebral hemisphere is concerned with space perception, that type of perception is a function of a more generalized hemispheral capacity for integrating data from several senses and several sources. This capacity not only enables the individual to interpret and relate to our perception of the external world (McFie, 1970), but to organize complex behavior based on integrating two or more different factors (Semmes, 1968) and to collate, compare, and contrast data with previous data (Bogen, 1969a). While these formulations may account for disorder in the right hemisphere interfering with decreased spatial perception, they do not offer a sufficient account for unilateral disregard.

In addition to the capacity to appose or compare preceptions and schemes (even while the left hemisphere is arriving at different results) Bogen and Bogen (1969) propose that the right hemisphere may very well have capacities not yet recognized, including some forms of creativity. The mode of right hemisphere neural integration proposed by Semmes (1968) is appropriate for supporting complex and creative activity. The right hemisphere is diffusely represented, as opposed to the focal representation of the left hemisphere. Focal or localized representation results in the kind of integration that makes possible such highly precise sensorimotor actions as speaking or writing. These actions require processes in similar units which are located for optimal integration. On the other hand, the diffuse representation of the right hemisphere results in more frequent convergence of unlike units which then allows for integration of dissimilar information.

This proposed mode of function of the right hemisphere is consistent with the observations of Hécaen (1967), who associated a lowering of intellectual vigilance with right hemisphere dysfunction. The postulated function may also help in interpreting the findings of Fitzhugh, Fitzhugh and Reitan (1962). These investigators studied a sample of 144 right-handed brain damaged epileptic subjects and found that sensorimotor data from the left hand were more closely related to intellectual level than those from the right hand.

These recent interpretations of brain function suggest that in the strong educational emphasis on left hemisphere function, such as language function, some equally important forms of learning may be neglected.

The discussion of this chapter suggests the necessity for good communication between the hemispheres for optimal functioning of the brain. The language center is usually in the left hemisphere, but for it to make maximum contribution to the reading process, for example, it must have free and easy access to nonlanguage auditory perception, to visual space perception, and to the orienting reflex and attentional mechanisms of the right hemisphere. The need for interhemispheral integration in reading as well as in other cognitive processes is brought out again by these proposed conditions which represent, at best, an oversimplification of the actual interhemispheral communication requirements.

One of the most well-recognized needs for transcallosal interhemispheric communication is that which unites the two halves of the visual fields. In relation to this type of interhemispheral integration, it is appropriate to consider the proposition of Mishkin (1962). Accepting as fact that visual mechanisms of the two hemispheres are integrated and that the right temporal lobe in man is dominant over the left temporal for visual functions, he suggests that there has been an asymmetrical development of the transcallosal structures with a strengthening of the pathway from the left visual cortex to the right temporal cortex. The arrangement would permit the right temporal cortex to integrate activity from the visual cortices of both hemispheres and to be dominant over the left for visual functions. For these functions to be available to the left hemisphere for interpretation into language requires communication back to the left hemisphere via some route, which may or may not involve the corpus callosum.

The possible effect of inadequate interhemispheral communication on learning is implied in a study by Sechzer (1970). Cats required at least twice as long to learn a visual or somatosensory task when only one hemisphere was learning the task as opposed to when both hemispheres had normal interhemispheric commication through the corpus callosum and with the optic chiasm unsectioned. This investigator suggested that the results might be explained on the basis of the amount of brain tissue available for learning. Furthermore, Sechzer points out, reducing the amount of brain tissue available for learning also reduces the amount available for memory storage during and after acquisition.

If these data from cats can be extended to visual and somatosensory learning in children, the right hemisphere enables functions that generally are focused in the right hemisphere but contribute to functions of the left hemisphere provided there is adequate communication between them via the corpus callosum. Furthermore, through its diffuse as opposed to focal neural organization, the right hemisphere may be able to contribute a type of collating and appositional processing of data that the left hemisphere usually cannot provide by itself but which is essential to optimal brain function. A disorder in the right hemisphere is hence inevitably influential in learning, memory, and higher conceptual processes usually associated with the left hemisphere. While transcortical interhemispheric communication is clearly important to optimum brain function, a question which arises from discussion in an earlier chapter is this: To what extent and in what way, if any, is interhemispheric transfer through the corpus callosum related to brain stem interhemispheric integration? The importance of the question and its answer may not be realized for some time.

The Intervention Program

No well-defined and tested treatment program for unilateral disregard in learning disabled children is offered. This lack is due, in part, to the fact that the problem has only recently and not frequently been recognized as a sensory integrative problem among this population. The symptoms described above, along with the short amount of experience with children with this problem, suggest the following principles and practice. These suggestions must be considered highly tentative and employed with caution and alertness to responses that indicate the technique is contraindicated.

The nature of sensory integration in general suggests initiating therapy by providing a "base" of tactile and vestibular stimuli through direct stimulation of the appropriate receptors. It is suggested that the criterion for determining the appropriateness of the procedure is the response of the child. If any type of stimulation is uncomfortable to or tends to disorganize the child, the amount and type should be changed until it is acceptable, then gradually increased and modified until a fair quantity and variety of stimuli are acceptable.

There is a logical basis for providing a large amount of stimuli on the left side of the body, especially the upper extremity. Vibration is occasionally acceptable and can be applied through commercial devices for that purpose. Emphasizing use of the left arm and leg in all of the scooter board and other activities will not only provide proprioceptive input but will elicit reflex and postural responses from that side of the body. These responses can also be elicited while the child is on the scooter, on balancing boards, and on the therapy ball, usually with the therapist holding the child's left hand, thus forcing that extremity to take care of the body's postural needs.

The possible role of the orienting reflex in unilateral disregard has led to exploration of the use of the rolling tube shown in Figure 7. The child is asked to roll especially to the left if disregard is in that direction. The eyes should lead the motion, followed by head, shoulders, and body. The rolling, of course, stimulates the vestibular system which, it is hypothesized, facilitates the orienting reflex. This activity should be used slowly, cautiously, and in restricted quantity, for it sometimes elicits considerable discomfort and anxiety in children with disregard to the left, a fact which is consistent with involvement of the limbic system in the orienting reflex.

Vestibular stimulation while the child is in the prone or quadruped position also seems appropriate and the child's tolerance to it is usually greater than to rolling. Lying on the scooter board and turning to the left, while either spinning or following a prescribed course, involves relating to the space of which there is a tendency toward disregard. It is hoped that the sensory input will facilitate the disordered attentional mechanism. A more advanced activity is sitting on the platform swing (Figure 9) and turning to the left, throwing balls into the box as one goes by. The intention of throwing to a given point directs attention to the left.

There may be some integrative value in the pattern of sensory input that arises from the quadrupedal position that can influence the disregard problem. The following activity offers that type of sensory input along with the directing of attention to the left. A device appropriate for hitting a one-inch cube or other small object is attached to the head of the child. A stick attached to a headband is appropriate. By rapidly turning his head the child hits the cube with the stick. He aims the cube toward a goal to his left. The turning of the head elicits the TNR, but if the child is organizing his response properly this activity may encourage the integration of that primitive reflex. If disregard is to the right, the child would hit the block to the right. It is interesting to postulate the influence that this constellation of sensory input and organization of motor response might have on the remediation of the problem of unilateral disregard.

Another activity that may hold some value is using a small beam of light, such as that from a flashlight, in a darkened room as a lure toward which the child pushes himself on a scooter board. A short flash of light is a strong stimulus for the orienting reflex and if placed to the left will have a good chance of attracting attention. Navigation in the dark reduces dependence on sight and requires strong reliance on and, it is hoped, enhancement of the somatosensory component of the body scheme for the direction of movements within a visualized environmental scheme.

Involving the hand in activity helps direct attention. The following task originally designed for advanced therapy to assist integration of the two sides of the body, may also be appropriate for unilateral disregard. A piece of paper at least two feet wide is taped to the floor. Three dots about one inch in diameter are drawn on the paper: one at the left border, one at the center, and one at the right border. While resting on knees and the non-dominant hand, the child draws a line with a crayon across the page through the dots. Part of the time the child keeps his eyes focused on one dot with the other dots seen only in peripheral vision while drawing a series of lines beginning at the dot on which he is focusing and ending on the far dot. Other times he keeps his eyes focused on the dot to which the line is drawn or on the center dot. Lines can be drawn either left to right or right to left. The task requires close attention to peripheral visual stimuli and often it is the peripheral stimulus which is overlooked in visual disregard. This task is fatiguing and should not be pursued for more than a few minutes at a time.

The possibility of disorder of visual space perception occurring as part of this syndrome should be considered. If present, the procedures suggested in the chapter on form and space perception would be an appropriate inclusion in the program.

Chapter 15

Auditory-Language Disorders

Among learning disabled children, language problems generally receive the greatest amount of attention. The reverse has been the case in the development of this theoretical system. Clinical observation followed by research results, however, are forcing a change in thinking regarding the sensory integrative foundations of auditory perception and language disorders. In a study of children whose only identified cause of academic problems lay in the auditory-language domain, as opposed to the somatosensory and visual domains, significant gains in reading were made over a matched control group (Ayres, 1972a). These results have led to an exploration of the possible means by which a non-language intervention program of sensory integration appears to increase reading skill. Were these the only data in support of non-language sensory integrative programs helping language disorders, the results might have been attributed to chance, even though that possibility was less than one in a hundred. Clinical observations, probably beginning with that of the Bobaths of England, consistently have been suggestive of language and other academic improvement concomitant with the utilization of certain types of neuromuscular and sensory integrative therapy. Explicit rationales to explain the neurophysiological bases have not been immediately clear.

In addition to describing the syndrome and its treatment through sensory integrative therapy, this chapter attempts to investigate the kinds of neural processes that might be involved. Of all the neurophysiology hypothesized in this book, that explored in relation to auditory-language problems represents the most tentative and immature and will no doubt require considerable expansion and revision as research and study clarify the relationship of sensory integrative processes to language development.

Nature of the Syndrome

Auditory-language dysfunction is the most easily identified type of sensory integrative dysfunction of those discussed in this book. Cognitive functions lend themselves to more reliable measurements than do somatosensory functions and the longer history of measurement of language has given it an advantage in the development of instruments for evaluation. Although a language problem, especially that seen in a learning disabled child, may be included in a discussion of disordered sensory integration, it is recognized that language itself includes additional processes, such as those of a syntactical or rhetorical nature, which extend beyond sensory integrative functions. It is the more elementary and fundamental aspects of auditory-language function which are under major consideration here. These aspects contain a large element of sensory integration. If Benton (1964) is correct, emphasizing the perceptual deficit origins of developmental language problems is an appropriate approach to some language problems, for he considers developmental aphasia of the receptive-expressive type a function of deficit of auditory perception.

The syndrome is most clearly identified with tests of auditory perception and various language functions. The majority — but not all — of the children scoring low on these tests and identified as learning disabled children also show patterns of deficits in other types of sensory integration, especially in postural and bilateral integration but also in praxis and visual perception. In these cases, the auditory-language problem is seen as part of a more extensive form of neural dysfunction.

In some children whose problems seem rather discretely auditory-language as opposed to appearing in connection with other syndromes, there are signs suggestive of lateralized dysfunction, such as lower standard scores of the right as the preferred hand than of the left hand and occasionally a tendency to prefer the left over the right in crossing the body's mid-line (Ayres, 1971). Reed (1967) found that ten-year-old children with poorer finger localization in the right opposed to the left hand read significantly less well than the group with a majority of left-hand errors. This relationship was not found at the six-year level. Luria (1966b) has attributed the procedure of sequencing, i.e., temporally organizing stimuli which arrive in a successive as opposed to a simultaneous manner with the left hemisphere, an attribute consistent with data collected by Ayres (1971). The association of these other sensory integrative problems with auditory-language problems are not frequent and not necessarily strong, so their help in establishing the presence of more generalized unilateral cerebral dysfunction is not great. Although there is little evidence to guide one, the possibility that auditory-language problems could stem either from left cerebral hemisphere dysfunction or from a more generalized dysfunction should not be overlooked, for their remediation problems may require different approaches.

Some Neural Bases of Audition and Language

As with the other senses, a brief look at the evolutionary development of the auditory sense contributes to building a rationale which attempts to account for the effectiveness of certain kinds of treatment. The auditory system of vertebrates evolved after the appearance of the vestibular system and out of what was part of that system, thus leading to postulating a close connection between the two systems, a connection which is a large determinant of the choice of treatment of language disorders. As man's brain evolved, the cortical auditory area did not increase in its capacity for auditory perception (many lower animals are more auditorially adept than man), but instead it developed a speech center. That center evolved topographically next to the sensory area for hearing and the motor and somatosensory areas for the lower face. Both phyletically and ontogenetically language development shows a dependence upon auditory processes. The latter therefore deserve particular attention.

Two neural concepts are particularly important in understanding audition as well as language disorders and their treatment through sensory integrative processes. The first concept emphasizes the role of the brain stem and other subcortical structures and the second concept focuses on the importance of connections between the cortical language area and other parts of the brain.

An earlier chapter explained how, as animals evolved, new systems were gradually added to the old, incorporating already established neural systems for sensory integration but maintaining a certain dependence upon them. If the concept is relevant to auditory-language development, this domain of human behavior may be in part dependent upon integration of auditory and related

motor responses of a more primitive type. The more primitive structures for auditory functions lie in the brain stem. It has been
pointed out that, in cats, most of the neural processes of sound
occurred in the brain stem, especially, and in other subcortical
locations. If man's auditory system is similar to that of a cat, auditory coding begins soon after stimuli enter the brain and many connections with other ongoing processes offer an opportunity for
further processing before the stimuli reach the cortex. At the brain
stem level the processes are not lateralized as to dominance in the
same sense that speech is lateralized. In other words, below the
cortex, both sides of the brain are involved in similar auditory
tasks. Although speech production in the adult requires cortical
action, the vocalizations at and soon after birth reflect brain stem
function, indicating presence of motor as well as sensory mechanisms at that level and serving as a reminder that the brain stem
carries mechanisms for well-integrated sensorimotor responses of a
primitive type.

The reticular system, the major integrating structure in the
brain stem, not only provides auditory processing to the extent
that the stimuli possibly verge on becoming percepts, but also
offers a major opportunity for integration of auditory information
with that from other sensory sources. A considerable number of
auditory fibers terminate in the reticular formation and presumably are involved in the total integrative activity there. How much
this function goes beyond initial arousal and organization of reflexes is speculation, just as most of this theory is. Observations of
intervention programs suggest that the reticular activity results in
organization far more complex than those elementary functions.

The mesencephalic reticular formation is the seat of considerable sensory convergence and it is to this area that many auditory
stimuli are sent as well as vestibular and possibly other proprioceptive information. The integration with other senses occurs, presumably, at convergent neurons as well as nuclei in the brain stem,
thalamus, and cortex. Auditory stimuli are among the most commonly reported modalities showing convergence, suggesting both
the importance and the means of establishing associations between
auditory stimuli and other sensory modalities. Vestibular and
acoustic stimuli are commonly found to activate the same neural
structure. It is conjectured that intersensory integration is an important contributant to the total auditory-language developmental
sequence and can be utilized effectively in the intervention program.

Another critical role of the brain stem and thalamic area in
auditory-language function is that which has been hypothesized

by many to be a major system for integrating cortical with subcortical information for final analysis, namely, the "centrencephalic
system," to use Penfield's term. In studying cats, Ades (1959)
found that brain stem and thalamic nuclei process sounds from
input that came from both above and below and both auditory
and non-auditory sources were involved. Myers (1967), whose work
was largely with lower primates, conjectured that the method of
organizing the different portions of the cortex for speech production is through systems projecting down to brain stem centers as
opposed to organizing them through association fibers in the pre-
central somatic motor cortex. It would seem necessary, however,
for the latter ultimately to be involved in the final movements of
the mouth and throat.

In response to conjecture of the brain's reliance on subcortical
connections, Geschwind (1967) has counter-suggested that animals
use the subcortical connections only when the normal transcortical
pathway is no longer available and that the callosal communication
is of very great importance in the language of man. General evidence from the study of man favors an interpretation that man's
speech relies on both subcortical as well as callosal communication.

Reports from Sperry and Gazzaniga (1967) on tests on the few
cases of human beings in which the corpus callosum has been
sectioned indicate that some visual, somatosensory, and language
information can still transfer from one hemisphere to the other,
such as that required for the left hemisphere to direct the left
hand in writing. In these right-handed individuals, however, verbal
expression was restricted to the information that was processed in
the left hemisphere. These cases suggested to the authors that it is
the executive and motor components of speech that are more
lateralized than the auditory components. It might also suggest
that the neural connections that were left intact following commissurotomy were not able to transfer information at the speech level
although apparently some kinds of information could be transferred.

These observations, then, are consistent with the conjecture that
the auditory contributants to learning and execution of language
are dependent, in part, upon mechanisms of the brain stem and
thalamus. The possibility still exists that language execution itself
may require the use of brain stem mechanisms, especially if higher
centers do not operate well without fairly normal related subcortical
functioning.

It is hypothesized at this time—and subject no doubt to change
in the future — that the subcortical mechanisms discussed above
help account for the enhanced reading scores of children with

auditory-language problems who received sensory integrative therapy emphasizing non-language sensory stimulation and integration of brain stem mechanisms.

The second major neural consideration in language functions is the need for the language area to be connected to all other related areas of the brain. The significance of the need for enhancing connections in the learning disabled child can only be conjecture, for the degree to which these connections are weak is only conjecture. The case of the individual who suffers brain damage as an adult is clearer. In these cases of aphasia, the condition has been called a "disconnection syndrome" (W. R. Russell, 1963; Geschwind, 1965), a term which implies the need for neural connections between speech and other areas.

One of the earliest insights into the involvement of lower brain centers in language was made by Penfield and Roberts (1959), who asserted that comprehension of speech occurred only after impulses were received in the higher brain stem and *both* cortical areas and while there was interaction between the higher brain stem and left hemisphere. Speech itself occurred after interaction between the higher brain stem and left hemisphere; the impulses traveled to both cortical motor areas directing muscles used in speech.

Many of the major students of language disorders (Penfield and Roberts, 1959; Luria, 1966a; Geschwind, 1965, 1967; W. R. Russell, 1963; and Myers, 1967) have stressed the fact that many different portions of the brain contribute to language functions, and adequate access to those areas is essential for optimum language development. Myers (1967), Penfield and Roberts (1959), Russell (1963), and Luria (1966a) all emphasize the involvement of many neural levels and both hemispheres in language. Luria's work (1966a) shows that lesions in cortical areas outside that usually designated as a speech area may also result in aphasia.

Full communication with neural information from other sensory modalities, especially visual, auditory, and somatosensory, is considered critical to speech by both Geschwind and Russell. Geschwind (1965) has stated "*that the development of speech itself depends on the ability to form stable intermodal associations,* particularly visual-auditory and tactile-auditory binds." Man's advanced (compared to lower animals) capacity to establish associations between the senses has contributed to his capacity to develop speech. Furthermore, according to Geschwind, the development of speech in turn assists in forming further intermodal associations.

Sensation may be of importance in another manner. The contribution of tactile and proprioceptive feedback from structures involved in the motor formulation of sounds and words are generally believed to be significant in language development, although they have only recently been under evaluation in the mouth area. Somatosensory and auditory feedback provides the only cues an individual has regarding the accuracy of the sounds he has given forth. Vision is of little use. The somatosensory feedback is believed to assist in developing the generalized ability for perception of sounds spoken by another person and silently, even semiconsciously, repeated by the child. Snyder (1971) has emphasized the role of the temporal patterning in auditory perception, and research (Ayres, 1972a) shows that one group of children with language disabilities who improved their reading test scores through sensory integrative therapy made their greatest auditory-language test score improvement in remembering a sequence of auditory stimuli.

Extrapolating some of the ideas from studies of adults and children to learning disorders in children, it is hypothesized (1) that disorders in integration of sensory modalities, especially of auditory, vestibular, and somatosensory stimuli, may easily interfere with language development and (2) that adequate communication between the two hemispheres is especially important to reading. Signs suggestive of inadequate interhemispheral communication in reading disabled children were pointed out in an earlier chapter. Just as we do not read by our eyes alone, neither do we hear and speak using only the auditory-language centers in the cerebral cortex.

One of the older concepts in theory of language disorders links it with dominant hand usage. The issues of the nature of the relationship and its degree of importance have neither disappeared nor been resolved, suggesting a complexity of interrelated function not yet conceptualized. As brain research and related theorizing yield new ideas, they can be used to broaden the understanding of the influence of the dominant hand on language.

Lassek (1957) points out that during most of man's evolution as man as opposed to as a lower animal, his survival was closely dependent upon acts of the hand. These critical acts became more and more skilled, both forcing and being the result of increased specialized function of the cerebral cortex.

Specialization of function and asymmetry of hemispheric function served the same end, namely, development of the left hemisphere's ability to direct the right hand in highly skilled motor acts. Such direction required the ability to interpret related sensory input precisely. The manual skill is believed to have evolved before speech. Basing her ideas on study of brain injured adults, Semmes (1968) considers the possibility that the hemispheric specialization of language *stems* from the fact that the left hemisphere is focally organized to control fine sensorimotor control. She feels that the asymmetry of the two hemispheres is not secondary to language. The studies support the early idea of a close connection between handedness and speech.

It would appear that there may be some rationale supporting the practice of stressing development of skilled manual ability in one hemisphere to support the development of speech as another skilled motor function. The appropriate time to place such stress, however, is after good interhemispheral communication has been established. The effectiveness of an intervention program that emphasized firm establishment of dominance of one hand presumably would be dependent upon enhancing focal function in the hemisphere in which speech had already developed. In the average child —who does not have a handedness problem anyway—assuming that speech is localized in the left hemisphere is fairly safe; such an assumption is less safe when considering a child with neurological problems that may have prevented the localization of speech in the left hemisphere.

The Intervention Program

Clinical observations of responses of children to sensory integrative therapy interpreted in connection with the neurological bases of auditory-language and other brain functions have led to the following recommendations, some of which are probably responsible for observed benefits and some of which possibly have contributed little. Further experimentation is necessary to obtain a more precise fit between problem and therapy.

If, as Worden and Livingston (1961) assert, the reticular formation is a transactional link for parts of the nervous system, then the auditory-language system is no exception to its organizing influence, even though reticular formation organization is far less specific than that of the cortex. Accordingly, very elementary, pre-language non-cognitive activity which elicits sensations from the body and reflex and adaptive responses to them appears to be the most appropriate initial therapy for language disorders. The greatest limitations of this type of therapy are its failure to impress the observer and the fact that the therapist cannot actually see sensory integration occurring. Sometimes observing a child's subsequent behavior helps formulate inferences as to whether neural integration in general has occurred. The teaching of language is not appropriate for therapy that is attempting to lay brain stem foundations. For the learning of words a more cognitive approach can follow.

The importance of intersensory integration to the development of language requires that the therapist forsake the common practice of focusing only on auditory stimuli, especially when attempting neural integration. Instead, he is advised to supply a considerable amount of somatosensory and, especially, vestibular stimuli. It is generally not necessary to supply auditory stimuli for association, for natural activity, especially that involving vestibular stimulation, usually elicits vocalization, often of a primitive type. This type of vocalization and the ordinary stimuli of conversation and that resulting from play are believed to be appropriate contributants to sensory integration at the brain stem level. The usual problem is avoiding offending non-participants with what to them is not therapeutic stimuli but just plain noise. While it might be argued that this type of vocalization is not teaching the child words he needs to know, the counter-argument is that the teaching of words is not appropriate for therapy that is attempting to organize the brain stem for the subsequent learning of words. The emitting and hearing of sounds and the most elementary forms of language communication along with somatosensory and vestibular stimulation is considered the appropriate combination for laying the intersensory modality base. A more cognitive approach can follow later, either during the same day if the child's age is appropriate or at a later time.

If the child shows any signs that vestibular stimuli are not making the normal synaptic connections, as evidenced by reduced or no nystagmus or vertigo following spinning, bombardment of the brain by vestibular stimuli from spinning in a net hammock or on a scooter board or trampoline is especially appropriate unless there are contraindications. Similarly, any deficits in other types of sensory integration should receive attention. Before efficient auditory associations are made with other sensory modalities, intrasensory integration must be adequate. Promoting sensory integration in general theoretically might also enable better communication between the cortical language area and the other areas of the brain which language authorities feel is essential to adequate speech. All of the activities which have been suggested in earlier chapters are appropriate to a greater or lesser degree for remediation of auditory-language problems, for all are directed toward normalizing sensory integration of one type or another. Further growth of understanding in this area will no doubt lead to greater specificity of procedure. At this stage, the most fruitful approaches seem to center around the use of vestibular stimuli and responses to them.

It is possible that the simultaneous bombardment of the brain by sensory input from various sources during simple gross activity provides not only an opportunity to promote intersensory integration but also brain stem processing of auditory stimuli *per se*. The processing conceivably could involve both corticifugal stimuli going down to a centrencephalic system as well as centripetal stimuli arriving from lower centers.

The role of purposive movement or adaptive motor responses in the integrative process subserving auditory and language functions is less easily hypothesized than the comparable role in the development of visual functions. One can only submit a few generalizations of brain function that may or may not be relevant, hoping that the passage of time will yield clarifying research.

As discussed earlier, purposive movement has assumed an important role throughout evolution in intra- and intermodality sensory integration. Herrick (1956) and Coghill (1929) placed considerable emphasis on the total motor reaction of the organism as a force in the evolution of the mind. As one looks at the evolutionary span during which the neural bases for intersensory modality integration were being laid down, it is clear that during the greater part of that time the motor patterns were executed with the quadruped position being primary during most non-resting motor output. All of the postural reflexes and reactions related to them, including the head righting reflex, the neck righting reflex, and some of the equilibrium reactions have close neurological connections with neural patterns for the quadruped posture. A good deal of the motor output among these vertebrates with quadruped ambulation was associated with auditory stimuli of survival value, such as fleeing from a sound that might presage a predator or detecting a prospective meal. It may be that all of these reactions originally established significantly strong relationships to the brain stem mechanisms concerned with audition. Any current human neural patterns that may remain from the pre-language, pre-bipedal evolutionary phase during which auditory and motor neural patterns were integrated and established most likely reside in the brain stem and possibly the thalamus as its upper end. To the extent that those sensorimotor patterns still reside in man's brain stem, to that extent they may be significant in man's current function.

The learning disabled children with auditory language problems and without noticeable disorder in postural mechanisms improved in reading scores following a program which involved considerable motor activity while using a scooter board in the prone position and many other pieces of apparatus designed to elicit postural reflexes and reactions. If these activities contributed to the children's enhanced neural integration subserving auditory-language processes, it may be for the above reasons.

A stronger argument can be made for the possible effectiveness of motor activity on language function that is immature because of inadequate interhemispheral integration, such as that found in the syndrome of dysfunction in postural and bilateral integration. In other words, if the reading problem is due to poor interhemispheral integration, enhancing that integration through methods proposed earlier will likely help language development.

It has been suggested that speech production is dependent upon connections between the language center in the left hemisphere and important parts of the brain, including the right hemisphere, where some aspects of auditory perception, such as tone quality and pattern discrimination, are most likely to receive some essential processing (cf. Milner, 1967, and Bogen, 1969b). If this is the case, then the need for adequate interhemispheral integration at the brain stem level is important for that reason.

No doubt the corpus callosum assumes an important role in interhemispheral communication regarding language. This role, it is suggested by Bogen and Bogen (1969), is associated with the highest and most complex brain activities and language is certainly one of these. It would seem likely that the familiar practice of using tactile and kinesthetic stimuli along with visual and auditory information as the child attempts the actual reading process might employ the transcallosal route for interhemispheral communication to a greater extent than most of the procedures recommended in this book. Similarly, the teaching of verbal concepts such as "under the table" or "between the boxes" by having the child act them out would be considered primarily a cortico-cortico activity combining right hemisphere visual space perception with left hemisphere language and some emphasis on utilization of brain stem sensorimotor and integrative mechanisms.

Just as it is important to remember that sensations from one modality can enhance perception in another, so also is it essential to recognize that they can interfere, especially if the reticular formation is not adept at inhibiting the imposing stimuli. Many individuals close their eyes to enable focusing on the hearing of a sound; tickling the back of the neck of someone speaking on the telephone would tax his attentive powers. When a child is being asked to concentrate very hard on interpretation of what a person is saying, simultaneous vestibular stimulation that threatens postural support would be inhibitory because the vestibular stimuli have survival priority, but if the child is spinning safely suspended in a net hammock, the resultant vestibular stimuli probably will enhance the processing of the sounds that automatically accompany a play situation.

Chapter 16

Hand Dominance and Lateralization
of Cerebral Function

Hand dominance and agreement between eye and hand dominance were among the first behavioral parameters to be considered significant indices of the status of neural functions related to learning disorders. The significance of a number of other parameters has now been clarified by research. The topic of dominance, while not central to the research on which this theoretical system is based, deserves some discussion in addition to that given in the previous chapter. Here the issue will be placed in a broader perspective.

Studies on eye and hand dominance are too numerous to be cited in detail; only a few typical examples will be mentioned. Professional observations such as those made by Critchley (1964), Hécaen and Ajuriaguerra (1964), and Zangwill (1960) have repeatedly linked reading problems with inadequate lateralization of cerebral function. Studying 250 randomly selected second-grade children, Balow and Balow (1964) found that strength of hand dominance, direction of dominance (right or left), or agreement between eye and hand dominance had no significant effect on reading.

On the other hand, Koos (1964) studied a group of primary public school children with intelligence quotients below the group median and demonstrated a linkage between reading achievement and mixed eye-hand dominance and left-right discrimination. Gottlieb, Doran and Whitley (1964) found that right-handed and right-sighted deaf children earned higher speech grades than did those with mixed eye-hand dominance. Somewhat similarly, Flick (1966) found that four-year-old boys with left-handedness and -eyedness had lower perceptual-motor ability and intelligence quotients than did those with other eye-hand dominance relationships.

When research results appear to conflict, a resolution of the difference in results often lies in a theoretical conceptualization more complex than that which previously has been developed. These studies, representative of many more, show that the relationship between learning disorders and eye-hand dominance probably is present in some children but its detection is easily obscured by the many variables operating in learning disorders, in establishing eye and hand dominance, and in any data collection procedure. While basic research has not greatly clarified the significance of the agreement between eye and hand dominance, slight advances have been made in understanding lateralization of function, especially skilled motor function.

Lateralization of Skilled Motor Function as a Developmental Process

The evolution process has moved toward localization and specialization of cortical function, resulting in one hemisphere's dominance for some functions and the other hemisphere's dominance for other functions. A significant difference between man's cerebral hemispheres and those of lower animals lies in organization of higher cognitive functions. In the lower animals the organization appears to be largely symmetrical, while in man functions are more asymmetrical and lateralized. The previous chapter presented some recent ideas as to the different kinds of organization promoting different functions of the two cerebral hemispheres. Emphasis was placed on organization differences as opposed to unilateral dominance. The studies of Hécaen (1967), Semmes (1968), and Teuber (1967) all point to the probability that the two hemispheres are concerned with the same function but that these functions are represented in a different manner, the left hemisphere having highly localized or focal representation for the functions it directs. As previously pointed out, the focal type of organization enables the development of fine skilled motor ability.

According to Semmes (1968), whose work is based on study of war veterans with penetrating brain injury, lesions in a focally represented left hemisphere result in more observable deficits than a comparable lesion in the right hemisphere. If right hemisphere lesions were massive, she suggests, the effect on behavior would be just as noticeable. The suggestion is certainly consistent with the work of Bogen (1969a, 1969b) and Bogen and Bogen (1969), who propose that the right hemisphere works as hard, as intricately, and with as much informational capacity as does the left and is dominant for certain higher functions, some of which are not yet recognized.

It may be, then, that what has been referred to as the desirability of establishment of hemisphere dominance is really the need for the lateralization of cerebral function resulting in localization and specialization of groups of neurons in the neocortex—probably the left—to facilitate speech and skilled motor function of the right hand. Someday the specialization of neurons in the right hemisphere may receive equal attention.

Although each infant apparently carries with him a hereditary predisposition toward lateralization of cerebral function, the actual process of establishing specialized cortical function is largely determined by the developmental process. Hand dominance is not evident until a child approaches school age, and definite ipsilaterality, according to a study by Belmont and Birch (1963) of bright normal children, is not established until ten years of age, although hand dominance is stabilized by age seven. They found that at the age of nine there is a critical break in the number of children who exhibit mixed handedness.

Lateralization of function is only one aspect of cerebral dominance. At this point of understanding of cerebral hemisphere dominance, it is believed that one hemisphere may generally dominate but sometimes the alternate one does and either hemisphere works better if it has the resources of the alternate hemisphere. This conjectured arrangement is supported by electroencephalographic studies of human beings and by reports on split-brain animal experiments, such as that by Sperry (1961), in which one hemisphere tended to dominate over the other but the dominance alternated. Hécaen and Ajuriaguerra (1964) have presented an opinion that bears consideration. They believe that poorly established laterality rather than a struggle for cerebral dominance is apt to be associated with reading disorders. They propose that lateralization begins in the motor domain and when the motor domain is not clearly established, the cortex tends toward ambilaterality but generally resembles that of a right-handed person. This type of reasoning has apparently been the basis for the therapeutic practice of encouraging hand dominance. Use of the hand, it would seem, is one of the more obvious methods of forcing lateralization of cerebral function directing fine motor skill. However, it leads to speculation about the developmental steps which may have been skipped in the process.

That biochemical changes in the cortex may occur as a result of the establishment of hand dominance is suggested by a study by Hydén and Egyhazi (1964) in which they analyzed the RNA increase and qualitative change in cortical neurons concerned with handedness in rats. When right-handed rats were forced to become left-handed, there was a significant change in the quantity and base composition of RNA in the motor sensory areas of the right cortex as compared to the left. That these changes were a function of learning was supported by the fact that no significant differences in right and left cortical RNA content and composition were found in right-handed rats not subject to the transfer experiments.

Failure to Establish Hand Dominance

Since establishing one hand as dominant is an aspect of development that holds some significance for the total sensory integrative process, an unusual delay in establishment of hand dominance, when accompanied by more interfering problems such as behavior or learning problems, deserves investigation of the underlying cause, for those factors which have interfered with development in the motor domain may account for those in other domains. It is proposed that the best way to approach a "handedness" problem is to investigate the possible underlying causative factors and ameliorate them insofar as is possible, in the hope that doing so will allow the brain to proceed with its normal maturational goal of establishlishing one hand as the dominant hand for skilled motor work.

It is believed that in some cases, the dysfunction underlying failure to establish one hand as the dominant hand is due to lateralized dysfunction in the brain or to the presence of more disorder on one side than on the other. It seems probable that dysfunction resulting from trauma is as apt to affect the left as the right cerebral hemisphere. If a child had a hereditary predisposition toward right-handedness and there was greater dysfunction in the left than in the right cerebral hemisphere, the degree of dexterity in the two hands might be equal or even favor the left, leading to a tendency for the child to use both hands equally and failure to establish dominance. As pointed out in a previous chapter, a tendency toward unilateral disregard may interfere with the establishment of dominance if the disregard is to the side with a hereditary predisposition toward dominance. The dysfunction may also interfere with establishment of eye dominance. If the right hand is chosen as the dominant hand, dominance will probably not be strong because of the adequacy of the left hand. If the left eye is chosen as dominant, mixed dominance will result. If coordination of the right hand is sufficiently impaired to cause the child to prefer his left as his dominant hand but conditions favor choosing his right eye as dominant, mixed dominance also results. Perhaps a more severe or generalized left hemisphere disorder would result in development of the left hand and eye as dominant. In this case the sensory integrative problem would likely be greater than when mixed eye-hand dominance is present. Such conditions have been found to explain satisfactorily a number of "handedness" or "dominance" problems.

Less frequently, differences in somatosensory perception of the two upper extremities make the right hand less satisfactory or comfortable to use, even though it is more skilled motorically, resulting in conflict over which hand to prefer for skilled work. In these cases, treatment to enhance somatosensory perception often relieves the problem and the child will then automatically show greater preference for his right hand.

One of the most frequent of the known causes for failure to establish strong unilateral dominance is the syndrome affecting postural and bilateral integration. When the two sides of the body fail to integrate their function, there is usually a tendency to avoid crossing the body's mid-line, each hand preferring to operate on its own side of the body. In extreme cases a child with this problem may draw a horizontal line on a chalkboard using his left hand for holding the chalk until he reaches his mid-line, then transferring the chalk to the right hand to continue the line to the right. A similar approach to performance on the Motor Accuracy and Space Visualization tests of the SCSIT and to visual motor tasks in general may be seen. This practice interferes with the normal development of a preferred hand for skilled work and often the left hand will show a higher standard score on the Motor Accuracy test than will the right hand, probably because of the more even division of tasks than is normal. Children with these problems generally have no resistance to using the right hand for writing and other skilled work as long as it does not necessitate extensive use of the right hand on the left side of extracorporeal space, for the right hand is generally superior in skill to the left hand. In addition to this fairly obvious interpretation of why this syndrome interferes with establishment of hand dominance, it is proposed that adequate interhemispheral integration normally precedes establishment of unilateral cerebral dominance for motor skills, the latter being in some way neurodevelopmentally dependent upon the former.

In these cases the therapist must avoid thinking that perhaps the child might be naturally predisposed to left-handedness, then emphasizing left hand dominance. Such a course of action is occasionally based on memory of the days when it was considered "dangerous" to force a child to use a non-dominant hand for writing. If the child does show greater skill with the left than right hand, there may be some basis for concern, but if the underlying problem is poor integration of the two sides of the body, concern and treatment should be directed toward the latter problem.

The conditions described above are probably not the only examples of sensory integrative dysfunction affecting the establishment of hand dominance. There are undoubtedly other factors that interfere simultaneously with learning and with hand dominance, both being results rather than causes of disorder. Furthermore, no attempt is made here to consider either all the implications of hand dominance when there is an inherent predisposition toward left-handedness without complicating sensory integrative dysfunction, or the implications of mixed eye-hand dominance. The special problems posed by the cerebral palsy child are also not under consideration.

Considerations in Selecting a Dominant Hand for a Child

When a child reaches the age where he is expected to write and he has not shown definite hand preference, a decision regarding his instruction is necessary. The process of writing should be delegated to one hand only. The decision should be based on a number of data, some of which are discussed below.

Determining the handedness in the child's family is necessary to estimate the probable hereditary predisposition of the child. The ease and naturalness with which a child uses his hands also reflects this predisposition. Both hands should be tested on the Motor Accuracy test and both raw, time adjusted, and standard scores compared. These data indicate which hand offers the greater skill and how each hand compares with the normative data.

Similarly comparison should be made of right and left hand scores on Kinesthesia, Manual Form Perception, Finger Identification, Graphesthesia, Tactile Localization, Crossing Mid-line of the Body and or right and left foot Standing Balance. Differences in defensive reaction to stimuli on the two sides of the body should be noted. Differences between extremities on Kinesthesia are found less frequently than differences in tactile perception. Consistent differences in scores between the right and left sides of the body should be present before significance is attached to them. The standard deviation scores of the two sides of the body help assay the relative degree of neural integration of the two cerebral hemispheres.

A thorough evaluation of those parameters involved in the syndrome interfering with postural mechanisms and coordinating function of the two sides of the body helps determine whether the dominance problem is related to those underlying symptoms. Another important consideration to add to these observances is the degree of hand preference the child has already established. To that degree cerebral organization and specialization have developed and to disturb that organization may be more disruptive than helpful. Furthermore, unrecognized factors need consideration even though their nature is not known.

Case Studies

F., a six-year-old kindergarten girl with a history of slow development, had failed to establish consistency in hand preference by the time the teacher was ready to introduce writing. Some abnormalities in language had been noted. Previously she had been identified as left-handed, -footed, and -eyed. F. was referred with the request to determine which hand should be taught to write. Although there was no familial evidence of left-handedness, the fact that F. used her left hand as frequently as her right hand and that during an earlier educational experience she had started to stutter led to the parental conjecture that she may naturally have been left-handed.

F.'s scores on the SCSIT fell grossly within normal limits. It was the examiner's impression that F. tried very hard at all of the test tasks and possibly solved some through cognitive rather than perceptual processes. She had a struggle with the concept of right versus left. In selecting the blocks for the formboard of the Space Visualization test, each time a left-hand block was chosen she picked it up with her left hand. Each time a right-hand block was chosen she picked that block up with her right hand. There were no exceptions. The right hand raw score on Motor Accuracy was 453 compared to 442 for the left hand, which indicated greater skill in the right hand; however, the right hand standard score was −0.3 compared to the left hand score of +0.2. She stood for fourteen seconds on her left foot and three seconds on her right foot when her eyes were open. With eyes closed, she was unable to stand on either foot alone. The left eye was preferred over the right but not strongly. No difference between right and left hand scores could be detected on somatosensory tests.

During Schilder's Arm Extension Test there was resistance to head turning, marked dropping of the arms, discomfort, and a report of feeling dizzy. She was unable to assume a prone extension position but did not evidence change in muscle tone during passive head turning while in the quadruped position. Muscle tone was low. Extraocular muscle control was irregular.

These findings identified two areas of dysfunction: a disorder of postural and bilateral integration and possibly some mild lateralized dysfunction in the left cerebral hemisphere. Although there were other problems, these were the two that had the most evidence bearing on the hand dominance question.

Without integration of function of the two sides of the body, probably related to inadequate development of postural mechanisms, each hand tended to function independently on its own side of the body, interfering with maturation of the right hand as the one performing skilled work regardless of location of that work. The skill of the two hands was closer together than is usually found in children of F.'s age, providing little support to development of the right hand as the dominant hand. It was recommended that F. be taught to write with her right hand and that treatment to enhance sensorimotor integration be undertaken.

Six and one-half-year-old G. was entering a class for educationally handicapped children, showing preference for his left hand as a writing hand but frequent and natural use of his right hand for many skilled unilateral tasks. Primitive postural mechanisms were poorly integrated into the nervous system. He preferred his right eye and right leg. Left leg standing balance was superior to the right leg balance, but both scores were below average. Space perception was poorly developed. Performance on Crossing the Midline of the Body test of the SCSIT indicated preference for the right hand over the left. The right hand standard score on crossed items only was +0.5 and the left hand standard score was −1.5, suggesting more normal use of the right than left hand for some sensorimotor tasks.

All scores on the language tests of the Illinois Test of Psycholinguistic Abilities were below average excepting that for Auditory Reception. The reading score of the Wide Range Achievement Test fell at the fourth month of kindergarten and the arithmetic score at the seventh month of kindergarten.

The right hand Motor Accuracy adjusted score was 434 and

the left 443, showing somewhat better coordination in the left hand when compared to the right. When the right hand score was compared with the less accurate hand normative data the resulting standard score was −0.1, which seemed a rather unlikely score of a child who was clumsy and awkward in task performance. When the right hand score was compared with the more accurate hand norms, the score was −1.9. The left hand score when compared to less accurate hand norms was +0.2 and when compared to more accurate hand norms was −1.2.

From these data it was hypothesized that G. was naturally predisposed to be right-handed, but that his dysfunction had affected his right hand more than his left. A standard score close to two standard deviations below the mean probably did represent his right hand coordination fairly well. G.'s left hand did not approximate the skill of a more accurate normal hand, but with the extra practice it received as a preferred hand it raised its level of performance beyond that expected of a non-dominant hand.

Because of G.'s accustomed use of the left hand and its better coordination relative to the right hand, the left hand was considered the better choice as a writing hand in spite of probable right hand hereditary predisposition.

Chapter 17

The Art of Therapy

The child must organize his own brain; the therapist can only provide the milieu conducive to evoking the drive to do so. Structuring that therapeutic environment demands considerable professional skill. Planning and executing movement provides one of the major means through which the brain produces and organizes stimuli, especially somatosensory and vestibular sensations. To a lesser degree, depending upon age, visual stimuli can be included among those organized through motor experience.

Movement which is not goal-directed usually is not as therapeutic as that which is more purposeful, and purposeful movement becomes therapeutic when a child makes a response which is adaptive, especially if it is more adaptive than any response previously evinced. Promoting a response which represents a more mature or integrated action than previous performance requires special understanding and ability on the part of the therapist. Such competence represents more than technical proficiency; it approaches an art.

The Internal Drive Toward Sensory Integration

The most therapeutic situation is that in which the child's inner urge for action and growth drives him toward a response that furthers maturation and integration. Within the domain of a child's sensorimotor function, these responses most frequently are either more effective postural or balancing responses or greater skill in motor planning, such as is required by the manipulation of objects. The latter includes playing with toys and solving visual puzzles.

When the optimum-for-growth situation is achieved, the child "turns on" and his obvious zest for experience signifies several things. It tells the therapist that the sensorimotor activity is at a developmental level appropriate to the maturation of the child's nervous system. The therapist can profit from noting this. It indicates that the experience is a "self-actualizing" one; it is growth-promoting, fulfilling, organizing, and integrating. It is the kind of experience that the average child continually seeks during the first few years of life. The average child finds it and grows from it; the child with poor sensory integration seems unable to create the situation necessary for normal maturation or to respond to it in a manner fostering maturation. He requires a situation especially tailored to meet his needs.

When a child does find himself in a situation that nurtures development of thwarted potential, his response clearly indicates that, at some level of consciousness, he recognizes the significance of the event. Often the child "takes over" the direction of the treatment in a generally constructive way. He may or may not be cooperative with others in his presence, including the therapist. Cooperation is not his objective; self-fulfillment is. Cooperation with the child then becomes the objective of the therapist. It is an important therapeutic objective. The child's response often is characterized by intense emotional involvement and excitement, perseverance with the task, a refusal to try anything else, a demand to be seen or heard but not directed, an urge to explore his capacity with variations of sensorimotor expressions, and resistance to the necessity for terminating the treatment period. Sometimes children act as though their lives depended upon the experience, and, indeed, to a certain extent, they do.

The realization of a latent potential becomes self-directing, and the more that self-direction can be tapped the greater and faster the neural organization. The ultimate goal of sensory integrative treatment is a being which wants to, can, and will direct himself meaningfully and with satisfaction in response to the environmental demands. The inner drive toward sensory integration exists in most, if not all, young children who come to the attention of a therapist. It often lies buried beneath many other needs which interfere. Enabling the child to gain contact with that drive is difficult, but necessary for maximum response to treatment.

Factors Promoting Self-Direction

Self-direction by a child requires ability on the part of the therapist to recognize the areas of sensory integrative dysfunction, to define them, to assess where the dysfunction lies relative to the developmental sequence, and then to reduce the demand being made on the child to a developmental level where an adaptive response is within the child's capacity. Making a demand for skilled sitting balance before righting reactions have been activated will be less apt to tap that internal drive toward normalcy than will asking the child to execute an equilibrium reaction while lying prone on a ball. The latter is an ontogenetically earlier response. Similarly, asking a child to manipulate a yo-yo when his body scheme is poorly developed will meet with little success unless yo-yos are the prevailing toy of his peers. In the latter case, developing a splinter skill with the toy may add to emotional adjustment.

Sensory integrative evaluations define the general area and degree of dysfunction, which, in turn, suggests the type of endeavor to present initially to the child. Watching the child's approach and response to equipment augments the information about his neurological organization. The same carpet-lined barrel lying on its side elicited three different responses from three children of the same age but of varying degrees of maturation of postural mechanisms. A girl with both poor motor planning and poorly developed postural mechanisms saw it as strictly a garbage can offering her no opportunities for use. One boy immediately crawled into it and started rolling; a third child jumped on top of it and tried to balance on it as he made it roll.

If a child cannot explore his own potential — and his dysfunction often makes it difficult for him to do so alone — the therapist must intervene, aiding, assisting, modifying, and suggesting, bringing out of the child that which he cannot quite bring out by himself. The capacity on the part of the therapist to adapt and innovate as the immediate situation requires contributes greatly in helping the child toward inner-directedness. The skill is one of the most valuable assets of a therapist.

The ability to provide freedom within structure that furthers exploration on the part of the child comes with comprehensive and deep understanding and grasp of the nature of sensory integrative dysfunction.

Knowledge of the general nature of the problem allows preparation for the treatment period with appropriate equipment and a general plan of action. Watching the child as he performs, seeing his mood, his emotional state, and his motor action guides the therapist in providing the optimum amount of freedom or gentle manipulation to foster the constructive involvement of the child in a task with the gusto as well as intent to achieve that leads him to a more advanced level of neural organization.

A balance of freedom and structure that maximizes constructive exploration is not easily achieved. Both freedom and structure contribute to the therapeutic situation and children require varying degrees of each. Free play does not inevitably, in itself, further sensory integration, but too rigid structure will inhibit the manifestation of potential. Noise and a little havoc often accompany exploration that is growth-promoting; the results are well worth it. Structure may push the child farther toward the therapeutic objective than he can reach alone, but too much will defeat its purpose.

The kind of involvement necessary to achieve the state wherein the child becomes effectively self-directing within the structure set by the therapist cannot be commanded; it must be elicited. Therein lies the art of therapy. The opportunity can be offered, encouragement given, suggestions proffered. Physical assistance may help, but unless the child wills to act upon the environment, he will not do so. Furthermore, he will not do so in a manner that can be called adaptive and growth-promoting and therefore therapeutic unless he finds it fulfilling to do so. Fulfillment comes with the right combination of challenge and success.

Many perceptual-motor tasks expected of a child of a given age are too difficult to be appropriate challenges for children with sensory integration problems. Facing a task without the possibility of success is not a challenge; it is confronting doom. Those who have encountered frequent failure have alternate ways of coping, some annoying, some camouflaging, and some clever. Children learn to avoid or to structure situations in which perceptual or motor skills beyond their capacity are required. The child who has difficulty turning to the left will move so as to enable him to turn to the right or he will cope by stopping the movement instead of turning. The child whose equilibrium reactions do not enable him to catch his balance easily will compensate by appearing to like to fall. "Crash" solutions to activities with motor demands inappropriate to the child's maturation of equilibrium reactions are common among young boys. Falling can be socially acceptable. It can even appear amusing to the child's peers. It is also a way of avoiding a challenge that may result in failure. It is the therapist's responsibility to enable the maintenance of equilibrium and the gaining of satisfaction from doing so.

Physical surroundings can foster the self-fulfilling properties of sensory integrative experience. Appropriate treatment apparatus is of first importance. It does not have to be elegant to be effective. More neural integration has been promoted by net hammocks, scooter boards, inner tubes and pieces thereof, and large therapy balls than by paper, pencils, and commercially prepared pictures, puzzles, diagrams, and the like. These latter media do have a place in treatment, however, in the later stages of a remedial program. An ideal situation places the child in a room devoid of all but two or three pieces of equipment offering opportunities for exploration appropriate to the state of neurological involvement. Additional alternate equipment is readily available to the therapist if the situation requires it. Floor and walls ideally are clean, smooth, and not too hard. Fewer injuries will occur on a wood than on a cement floor. Mats are available to place as needed for protection. Freedom to explore and respond is possible within a limited, flexible structure.

There is nothing quite as stimulating as the introduction of a new piece of equipment. Excitement stimulates effort. Novelty promotes exploration. The response of one child stimulates effort on the part of another. Suggestions become more acceptable. When the equipment has lost its charm, its absence for a few weeks may renew it.

Large quantities of simple, versatile equipment that makes possible the attainment of an objective through many different approaches keep vigor in a therapeutic program. They also require considerable storage area.

The Child's Response to Guided Exploration

Certain sensory experiences are a necessary part of the total development of the child. It is believed that there are inherent designs within the brain that normally activate the experiences that produce the sensory patterns critical to normal development. Just as a child needs certain relationships with parents and peers to develop normally in the interpersonal domain, he needs certain sensory experiences to develop intrapersonally.

When these experiences are achieved, even belatedly, not only is the strengthened sensory integration providing, it is hoped, a better foundation for learning, it is providing a better foundation for emotional development. It is hypothesized that the relation of the sensory input to the neurological substrate of emotional development is responsible for the feeling of fulfillment experienced by many children during sensory integrative therapy.

The extent to which a child's potential is realized through his sensory experience is usually reflected in his enthusiasm for treatment. The response should not be interpreted merely as the child's feeling better about himself because he can now engage more effectively in the activities expected of a child his age. If such ability accrues, it is a bonus from which there may be additional satisfaction, but motor skill is neither the objective nor the most important end product of sensory integrative treatment. The goal is sensory stimulation in order to strengthen neural integration, especially that neural integration that underlies learning and behavior. Responses of children suggest that the goal is realized in many but not all children. It is important to bear in mind that while neurological organization may be augmented at least temporarily, it is not always entirely maintained and probably never completely normalizes the underlying dysfunction.

Although a great deal is known, on a factual level, about the manner in which the brain of a lower animal functions, even more is unknown about how the human brain functions. Watching a child with a brain that does not function in an altogether normal manner and observing how he occasionally enters constructively into a sensorimotor act with a zest that hardly has bounds, leads a therapist to consider the possibility that the reaction of the child is a better guide to therapy than all the facts and hypotheses at hand. The child's brain is operating on the basis of all that is known as well as not known; furthermore, it is operating on the basis of what is functioning normally within his brain as well as that which deviates from the norm. His brain holds the answer to the question, "Of what should therapy consist?" Watching the expressions of that brain in its most constructive moments can help answer the question.

On the other hand, a negative response on the part of the child to the treatment situation is a signal to the therapist to stop and analyze the situation. The first question to ask is, "Is the developmental level of the activity too advanced for the degree of sensorimotor integration of the child?" The answer to the question is sometimes found by providing activities of a developmentally earlier nature. If the child shows a more accepting response, the former challenge was probably too great for him. The ability of a child to walk in a fairly normal manner is not necessarily an indication that he has the sensory integration necessary to accomplish all sensorimotor actions that normally mature ontogenetically before walking appears. A child with a poorly integrated tonic labyrinthine reflex may still learn to walk on a rolling barrel even though he learns it as a splinter skill. Development in the child with learning disorders is irregular and spotty rather than delayed or stopped at a specific point.

A negative response also may be evoked in a competitive situation where the peer is more successful. Discomfort can result from being reminded of inadequacies. Some children respond negatively to the very sight of a jump rope because of failure experience in the usual school situation, but the same child may tackle a complicated unfamiliar scooter activity requiring comparable sensory organization. The following account illustrates another type of negative response resulting from the therapist's misjudging the situation. An anxious child was introduced to an obstacle course which the therapist thought was appropriate for the child's central integrative state. Apparently the child held a different opinion, for as soon as he saw the situation he crawled into the barrel lying on its side and repeatedly rolled through the obstacle course equipment, rendering it useless and, of course, benign.

Any individual can bring hostility to the treatment situation from another unrelated situation. Allowing the release of hostility through activity may clear the way for establishment of other objectives. Kicking and smashing cardboard cartons and hitting balloons until they break can reduce the hostility level. Whatever the cause of a negative or indifferent response, a wise course of action is to introduce a less demanding therapeutic task that carries more assurance of success.

The child's sense of fulfillment radiates as he experiences himself interacting effectively with the world of objects, or as he pits himself against gravity and finds that it is not quite the ruthless master it was a short time before, or as he finds his body bringing him satisfying sensation. He no longer is the impotent organism shoved about by environmental forces; he can act effectively on the world. He is more of a whole being. Children may perform tasks for rewards, but there is no reward that has quite the enduring qualities that success holds. It is one of the most effective operant conditioners.

The internal and inherent drive or urge toward normal sensorimotor development and expression appears directly associated with the actual integrative process. That drive is far stronger, more obvious, and more freely expressed under certain conditions than under others. The situation which is most apt to draw forth the inner drive toward maturing is that in which the activity can be executed in a fairly normal manner but previously had been more difficult or not attempted. Rolling inside of a barrel is fun for the child of six to ten years of age whose equilibrium reactions are just adequate to make the barrel roll, but when the task is no longer a challenge to be mastered, it is often seen as juvenile. Boys in their teens have found scooter boards emotionally acceptable. Balancing on equilibrium boards has been fun for adolescents even though such boards are usually "outgrown" by the average child of eight. A child finds an activity fulfilling his potential if it meets his level of development in some domain.

These observations that the degree of gratification of a task is directly related to the degree to which it fits a developmental need have been particularly obvious in the treatment of immature postural mechanisms. In this domain, the developmental sequence is fairly evident and each successive step is more dependent upon previous development than is the case in some other neural subsystems. The concept also has been seen in the development of the capacity to motor plan. Riding a scooter board under a rubber strip and catching it with one flexed leg may fascinate an eight-year-old apraxic girl while others her age are content with nothing less than discovering complex variations of pease porridge hot, cat's cradles with strings, and Chinese jump rope.

Mere activity, in itself, does not necessarily further better sensory integration. If it did, the hyperactive child would be the better organized child. The action must represent direction and effort that is more mature than that previously possible. Desire and will to accomplish the difficult must be present. Without these elements, the movement may be just an expression of a nervous system that says "move — never mind how." That is the type of message that is apt to be sent by the brain of a child with poor sensory integration. Directions of the better organized brain would be "move in a manner that results in effective interaction of body and environment."

When a child has just mastered an adaptive response to a pattern of sensory input, he often will pursue that task with considerable zest and excitement, seeming to be almost compelled to repeat and repeat the task as a fulfilling and maturing experience. Structured permissiveness enables such a course of action which generally is considered a highly therapeutic experience. Since children with learning disorders sometimes are unable to stop themselves at an appropriate time, the therapist occasionally may need to intervene. By way of example, a child who had recently learned to perceive which direction he was falling and to catch himself appropriately was exuberantly playing with the large therapy ball.

He repeatedly ran to the ball, threw himself on it and fell to the side of the ball, catching himself. The therapist stood to one side, watching but neither directing nor talking. The child finally fell exhausted to the ground, saying, "*When* are we going to stop?" In this case it would have been advisable for the therapist to stop the child before he had driven himself to a state of exhaustion. The next time the child was presented with the ball, he first rejected it, then quickly added, "I half like it and half don't."

Disadvantages of Structured Exploration

The unsophisticated professional person can easily misinterpret sensory integrative therapy. Only the trained eye can begin to recognize the effect of the interaction of child and activity on the child's sensory system, and even the trained eye can hardly begin to fathom all that is occurring in the child's brain. Direct, forthright exercises are more easily analyzed. They are usually more impressive because that which is observed seems directly related to the end product. Regimented control often wins respect in this society, whereas the permissive atmosphere may give the impression that the child is just "fooling around." The most effective therapy is often the least convincing to those not intimately involved in the child's welfare. Furthermore, determination of the amount of increased integration resulting from therapy is particularly difficult, for it appears in behavior apparently unrelated to the activity, such as ability to sit in class more quietly, a reduced tendency to lose emotional control in the evening, and a slightly increased ability to learn academic material. Movement is obvious; sensory input is subtle and easily camouflaged by the strong visual stimulus of motion. Courage and convictions are required of the therapist who would administer sensory integrative therapy.

The child's emotional involvement in perceptual-motor activity carries a significant message, but it does not necessarily say the brain is being advanced toward a more mature level of organization. If such advancement is not made, the situation is not therapeutic, although the activity may provide general emotional and physiological benefits. Recognizing and assessing the maturation value of activity requires skilled professional judgment.

The unsophisticated person can also be deceived into thinking that achieving a fulfilling sensory integrative situation is simple and that the therapist need only sit back while the children determine their treatment "willy-nilly." The most effective treatment appears simple, but it is simplicity that is the result of careful work and preparation. It is possible, of course, for the therapist to fool himself as well as others. Almost any activity can be named "eye-hand coordination training." Naming it does not make it anything more than practice.

It would be far easier and more impressive to provide treatment through methods that appear more scientific, such as placing a child on a table, attaching some apparatus, and turning some knobs to start the apparatus working on the child. Such a procedure would avoid most of the disadvantages of using a natural procedure, but that is not the way to further neural integration. The brain must organize itself and must do so through receiving information from self and environment, integrating that information for use, and then using it for adaptive action upon the environment. Society may respond more favorably to the spotless chrome-clad treatment office, but sensorimotor integration proceeds best with simple, unimpressive, often makeshift equipment which, furthermore, is often generously sprinkled with dirt carried in from playground or street on shoes or pants cuffs.

Another limitation of a permissive situation lies in the fact that the child with poor neural integration usually has many emotional problems and will take advantage of the permissiveness for their expression. In this case a revised plan with more direction and structure with considerable support may be required.

Similarities between Psychotherapy and Sensory Integrative Therapy

The art of sensory integrative therapy is analogous in many ways to the art of psychotherapy. Considering the similarities helps to clarify the nature of sensory integrative therapy and promote a better grasp of its underlying philosophy. In each instance, it is the child who must change within himself; the therapist can only promote and guide. The therapist prepares a setting based on the appraisal of the child's behavior and responds to the patient according to the patient's response to that setting. Both types of treatment aspire toward emotional integration, although by different routes. A close analogy lies in the attitude of the therapist. In each case the therapist can, if he chooses, "feel with" the patient. He can offer empathy so close that the experience actually becomes one of his own. Without losing objective judgment, the emotional involvement helps to avoid the passing of negative judgment. The therapist, in each case, can share the joy that comes with increased maturation and the understanding at having to discontinue a fulfilling experience. Patient and therapist work together and the togetherness is often felt quite consciously by the therapist.

Much of the time both the sensory and the psychotherapeutic situation are dealing with semi- or non-conscious experiences. The psychotherapist thinks in terms of subconscious psychic complexes and dynamics; the sensory integrative therapist includes many subcortical integrative mechanisms in his thinking and treatment planning. While one therapist is considering the Oedipus complex, the other is considering brain stem integrating processes. In both cases the underlying mechanisms are recognized, their effect on behavior analyzed, and methods of dealing with them contemplated.

Both fields utilize constructs as a basis for understanding behavior. At this stage in the development of each type of therapy, the theories of personality structure seem more acceptable to society than do those of sensory integrative function. Familiarity may be a determining factor. It cannot be said that personality theories are more objectively based on scientific fact.

In working with children, each field usually chooses to employ a play-like situation replicating those life experiences in which natural maturation was not experienced. In each case the therapist structures a situation within which the child is given freedom to follow inner dictates toward health. In neither instance can the better integration be forced; it can only be cultivated.

As the natural developmental association between sensory input and psychic experience becomes better understood, the two forms of therapy may profit from joining forces. What is rocking and being cuddled other than tactile and vestibular stimulation plus an interpersonal relationship? Are not the neural traces for the sensory and the social aspects of the experience laid down as one in the brain? Are not many of a child's important emotional experiences in the first five years of life closely associated on an experiential and therefore neurological basis with their sensorimotor equivalents?

List of References

Aarons, Louis; and Goldenberg, Louis. Galvanic stimulation of the vestibular system and perception of the vertical. Perceptual and Motor Skills, 1964, 19, 59-66.

Abercrombie, M. L. J. Eye movements, perception and learning. In V. H. Smith (Ed.), Visual Disorders and Cerebral Palsy, Little Club Clinics in Developmental Medicine, No. 9. London: William Heinemann Medical Books, 1963.

Abercrombie, M. L. J. Some notes on spatial disability: movement, intelligence quotient and attentiveness. Developmental Medicine and Child Neurology, 1968, 10, 206-213.

Abercrombie, M. L. J. Eye movements and perceptual development. In P. Gardiner; R. MacKeith; and V. Smith (Eds.), Aspects of Developmental and Paediatric Ophthalmology. Clinics in Developmental Medicine No. 32. London: William Heinemann Medical Books, 1969.

Abercrombie, M. L. J.; Gardiner, P. A.; Hansen, E.; Jonckheere, J.; Lindon, R. L.; Solomon, G., and Tyson, M. C. Visual, perceptual, and visuomotor impairment in physically handicapped children. Perceptual and Motor Skills, 1964, 18, 561-625.

Abercrombie, M. L. J.; and Tyson, M. C. Body image and Draw-a-Man test in cerebral palsy. Developmental Medicine and Child Neurology, 1966, 8, 9-15.

Abuladze, K. S. Central inhibition of reflexes and the problem of the coupled activity of cerebral hemispheres. In E. A. Asratyan (Ed.), Progress in Brain Research, Vol. 22, Brain Reflexes. New York: Elsevier Pub. Co., 1968.

Adams, Sandra L. The effect of somatic sensory stimulation on kinesthetic perception. Unpublished master's thesis, Department of Physical Therapy, University of Southern California, 1965.

Ades, Harlow. Central auditory mechanisms. In J. Field; H. W. Magoun; and V. E. Hall (Eds.), Handbook of Physiology, Section 1: Neurophysiology, Vol. I. Washington, D. C.: American Physiological Society, 1959.

Adey, W. R. Studies of hippocampal electrical activity during approach learning. In J. F. Delafresnaye (Ed.), Brain Mechanisms and Learning. Oxford: Blackwell Scientific Publications, 1961.

Adey, W. Ross. Hippocampal mechanisms in processes of memory: thoughts on a model of cerebral organization in learning. In M. A. B. Brazier (Ed.), Brain Function, Vol. II, RNA and Brain Function, Memory and Learning. Berkeley and Los Angeles: University of California Press, 1964.

Akelaitis, Andrew J. Studies on the corpus callosum: VII. Study of language functions (tactile and visual lexia and graphia) unilaterally following section of the corpus callosum. Journal of Neuropathology and Experimental Neurology, 1943, 2, 226-262.

Akelaitis, Andrew J. A study of gnosis, praxis and language following section of the corpus callosum and anterior commissure. Journal of Neurosurgery, 1944, 1, 94-102.

Albe-Fessard, D.; and Fessard, A. Thalamic integration and their consequences at the telencephalic level. In G. Moruzzi; A. Fessard; and H. Jasper (Eds.), Progress in Brain Research, Vol. I, Brain Mechanisms. New York: Elsevier Publishing Co., 1963.

Albe-Fessard, Denise; Liebeskind, John; and Lamarre, Yves. Projection au niveau du cortex somato-moteur du Singe d'afférences provenant des récepteurs musculaires. Comptes Rendus Hebdomadaires des Séances de l'Academie des Sciences (Paris), 1965, 261, 3891-3894.

Ames, Louise B.; and Ilg, Frances L. The developmental point of view with special reference to the principle of reciprocal neuromotor interweaving. Journal of Genetic Psychology, 1964, 105, 195-209.

Andersson, Sven A. Projection of different spinal pathways to the second somatic sensory area in cat. Acta Physiologica Scandinavica, 1962, 56, 1-74, supplementum 194.

Anokhin, P. K. A new conception of the physiological architecture of conditioned reflex. In J. F. Delafresnaye (Ed.), Brain Mechanisms and Learning. Oxford: Blackwell Scientific Publications, 1961.

Armstrong, Donna May. The effect of light touch, sensory stimulation upon tactile discrimination. Unpublished master's thesis, Department of Physical Therapy, University of Southern California, 1968.

Ayres, A. Jean. Occupational therapy directed toward neuromuscular integration. In H. S. Willard and C. S. Spackman (Eds.), Occupational Therapy, 3rd ed. rev. Philadelphia: J. B. Lippincott Co., 1963.

Ayres, A. Jean. Tactile functions: their relation to hyperactive and perceptual motor behavior. American Journal of Occupational Therapy, 1964, 18, 6-11.

Ayres, A. Jean. Patterns of perceptual-motor dysfunction in children: a factor analytic study. Perceptual and Motor Skills, 1965, 20, 335-368.

Ayres, A. J. Interrelations among perceptual-motor abilities in a group of normal children. American Journal of Occupational Therapy, 1966a, 20, 288-292.

Ayres, A. Jean. Interrelationships among perceptual-motor functions in children. American Journal of Occupational Therapy, 1966b, 20, 68-71.

Ayres, A. Jean. Deficits in sensory integration in educationally handicapped children. Journal of Learning Disabilities, 1969a, 2, 160-168.

Ayres, A. Jean. Relation between Gesell developmental quotients and later perceptual-motor performance. American Journal of Occupational Therapy, 1969b, 23, 11-17.

Ayres, A. Jean. Characteristics of types of sensory integrative dysfunction. American Journal of Occupational Therapy, 1971, 25, 329-334.

Ayres, A. Jean. Improving academic scores through sensory integration. Journal of Learning Disabilities, 1972a, 5, 338-343.

Ayres, A. Jean. Southern California Sensory Integration Tests. Los Angeles: Western Psychological Services, 1972b.

Ayres, A. Jean. Types of sensory integrative dysfunction among disabled learners. American Journal of Occupational Therapy, 1972c, 26, 13-18.

Ayres, A. Jean; and Heskett, Wm. M. A Therapeutic Activity for Perceptual Motor Dysfunction, 1970a. Film available from Film Distribution, Department of Cinema, University of Southern California, Los Angeles.

Ayres, A. Jean; and Heskett, Wm. M. Clinical Observations of Disorders in Postural and Bilateral Integration, 1970b. Film available from Film Distribution, Department of Cinema, University of Southern California, Los Angeles.

Ayres, A. Jean; and Reid, W. The self-drawing as an expression of perceptual-motor dysfunction. Cortex, 1966, 2, 254-265.

Balow, I. H.; and Balow, Bruce. Lateral dominance and reading achievement in the second grade. American Educational Research Journal, 1964, 1, 139-143.

Barlow, H. B. Possible principles underlying the transformations of sensory messages. In W. A. Rosenblith (Ed.), Sensory Communication. New York: John Wiley & Sons, 1961.

Beery, Judith W. Matching of auditory and visual stimuli by average and retarded readers. Child Development, 1967, 38, 827-833.

Belmont, I.; Birch, H. G.; and Karp, E. The disordering of intersensory and intrasensory integration by brain damage. Journal of Nervous and Mental Disease, 1965, 141, 410-418.

Belmont, Lillian; and Birch, Herbert G. Lateral dominance and right-left awareness in normal children. Child Development, 1963, 34, 253-270.

Belmont, Lillian; and Birch, Herbert G. Lateral dominance, lateral awareness, and reading disability. Child Development, 1965, 36, 57-71.

Bennett, Edward L.; Diamond, Marian C.; Krech, David; and Rosenzweig, Mark R. Chemical and anatomical plasticity of brain. Science, 1964, 146, 610-619.

Benton, Arthur L. Developmental aphasia and brain damage. Cortex, 1964, 1, 40-52.

Bergès, Jean; and Lézine, Irène. The imitation of gestures. Clinics in Developmental Medicine No. 18. London: William Heinemann Medical Books, 1965.

Birch, Herbert G.; and Belmont, Ira. Perceptual analysis and sensory integration in brain-damaged persons. Journal of Genetic Psychology, 1964, 105, 173-179.

Birch, H. G.; and Belmont, L. Auditory-visual integration in normal and retarded readers. American Journal of Orthopsychiatry, 1964, 34, 852-861.

Birch, H. G.; and Belmont, L. Auditory-visual integration, intelligence and reading ability in school children. Perceptual and Motor Skills, 1965, 20, 295-305.

Birch, Herbert G.; and Lefford, Arthur. Intersensory development in children. Monographs of the Society for Research in Child Development, 1963, 28, No. 5, Serial No. 89.

Birch, Herbert; and Lefford, Arthur. Visual differentiation, intersensory integration, and voluntary motor control. Monographs of the Society for Research in Child Development, 1967, 32, No. 2, Serial No. 110.

Bishop, George H. The relation between nerve fiber size and sensory modality: phylogenetic implications of the afferent innervation of cortex. Journal of Nervous and Mental Disease, 1959, 128, 89-114.

Black, Perry; and Myers, Ronald E. A neurological investigation of eye-hand control in the chimpanzee. In E. G. Ettlinger (Ed.), Ciba Foundation Study Group No. 20. Functions of the Corpus Callosum. London: J. & A. Churchill Ltd., 1965.

Blitz, Bernard; Dinnerstein, Albert J.; and Lowenthal, Milton. Attenuation of experimental pain by tactile stimulation: effect of vibration at different levels of noxious stimulus intensity. Perceptual and Motor Skills, 1964, 19, 311-316.

Bobath, K.; and Bobath, B. The facilitation of normal postural reactions and movements in the treatment of cerebral palsy. Physiotherapy (England), 1964, 50, 246-262.

Bobath, Karel. The Motor Deficit in Patients with Cerebral Palsy. Clinics in Developmental Medicine No. 23. London: William Heinemann Medical Books, Ltd., 1966.

Bobath, K.; and Bobath, Berta. Tonic reflexes and righting reflexes in diagnosis and assessment of cerebral palsy. Cerebral Palsy Review, 1955, 16, No. 5, 3-10, 26.

Bobath, Karel; and Bobath, Berta. Control of motor function in the treatment of cerebral palsy. Physiotherapy (England), October, 1957.

Bogen, Joseph E. The other side of the brain I: dysgraphia and dyscopia following cerebral commissurotomy. Bulletin of the Los Angeles Neurological Societies, 1969a, 34, 73-105.

Bogen, Joseph E. The other side of the brain II: an appositional mind. Bulletin of the Los Angeles Neurological Societies, 1969b, 34, 135-162.

Bogen, Joseph E.; and Bogen, Glenda M. The other side of the brain III: the corpus callosum and creativity. Bulletin of the Los Angeles Neurological Societies, 1969, 34, 191-220.

Bortner, Morton; and Birch, Herbert G. Perceptual and perceptual-motor dissociation in cerebral palsied children. Journal of Nervous and Mental Disease, 1962, 134, 103-108.

Brain, Lord. Some reflections on brain and mind. Brain, 1963, 86, 381-402.

Brazier, Mary A. B. Expanding concepts in neurophysiology. Archives of Neurology and Psychiatry, 1952, 67, 545-549.

Brazier, Mary A. B. Stimulation of the hippocampus in man using implanted electrodes. In M. A. B. Brazier (Ed.), Brain Function, Vol. II, RNA and Brain Function Memory and Learning. Berkeley and Los Angeles: University of California Press, 1964.

Brazier, Mary A. B.; Killam, Keith F.; and Hance, A. James. The reactivity of the nervous system in the light of the past history of the organism. In W. A. Rosenblith (Ed.), Sensory Communication. New York: John Wiley & Sons, 1961.

Breinin, Goodwin M. Electromyographic evidence for ocular muscle proprioception in man. Archives of Ophthalmology, 1957, 57, 176-180.

Bremer, F. Neurophysiological correlates of mental unity. In J. C. Eccles (Ed.), Brain and Conscious Experience. New York: Springer-Verlag, 1966.

Brenner, May W.; and Gillman, Selma. Visuomotor ability in school children — a survey. Developmental Medicine and Child Neurology, 1966, 8, 686-703.

Bridgman, Charles S.; and Smith, Karl U. Bilateral neural integration in visual perception after section of the corpus callosum. Journal of Comparative Neurology, 1945, 83, 57-68.

Brodal, Alf. Anatomical organization and fiber connections of the vestibular nuclei. In W. S. Fields and B. R. Alford (Eds.), Neurological Aspects of Auditory and Vestibular Disorders. Springfield, Ill.: Charles C Thomas, 1964.

Bryden, M. P. Tachistoscopic recognition, handedness and cerebral dominance. Neuropsychologia, 1965, 3, 1-8.

Buchwald, Jennifer S.; and Eldred, Earl. Conditioned responses in the gamma efferent system. Journal of Nervous and Mental Disease, 1961, 132, 146-152.

Buser, P.; and Imbert, M. Sensory projections to the motor cortex in cats: a microelectric study. In W. A. Rosenblith (Ed.), Sensory Communication. New York: John Wiley & Sons, 1961.

Carpenter, M. B. Ascending vestibular projections and conjugate horizontal eye movements. In W. S. Fields and B. R. Alford (Eds.), Neurological Aspects of Auditory and Vestibular Disorders. Springfield, Ill.: Charles C Thomas, 1964.

Casler, Lawrence. Maternal deprivation: a critical review of the literature. Monographs of the Society for Research in Child Development, 1961, 26, No. 2, Serial No. 80.

Casler, Lawrence. The effects of extra tactile stimulation on a group of institutionalized infants. Genetic Psychology Monographs, 1965, 71, 137-175.

Clements, Sam D.; and Peters, John E. Minimal brain dysfunction in the school age child. Archives of General Psychiatry, 1962, 6, 185-197.

Coghill, G. E. Anatomy and the Problem of Behavior. Cambridge: Cambridge University Press, 1929.

Cohen, Leonard. Role of eye and neck proprioceptive mechanisms in body orientation and motor coordination. Journal of Neurophysiology, 1961, 24, 2-11.

Cohn, Robert. On certain aspects of the sensory organization of the human brain: II. A study of rostral dominance in children. Neurology, 1951, 119-122.

Cole, M.; and Kraft, M. B. Specific learning disability. Cortex, 1964, 1, 302-313.

Coleman, Richard I.; and Deutsch, Cynthia P. Lateral dominance and right-left discrimination: A comparison of normal and retarded readers. Perceptual and Motor Skills, 1964, 19, 43-50.

Corkin, Suzanne. Tactually-guided maze learning in man: effects of unilateral cortical excisions and bilateral hippocampal lesions. Neuropsychologia, 1965, 3, 339-351.

Craddock, Samuel N., Jr.; and Thompson, Robert. A discrete inter-pedunculo-central tegmental region critical for retention of visual discrimination habits in the white rat. Journal of Comparative and Physiological Psychology, 1971, 76, 39-50.

Critchley, Macdonald. Developmental Dyslexia. London: William Heinemann Medical Books, 1964.

Crosby, Elizabeth C.; Humphrey, Tryphena; Lauer, Edward W.; et al. Correlative Anatomy of the Nervous System. New York: Macmillan Co., 1962.

Culbertson, F. M.; and Gunn, R. C. Comparison of the Bender Gestalt Test and Frostig Test in several clinical groups of children. Journal of Clinical Psychology, 1966, 22, 439.

Dember, William N. Visual Perception: The Nineteenth Century. New York: John Wiley & Sons, 1964.

Denny-Brown, D. The midbrain and motor integration. Proceedings of the Royal Society of Medicine, 1962, 55, 527-538.

Denny-Brown, Derek; and Chambers, R. A. The parietal lobe and behavior. Research Publication, Association for Research in Nervous and Mental Diseases, 1958, 36, 35-117.

Diamond, I. T. The sensory neocortex. In W. D. Neff (Ed.), Contributions to Sensory Physiology, Vol. 2. New York: Academic Press, 1967.

Doty, Robert. Conditioned reflexes elicited by electrical stimulation of the brain in Macaques. Journal of Neurophysiology, 1965, 28, 623-640.

Doty, Robert W. On butterflies in the brain. Abstract for Symposium on Higher Nervous Activity, IVth World Congress of Psychiatry, Madrid, September, 1966.

Ebner, Ford F.; and Myers, Ronald E. Direct and transcallosal induction of touch memories in the monkey. Science, 1962, 138, 51-52.

Eccles, J. C. Conscious experience and memory. In J. C. Eccles (Ed.), Brain and Conscious Experience. New York: Springer-Verlag, 1966.

Eccles, J. C. The effects of use and disuse on synaptic function. In J. F. Delafresnaye (Ed.), Brain Mechanisms and Learning. Oxford: Blackwell Scientific Publications, 1961.

Eccles, J. C.; Ito, M.; and Szentágothai, J. The Cerebellum as a Neuronal Machine. New York: Springer-Verlag, 1967.

Eccles, Rosamond M.; and Lundberg, A. Synaptic actions in moto-neurones by afferents which may evoke the flexion reflex. Archives Italiennes de Biologie, 1959, 97, 199-221.

Eells, Janet F. Inconsistency of early handling and its effect upon emotionality in the rat. Journal of Comparative and Physiological Psychology, 1961, 54, 690-693.

Eldred, Earl. Functional implications of dynamics and static components of the spindle response to stretch. American Journal of Physical Medicine, 1967a, 46, 129-140.

Eldred, Earl. Peripheral receptors: their excitation and relation to reflex patterns. American Journal of Physical Medicine, 1967b, 46, 69-87.

Ellinwood, E. H., Jr. Amphetamine psychosis: II. Theoretical implications. Journal of Neuropsychiatry (Belgium), 1968, 4, 45-54.

Ernhart, Claire B.; Graham, Frances K.; Eichman, Peter L.; Marshall, John M.; and Thurston, Don. Brain injury in the preschool child: some developmental considerations: II. Comparison of brain injured and normal children. Psychological Monographs, 1963, 77, 11, 17-33, Whole No. 574.

Evarts, E. V.; and Thach, W. T. Motor mechanisms of the CNS: cerebrocerebellar interrelations. Annual Review of Physiology, 1969, 31, 451-498.

Fair, Charles M. The organization of memory functions in the vertebrate nervous system. Neurosciences Research Program Bulletin, 1965, 3, No. 1, 27-62.

Fangel, Christian; and Kaada, Birger R. Behavior "attention" and fear induced by cortical stimulation in the cat. Electroencephalography and Clinical Neurophysiology, 1960, 12, 575-588.

Fay, Temple. The use of pathological and unlocking reflexes in the rehabilitation of spastics. American Journal of Physical Medicine, 1954, 33, 347-352.

Fay, Temple. The origin of human movement. American Journal of Psychiatry, 1955, 3, 644-652.

Fessard, A. The role of neuronal networks in sensory communications within the brain. In W. A. Rosenblith (Ed.), Sensory Communication. New York: John Wiley & Sons, 1961.

Fink, Max; Green, Martin; and Bender, M. B. The face-hand test as a diagnostic sign of organic mental syndrome. Neurology, 1952, 2, 46-58.

Fink, Max; Green, Martin A.; and Bender, Morris B. Perception of simultaneous tactile stimuli by mentally defective subjects. Journal of Nervous and Mental Disease, 1953, 117, 43-49.

Fiorentino, M. R. Reflex Testing Methods for Evaluating C.N.S. Development. Springfield, Ill.: Charles C Thomas, 1963.

Fish, Barbara. The maturation of arousal and attention in the first months of life: A study in ego development. Journal of the American Academy of Child Psychiatry, 1963, 2, 253-270.

Fisher, Seymour. Sex differences in body perception. Psychological Monographs, 1964, 78, No. 14, Whole No. 591.

Fitzhugh, L. C.; Fitzhugh, K. B.; and Reitan, R. M. Sensorimotor deficits of brain-damaged Ss in relation to intellectual level. Perceptual and Motor Skills, 1962, 15, 603-608.

Flick, Grad L.   Sinistrality revisited: A perceptual-motor approach. Child Development, 1966, 37, 613-622.

Fox, Julia V. D.   Cutaneous stimulation: effects on selected tests of perception. American Journal of Occupational Therapy, 1964, 18, 53-55.

Fox, Julia V. D.   Improving tactile discrimination of the blind. American Journal of Occupational Therapy, 1965, 19, 5-11.

Fredrickson, J. M.; Figge, U.; Scheid, P.; and Kornhuber, H. H.   Vestibular nerve projection to the cerebral cortex of the rhesus monkey. Experimental Brain Research, 1966, 2, 318-327.

French, J. D.   The reticular formation. In J. Field, H. W. Magoun, and V. E. Hall (Eds.), Handbook of Physiology, Section 1: Neurophysiology. Vol. II. Washington, D. C.: American Physiological Society, 1960.

French, John D.; Hernández-Peón, Raúl; and Livingston, R. B.   Projections from cortex to cephalic brain stem (reticular formation) in monkey. Journal of Neurophysiology, 1955, 18, 74-95.

Gabor, Andrew J.; and Peele, Talmadge L.   Alterations in behavior following stimulation of the claustrum of the cat. Electroencephalography and Clinical Neurophysiology, 1964, 17, 513-519.

Ganz, Leo; and Wilson, Paul D.   Innate generalization of a form discrimination without contouring eye movements. Journal of Comparative and Physiological Psychology, 1967, 63, 258-269.

Garfield, John C.   Motor impersistence in normal and brain-damaged children. Neurology, 1964, 14, 623-630.

Gazzaniga, M. S.   Interhemispheric communication of visual learning. Neuropsychologia, 1966, 4, 183-189.

Gellhorn, Ernst.   Cerebral interaction: simultaneous activation of specific and unspecific systems. In D. E. Sheer (Ed.), Electrical Stimulation of the Brain. Austin, Texas: University of Texas Press, 1961.

Gellhorn, E.   Motion and emotion: the role of proprioception in the physiology and pathology of the emotions. Psychological Review, 1964, 71, 457-472.

Gernandt, Bo E.   Somatic and autonomic motor outflow to vestibular function. In W. S. Fields and B. R. Alford (Eds.), Neurological Aspects of Auditory and Vestibular Disorders. Springfield, Ill.: Charles C Thomas, 1964.

Gerstmann, Josef.   Syndrome of finger agnosia, disorientation for right and left, agraphia and acalculia. Archives of Neurology and Psychiatry, 1940, 44, 398-408.

Geschwind, Norman.   Disconnexion syndromes in animals and man. Brain, 1965, 88, 237-294, 585-644.

Geschwind, Norman.   Brain mechanisms suggested by studies of hemispheric connections. In C. H. Millikan (chairman) and F. L. Darley (Eds.), Brain Mechanisms Underlying Speech and Language. New York: Grune and Stratton, 1967.

Gesell, Arnold, et al.   The First Five Years of Life. New York: Harper and Row, 1940.

Ghent, Lila. Developmental changes in tactual thresholds on dominant and nondominant sides. Journal of Comparative and Physiological Psychology, 1961, 54, 670-673.

Gibson, Eleanor J. Development of perception: discrimination of depth compared with discrimination of graphic symbols. In J. C. Wright and J. Kagan (Eds.), Basic Cognitive Processes in Children. Monographs of the Society for Research in Child Development, 1963, 28, No. 2, Serial No. 86.

Gibson, Eleanor J. The development of perception as an adaptive process. American Scientist, 1970, 58, 98-107.

Gibson, J. J. The Senses Considered as Perceptual Systems. Boston: Houghton Mifflin, 1966.

Gleitman, Henry. Place-learning. Scientific American, 1963, 209, 116-122.

Glickstein, Mitchell; and Sperry, R. W. Intermanual somesthetic transfer in split-brain rhesus monkeys. Journal of Comparative and Physiological Psychology, 1960, 53, 322-327.

Goins, Jean T. Visual perception abilities and early reading progress. Supplementary Educational Monographs No. 87. University of Chicago Press, 1958.

Gooddy, W.; and Reinhold, M. Some aspects of human orientation in space. Brain, 1952, 75, 472-509.

Gordon, Malcolm W. Role of adaptive enzyme formation in morphogenesis. In S. R. Korey and J. I. Nurnberger (Eds.), Progress in Neurobiology: I. Neurochemistry. New York: Paul B. Hoeber, 1956.

Gottlieb, Gilbert; Doran, Carter; and Whitley, Sarah. Cerebral dominance and speech acquisition in deaf children. Journal of Abnormal and Social Psychology, 1964, 69, 182-189.

Granit, Ragnar. Sensory mechanisms in perception. In J. C. Eccles (Ed.), Brain and Conscious Experience. New York: Springer-Verlag, 1966.

Green, John D. The rhinencephalon and behavior. In G. E. W. Wolstenholme and C. M. O'Connor (Eds.), Ciba Foundation Symposium on the Neurological Basis of Behaviour. London: J. & A. Churchill, 1958.

Griffin, Martha A. A study of the sensory stimulus of touch and its immediate performance effects on two tests of tactile perception. Unpublished master's thesis, Department of Occupational Therapy, University of Southern California, 1964.

Guzmán-Flores, C.; Buendía, N.; Anderson, C.; and Lindsley, D. B. Cortical and reticular influences upon evoked responses in dorsal column nuclei. Experimental Neurology, 1962, 5, 37-46.

Halnan, C. R. E.; and Wright, Gordon H. Tactile localization. Brain, 1960, 83, 677-700.

Halstead, Ward C. Brain and Intelligence: A quantitative study of the frontal lobes. Chicago: University of Chicago Press, 1947.

Hamilton, Charles R. Effects of brain bisection on eye-hand coordination in monkeys wearing prisms. Journal of Comparative and Physiological Psychology, 1967, 64, 434-443.

Harlow, Harry. The nature of love. American Psychologist, 1958, 13, 673-685.

Head, Henry. Studies in Neurology, Vol. II. London: Oxford University Press, 1920.

Hebb, D. O. Organization of Behavior. New York: John Wiley & Sons, 1949.

Hécaen, H. Clinical symptomatology in right and left hemispheric lesions. In V. B. Mountcastle (Ed.), Interhemispheric Relations and Cerebral Dominance. Baltimore: Johns Hopkins Press, 1962.

Hécaen, Henry. Brain mechanisms suggested by studies of parietal lobes. In C. H. Millikan (chairman) and F. L. Darley (Eds.), Brain Mechanisms Underlying Speech and Language. New York: Grune and Stratton, 1967.

Hécaen, Henry; and Ajuriaguerra, Julian de. Left-Handedness: Manual Superiority and Cerebral Dominance. New York: Grune and Stratton, 1964.

Held, Richard. Dissociation of visual functions by deprivation and rearrangement. Psychologische Forschung, 1968, 31, 338-348.

Held, Richard; and Hein, Alan. Movement-produced stimulation in the development of visually guided behavior. Journal of Comparative and Physiological Psychology, 1963, 56, 872-876.

Held, Richard; and Rekosh, Jerold. Motor-sensory feedback and the geometry of visual space. Science, 1963, 141, 722-723.

Hernández-Peón, Raúl. Reticular mechanisms of sensory control. In W. A. Rosenblith (Ed.), Sensory Communication. New York: John Wiley & Sons, 1961.

Hernández-Peón, Raúl; Scherrer, Harold; and Jouvet, Michael. Modification of electrical activity in cochlear nucleus during "attention" in unanesthetized cats. Science, 1956, 123, 331-332.

Herrick, C. Judson. The functions of the olfactory parts of the cerebral cortex. Proceedings of the National Academy of Sciences, 1933, 19, 7-14.

Herrick, C. Judson. The Evolution of Human Nature. Austin: University of Texas Press, 1956.

Hershenson, Maurie. Visual discrimination in the human newborn. Journal of Comparative and Physiological Psychology, 1964, 58, 270-276.

Hrbek, A.; Prechtl, H. F. R.; Hrbkova, M.; Lenard, H. G.; and Grant, D. Kerr. Proprioceptive evoked potential in newborn infants and adults. Developmental Medicine and Child Neurology, 1968, 10, 164-167.

Huss, Joy. Application of the Rood techniques to treatment of the physically handicapped child. In W. L. West (Ed.), Occupational Therapy for the Multiply Handicapped Child. Proceedings of the Conference on Occupational Therapy for the Multiply Handicapped Child, Center for Continuing Education, Chicago, 1965.

Hyde, Jane E.; and Eliasson, Sven G. Brainstem induced eye movement in cats. Journal of Comparative Neurology, 1957, 108, 139-172.

Hydén, Holger. Satellite cells in the nervous system. Scientific American, 1961, 205, No. 6, 62-70.

Hydén, H.; and Egyhazi, E. Nuclear RNA changes of nerve cells during a learning experiment in rats. Proceedings of the National Academy of Sciences, 1962, 48, 1366-1373.

Hydén, H.; and Egyhazi, E. Glial RNA changes during a learning experiment in rats. Proceedings of the National Academy of Sciences, 1963, 49, 618-624.

Hydén, H.; and Egyhazi, E. Changes in RNA content and base composition in cortical neurons of rats in a learning experiment involving transfer of handedness. Proceedings of the National Academy of Sciences, 1964, 52, 1030-1035.

Ingram, T. T. S.; Mason, A. W.; and Blackburn, I. A retrospective study of 82 children with reading disability. Developmental Medicine and Child Neurology, 1970, 12, 271-281.

Jaffe, Joseph; and Bender, M. B. The factor of symmetry in the perception of two simultaneous cutaneous stimuli. Brain, 1952, 75, 167-176.

Jasper, H. H. Pathophysiological studies of brain mechanisms in different states of consciousness. In J. C. Eccles (Ed.), Brain and Conscious Experience. New York: Springer-Verlag, 1966.

Jongkees, L. B. W. The examination of the vestibular organ. In Y. Zotterman (Ed.), Progress in Brain Research, Vol. 23, Sensory Mechanisms. New York: Elsevier Publishing Co., 1967.

Joynt, R. J.; Benton, A. L.; and Fogel, M. L. Behavioral and pathological correlates of motor impersistence. Neurology, 1962, 12, 876-881.

Jung, Richard. Neuronal integration in the visual cortex and its significance for visual information. In W. A. Rosenblith (Ed.), Sensory Communication. New York: John Wiley & Sons, 1961.

Jung, R.; Kornhuber, H. H.; and DaFonseca, J. S. Multisensory convergence on cortical neurons. In G. Moruzzi, A. Fessard and H. H. Jasper (Eds.), Progress in Brain Research, Vol. I. Brain Mechanisms. New York: Elsevier Publishing Co., 1963.

Kaada, B. R. Somato-motor, autonomic and electrocorticographic responses of electrical stimulation of "rhinencephalic" and other structures in primates, cat and dog. Acta Physiologica Scandinavica, 1951, 24, Supplement 83.

Kabat, Herman; and Knott, Margaret. Principles of neuromuscular reeducation. Physical Therapy Review, 1948, 28, 107-111.

Karamyan, A. I. On the evolution of the integrative activity of the central nervous system in the phylogeny of vertebrates. In E. A. Asratyan (Ed.), Progress in Brain Research, Vol. 22, Brain Reflexes. New York: Elsevier Publishing Co., 1968.

Kasatkin, N. I. Ontogeneses of brain function. Acta Universitatis Carolinae Medica, 1962, 8, 657-664.

Kempinsky, W. H.; and Ward, Arthur A. Effect of section of vestibular nerve upon cortically induced movement in cat. Journal of Neurophysiology, 1950, 13, 295-304.

Kephart, Newell C. The Slow Learner in the Classroom. Columbus, Ohio: Charles E. Merrill Books, Inc., 1960.

Kephart, Newell C. Learning Disability: An Educational Adventure. West Lafayette, Ind.: Kappa Delta Pi Press, 1968.

Kerr, D. I. B.; and Hagbarth, K.-E. An investigation of olfactory centrifugal fiber system. Journal of Neurophysiology, 1955, 18, 362-374.

King, Robert B.; Meagher, John N.; and Barnett, Joseph C. Studies of trigeminal nerve potentials. Journal of Neurosurgery, 1956, 13, 176-183.

Kinsbourne, M.; and Warrington, Elizabeth K. The developmental Gerstmann syndrome. Archives of Neurology, 1963, 8, 490-501.

Klüver, Heinrich; and Bucy, Paul C. Preliminary analysis of functions of the temporal lobes in monkeys. Archives of Neurology and Psychiatry, 1939, 42, 979-1000.

Koos, Eugenia M. Manifestations of cerebral dominance and reading retardation in primary- grade children. Journal of Genetic Psychology, 1964, 104, 155-165.

Kraft, M. B. The face-hand test. Developmental Medicine and Child Neurology, 1968, 10, 214-219.

Krauthamer, G. M.; and Albe-Fessard, D. Electrophysiological studies of the basal ganglia and striopallidal inhibition of non-specific afferent activity. Neuropsychologia, 1964, 2, 73-83.

Kuroki, Teruo. Arrest reaction elicited from the brain stem. Folia Psychiatrica et Neurologica Japonica, 1958, 12, 317-340.

Lamarre, Y.; and Liebeskind, J. C. Projections des afférences d'origine musculaire au niveau du cortex sensori-motor chez le Singe. Journal de Physiologie (Paris), 1965, 57, 259.

Lashley, K. S. Brain Mechanisms and Intelligence. Chicago: University of Chicago Press, 1929.

Lassek, A. M. The Human Brain from Primitive to Modern. Springfield, Ill.: Charles C Thomas, 1957.

Lebowitz, Martin H.; Colbert, Edward G.; and Palmer, James O. Schizophrenia in children. American Journal of Diseases of Children, 1961, 102, 25-27.

Lesný, Ivan. A more sensitive way of eliciting the Moro response by pinching the epigastrium. Developmental Medicine and Child Neurology, 1967, 9, 212-215.

Levine, S. Some effects of stimulation in infancy. In S. A. Barnett (Ed.), Lessons from Animal Behavior for the Clinician. Little Club Clinics in Developmental Medicine, No. 7, 1962.

Levine, Seymour; and Alpert, Morton. Differential maturation of the central nervous system as a function of early experience. A. M. A. Archives of General Psychiatry, 1959, 1, 403-405.

Lindsley, Donald B. The reticular activating system and perceptual integration. In D. E. Sheer (Ed.), Electrical Stimulation of the Brain. Austin: University of Texas Press, 1961.

Livanov, M. N.; Gavrilova, N. A.; and Aslonov, A. S. Intercorrelations between different cortical regions of human brain during mental activity. Neuropsychologia, 1964, 2, 281-289.

Luria, A. R. Higher Cortical Functions in Man. New York: Basic Books, 1966a.

Luria, A. R. Human Brain and Psychological Processes. New York: Harper and Row, 1966b.

Lyle, J. G. Reading retardation and reversal tendency: a factorial study. Child Development, 1969, 40, 833-843.

McCleary, Robert A. Type of response as a factor in interocular transfer in the fish. Journal of Comparative and Physiological Psychology, 1960, 53, 311-321.

McDonald, Eugene T.; and Aungst, Lester F. Studies in oral sensory motor function. In J. F. Bosma (Ed.), Symposium on Oral Sensation and Perception. Springfield, Ill.: Charles C Thomas, 1966.

McFarland, J. H.; Werner, H.; and Wapner, S. The effects of postural factors and the distribution of tactual sensitivity and the organization of tactual kinaesthetic space. Journal of Experimental Psychology, 1962, 63, 148-154.

McFie, John. 'The other side of the brain.' Developmental Medicine and Child Neurology, 1970, 12, 514-515.

McGraw, M. B. The Neuromuscular Maturation of the Human Infant. New York: Hafner Publishing Co., 1963. First published 1945.

MacKay, D. M. Interactive processes in visual perception. In W. A. Rosenblith (Ed.), Sensory Communication. New York: John Wiley & Sons, 1961.

McKinney, John P. Hand schema in children. Psychonomic Science, 1964, 1, 99-100.

MacLean, Paul D. The limbic system ("visceral brain") and emotional behavior. Archives of Neurology and Psychiatry, 1955, 73, 130-134.

Magoun, H. W. The ascending reticular activating system. In P. Bard (Ed.), Patterns of Organization in the Central Nervous System, Vol. 30. Baltimore: William and Wilkins Co., 1952a.

Magoun, H. W. An ascending reticular activating system in the brain stem. Archives of Neurology and Psychiatry, 1952b, 67, 145-154.

Magoun, H. W. The Waking Brain. Springfield, Ill.: Charles C Thomas, 1958.

Magoun, H. W. Recent contributions to the electrophysiology of learning. Annals of the New York Academy of Sciences, 1961, 92, 818-829.

Maslow, Phyllis; Frostig, Marianne; Lefever, D. Welty; and Whittlesey, John R. B. The Marianne Frostig developmental test of visual perception, 1963 standardization. Perceptual and Motor Skills, 1964, 19, 463-499.

Mason, W. A.; Harlow, H. F.; and Rueping, H. R. The development of manipulatory responsiveness in the infant rhesus monkey. Journal of Comparative Physiological Psychology, 1959, 52, 555-558.

Mello, Nancy K. Interhemispheric reversal of mirror-image oblique lines after monocular training in pigeons. Science, 1965, 148, 252-254.

Melzack, Ronald. Effects of early perceptual restriction on simple visual discrimination. Science, 1962, 137, 978-979.

Melzack, R.; and Burns, S. K. Neurophysiological effects of early sensory restriction. Experimental Neurology, 1965, 13, 163-175.

Melzack, R.; Konrad, K. W.; and Dubrovsky, B. Prolonged changes in central nervous system activity produced by somatic and reticular stimulation. Experimental Neurology, 1969, 25, 416-428.

Melzack, Ronald; and Wall, Patrick D. Pain mechanisms: a new theory. Science, 1965, 150, 971-979.

Milani-Comparetti, A.; and Gidoni, E. A. Routine developmental examination in normal and retarded children. Developmental Medicine and Child Neurology, 1967, 9, 631-638.

Milner, Brenda. Laterality effects in audition. In V. B. Mountcastle (Ed.), Interhemispheric Relations and Cerebral Dominance. Baltimore: Johns Hopkins Press, 1962.

Milner, Brenda. Visually-guided maze learning in man: effects of bilateral hippocampal, bilateral frontal, and unilateral cerebral lesions. Neuropsychologia, 1965, 3, 317-338.

Milner, Brenda. Brain mechanisms suggested by studies of temporal lobes. In C. H. Millikan (chairman) and F. L. Darley (Eds.), Brain Mechanisms Underlying Speech and Language. New York: Grune and Stratton, 1967.

Mishkin, M. A. A possible link between interhemispheric integration in monkeys and cerebral dominance in man. In V. B. Mountcastle (Ed.), Interhemispheric Relations and Cerebral Dominance. Baltimore: Johns Hopkins Press, 1962.

Morrell, Frank. Modification of RNA as a result of neural activity. In M. A. B. Brazier (Ed.), Brain Function, Vol. II. RNA and Brain Function Memory and Learning. Berkeley and Los Angeles: University of California Press, 1964.

Moruzzi, G.; and Magoun, H. W. Brain stem reticular formation and activation of the EEG. Electroencephalography and Clinical Neurophysiology Journal, 1949, 1, 455-473.

Mountcastle, Vernon B. Modality and topographic properties of single neurons of cat's somatic sensory cortex. Journal of Neurophysiology, 1957, 20, 408-434.

Mountcastle, Vernon B. Some functional properties of the somatic afferent system. In W. A. Rosenblith (Ed.), Sensory Communication. New York: John Wiley & Sons, 1961.

Mountcastle, V. B.; and Powell, T. P. S. Central nervous mechanisms subserving position sense and kinesthesis. Bulletin of the Johns Hopkins Hospital, 1959, 105, 173-200.

Myers, Ronald E. Visual defects after lesions of brain stem tegmentum in cats. Archives of Neurology, 1964, 11, 73-90.

Myers, Ronald E. Cerebral connectionism and brain function. In C. H. Millikan (chairman) and F. L. Darley (Eds.), Brain Mechanisms Underlying Speech and Language. New York: Grune and Stratton, 1967.

Myers, Ronald E.; Sperry, R. W.; and McCurdy, Nancy M. Neural mechanisms in visual guidance of limb movement. Archives of Neurology, 1962, 7, 195-202.

Neff, William D.; and Goldberg, Jay M. Higher functions of the nervous system. Annual Review of Physiology, 1960, 22, 499-524.

Nelson, L. R.; and Lende, R. A. Interhemispheric responses in the opossum. Journal of Neurophysiology, 1965, 28, 189-199.

Noback, Charles R.; and Moskowitz, Norman. The primate nervous system: functional and structural aspects in phylogeny. In J. Buettner-Janusch (Ed.), Evolutionary and Genetic Biology of Primates, Vol. I. New York: Academic Press, 1963.

Norton, Yvonne de S. A concept: structuro-functional development leading toward early cognito-perceptual behavior. American Journal of Occupational Therapy, 1970, 24, 34-43.

Olds, J.; and Olds, M. E. Interference and learning in paleocortical systems. In J. F. Delafresnaye (Ed.), Brain Mechanisms and Learning. Oxford: Blackwell Scientific Publications, 1961.

Orbach, J.; and Chow, Kao Liang. Differential effects of resections of somatic areas I and II in monkeys. Journal of Neurophysiology, 1959, 22, 195-203.

Ornitz, Edward M. Vestibular dysfunction in schizophrenia and childhood autism. Comprehensive Psychiatry, 1970, 11, 159-173.

Painter, G. The effect of a rhythmic and sensory motor activity program on perceptual motor spatial abilities of kindergarten children. Exceptional Children, 1966, 33, 113-116.

Papoušek, Hanuš. The development of higher nervous activity in children in the first half-year of life. Monographs of the Society for Research in Child Development, 1965, 30, Serial No. 100.

Penfield, Wilder. Speech, perception and the uncommitted cortex. In J. C. Eccles (Ed.), Brain and Conscious Experience. New York: Springer-Verlag, 1966.

Penfield, Wilder; and Roberts, Lamar. Speech and Brain Mechanisms. Princeton: Princeton University Press, 1959.

Phillips, C. G. Changing concepts of the precentral motor area. In J. C. Eccles (Ed.), Brain and Conscious Experience. New York: Springer-Verlag, 1966.

Piaget, Jean. The Origins of Intelligence in Children. New York: International Universities Press, 1952.

Poggio, G. F.; and Mountcastle, V. B. A study of the functional contributions of the lemniscal and spinothalamic systems to somatic sensibility. Bulletin of the Johns Hopkins Hospital, 1960, 106, 266-316.

Pollack, Max; and Gordon, Edmund. The face-hand test in retarded and nonretarded emotionally disturbed children. American Journal of Mental Deficiency, 1959-1960, 64, 758-760.

Prechtl, H. F. R.; and Stemmer, Ch. J. The choreiform syndrome in children. Developmental Medicine and Child Neurology, 1962, 4, 119-127.

Prescott, James W. A developmental neural-behavioral theory of social-ization. Paper presented at the 1970 Conference of the American Psychological Association. Miami Beach, Florida, 1970.

Pribram, Karl H. Limbic system. In D. E. Sheer (Ed.), Electrical Stimulation of the Brain. Austin: University of Texas Press, 1961.

Punwar, Alice. Spatial visualization, reading, spelling, and mathematical abilities in second- and third-grade children. American Journal of Occupational Therapy, 1970, 24, 495-499.

Reed, James C. Lateralized finger agnosia and reading achievement at ages 6 and 10. Child Development, 1967, 38, 213-220.

Richter, Derek. Protein metabolism in relation to cerebral growth and development. In Ultrastructure and Metabolism of the Nervous System. Vol. XL: Research Publications, Association for Research in Nervous and Mental Disease, 1962.

Riddoch, G.; and Buzzard, E. F. Reflex movements and postural re-actions in quadriplegia and hemiplegia with special reference to those of the upper limb. Brain, 1921, 44, part 4, 397-489.

Riesen, Austin H. Excessive arousal effects of stimulation after early sensory deprivation. In P. Solomon *et al.* (Eds.), Sensory De-privation. Cambridge: Harvard University Press, 1961a.

Riesen, A. H. Studying perceptual development using the technique of sensory deprivation. Journal of Nervous and Mental Disease, 1961b, 132, 21-25.

Roach, Eugene G.; and Kephart, Newell C. The Purdue Perceptual-motor Survey. Columbus, Ohio: Charles E. Merrill Books, 1966.

Roberts, Tristan D. M. Neurophysiology of Postural Mechanisms. New York: Plenum Press, 1967.

Rood, Margaret S. Neurophysiologic reactions as a basis for physical therapy. The Physical Therapy Review, 1954, 34, 444-449.

Rose, Jerzy E.; and Mountcastle, Vernon B. Touch and kinesthesis. In J. Field, H. W. Magoun and V. E. Hall (Eds.), Handbook of Physiology, Section 1, Vol. I. Washington, D. C.: American Physi-ological Society, 1959.

Rosenblith, Judy F. Judgments of simple geometric figures by children. Perceptual and Motor Skills, 1965, 21, 947-990.

Rosenzweig, Mark R. Environmental complexity, cerebral change, and behavior. American Psychologist, 1966, 21, 321-332.

Rosenzweig, Mark R.; Krech, David; Bennett, Edward L.; and Diamond, Marion C. Effects of environmental complexity and training on brain chemistry and anatomy: A replication and extension. Journal of Comparative and Physiological Psychology, 1962, 55, 429-437.

Ruch, T. C.; and Shenkin, H. A. The relation of area 13 on orbital surface of frontal lobes to hyperactivity and hyperphagia in mon-keys. Journal of Neurophysiology, 1943, 6, 349-360.

Russell, Glen V. Interrelationships within the limbic and centrence-phalic systems. In D. E. Sheer (Ed.), Electrical Stimulation of the Brain. Austin: University of Texas Press, 1961.

Russell, I. S.; and Ochs, S. One-trial interhemispheric transfer of a learning engram. Science, 1961, 133, 1077-1078.

Russell, W. Ritchie. The physiology of memory. Proceedings of the Royal Society of Medicine, 1958, 51, 9-15.

Russell, W. Ritchie. Brain: Memory Learning. Oxford: Clarendon Press, 1959.

Russell, W. Ritchie. Some anatomical aspects of aphasia. Lancet, 1963, Issue No. 7292, 1173-1177.

Rutledge, L. T. Facilitation: Electrical response enhanced by conditional excitation of cerebral cortex. Science, 1965, 148, 1246-1248.

Rutter, Michael. The concept of dyslexia. In P. Wolff and R. MacKeith (Eds.), Planning for Better Learning, Clinics in Developmental Medicine No. 33, 1969.

Rutter, Michael; Graham, Philip; and Birch, Herbert G. Interrelations between the choreiform syndrome, reading disability and psychiatric disorder in children of 8-11 years. Developmental Medicine and Child Neurology, 1966, 8, 149-159.

Sandifer, Paul. Cogan's apraxia as a cause of reading difficulty. In Visual Disorders and Cerebral Palsy, Little Club Clinics in Developmental Medicine, No. 9. London: William Heinemann Medical Books, 1963.

Scheibel, Madge; and Scheibel, Arnold. Some structural and functional substrates of development in young cats. In W. A. Himwich and H. E. Himwich (Eds.), Progress in Brain Research, 1964, 9, 6-25.

Schiffman, H. R.; and Walk, R. D. Behavior on the visual cliff of monocular as compared to binocular chicks. Journal of Comparative and Physiological Psychology, 1963, 56, 1064-1068.

Schilder, Paul. The vestibular apparatus in neurosis and psychosis. Journal of Nervous and Mental Disease, 1933, 78, 1-23, 139-164.

Schilder, Paul. Brain and Personality. New York: International Universities Press, 1951.

Schilder, Paul. Contributions to Developmental Neuropsychiatry. New York: International Universities Press, 1964.

Schopler, Eric. Early infantile autism and receptor processes. Archives of General Psychiatry, 1965, 13, 327-335.

Schwartz, Marvin; and Shagass, Charles. Reticular modification of somatosensory cortical recovery function. Electroencephalography and Clinical Neurophysiology (Amsterdam), 1963, 15, 265-271.

Sechzer, J. A. Prolonged learning and split-brain cats. Science, 1970, 169, 889-892.

Segundo, J. P.; and Machne, Xenia. Unitary responses to afferent volleys in lenticular nucleus and claustrum. Journal of Neurophysiology, 1956, 19, 325-339.

Semans, Sarah. The Bobath concept in treatment of neurological disorders. American Journal of Physical Medicine, 1967, 46, 732-785.

Semmes, Josephine. A non-tactual factor in astereognosis. Neuropsychologia, 1965, 3, 295-315.

Semmes, Josephine. Hemispheric specialization: a possible clue to mechanism. Neuropsychologia, 1968, 6, 11-26.

Semmes, Josephine. Protopathic and epicritic sensation: a reappraisal. In A. L. Benton (Ed.), Contributions to Clinical Neuropsychology. Chicago: Aldine Publishing Co., 1969.

Semmes, Josephine; and Mishkin, Mortimer. A search for the cortical substrate of tactual memories. In E. G. Ettlinger (Ed.), Ciba Foundation Study Group No. 20. Functions of the Corpus Callosum. London: J. & A. Churchill, 1965.

Semmes, Josephine; Weinstein, Sidney; Ghent, Lila; and Teuber, Hans-Lukas. Somatosensory Changes after Penetrating Brain Wounds in Man. Cambridge: Harvard University Press, 1960.

Semmes, Josephine; Weinstein, Sidney; Ghent, Lila; and Teuber, Hans-Lukas. Spatial orientation in man after cerebral injury: I. Analysis by locus of lesion. Journal of Psychology, 1955, 39, 227-244.

Sheer, D. E. Emotional facilitation in learning situations with subcortical stimulation. In D. E. Sheer (Ed.), Electrical Stimulation of the Brain. Austin: University of Texas Press, 1961.

Sherrington, Charles S. The Integrative Action of the Nervous System. New Haven: Yale University Press, 1906.

Sherrington, Charles. Man on His Nature. Garden City, N. Y.: Doubleday and Co., 1955. First published 1940.

Shimamoto, T.; and Verzeano, M. Relations between caudate and diffusely projecting thalamic nuclei. Journal of Neurophysiology, 1954, 17, 278-288.

Silver, A. A.; and Hagin, R. Specific reading disability: delineation of the syndrome and relationship to cerebral dominance. Comprehensive Psychiatry, 1960, 1, 126-134.

Silver, A. A.; and Hagin, R. A. Specific reading disability: follow-up studies. American Journal of Orthopsychiatry, 1964, 34, 95-102.

Silverstein, A. B. Variance components in the developmental test of visual perception. Perceptual and Motor Skills, 1965, 20, 973-976.

Siminoff, R. Functional organization of hairy skin in response to sensory stimuli. Experimental Neurology, 1965, 13, 331-350.

Smith, Karl U. with Ansell, Sherman and Smith, W. M. as research collaborators. Sensory feedback analysis in medical research. American Journal of Physical Medicine, 1963, 42, 228-262.

Smith, O. W.; and Smith, P. C. Developmental studies of spatial judgments by children and adults. Perceptual and Motor Skills, 1966, 22, 3-73.

Smythies, J. R. Brain Mechanisms and Behavior. New York: Academic Press, 1970.

Snyder, Lynn S. Language impairment in children with perceptual-motor dysfunction. American Journal of Occupational Therapy, 1971, 25, 105-108.

Sokolov, Ye. N. Perception and the Conditioned Reflex. New York: Macmillan Co., 1963.

Solomon, Joseph C. Passive motion and infancy. American Journal of Orthopsychiatry, 1959, 29, 650-651.

Solomon, Philip, *et al.* Sensory Deprivation. Cambridge: Harvard University Press, 1961.

Sperry, R. W. Neurology and the mind-brain problem. American Scientist, 1952, 40, 291-312.

Sperry, R. W. Physiological plasticity and brain circuit theory. In H. F. Harlow and C. N. Woolsey (Eds.), Biological and Biochemical Bases of Behavior. Madison: University of Wisconsin Press, 1958.

Sperry, R. W. Some developments in brain lesion studies of learning. Federation Proceedings, 1961, 20, Part I, 609-616.

Sperry, R. W.; and Gazzaniga, M. S. Language following surgical disconnection of the hemispheres. In C. H. Millikan (chairman) and F. L. Darley (Ed.), Brain Mechanisms Underlying Speech and Language. New York: Grune and Stratton, 1967.

Sprague, James M.; and Chambers, W. W. Control of posture by reticular formation and cerebellum in the intact anesthetized and unanesthetized and in the decerebrated cat. American Journal of Physiology, 1954, 176, 52-64.

Sprague, J. M.; Chambers, W. W.; and Stellar, E. Attentive, affective, and adaptive behavior in the cat. Science, 1961, 133, 165-173.

Sprague, J. M.; Levitt, M.; Robson, K.; Liu, C. N.; Stellar, E.; and Chambers, W. W. A neuroanatomical and behavioral analysis of the syndromes resulting from midbrain lemniscal and reticular lesions in the cat. Archives Italiennes de Biologie, 1963, 101, 225-295.

Sprague, James M.; and Meikle, Thomas H., Jr. The role of the superior colliculus in visually guided behavior. Experimental Neurology, 1965, 11, 115-146.

Sprague, J. M.; Stellar, Eliot; and Chambers, W. W. Neurological basis of behavior in the cat. Science, 1960, 132, 1498.

Stewart, M. A.; Pitts, F. N.; Craig, A. G.; and Dieruf, W. The hyperactive child syndrome. American Journal of Orthopsychiatry, 1966, 36, 861-867.

Stockmeyer, Shirley A. An interpretation of the approach of Rood to the treatment of neuromuscular dysfunction. American Journal of Physical Medicine, 1967, 46, 900-956.

Teuber, Hans-Lukas. Effects of brain wounds implicating right or left hemisphere in man. In V. B. Mountcastle (Ed.), Interhemispheric Relations and Cerebral Dominance. Baltimore: Johns Hopkins Press, 1962.

Teuber, H.-L. Alterations of perception after brain injury. In J. C. Eccles (Ed.), Brain and Conscious Experience. New York: Springer-Verlag, 1966.

Teuber, Hans-Lukas. Lacunae and research approaches to them. I. In C. H. Millikan (chairman) and F. L. Darley (Ed.), Brain Mechanisms Underlying Speech and Language. New York: Grune and Stratton, 1967.

Thompson, Robert; Lukaszewska, Irena; Schweigert, Arlene; and Mc-
New, J. J. Retention of visual and kinesthetic discriminations in rats
following pretecto-diencephalic and ventral mesencephalic damage.
Journal of Comparative and Physiological Psychology, 1967, 63,
458-468.

Thompson, Robert; and Myers, Ronald E. Brainstem mechanisms underlying visually guided responses in the rhesus monkey. Journal of
Comparative and Physiological Psychology, 1971, 74, 479-512.

Trevarthen, C. B. Double visual learning in split-brain monkeys. Science,
1962, 136, 258-259.

Trevarthen, C. Functional interactions between the cerebral hemispheres
of the split-brain monkey. In E. G. Ettlinger (Ed.), Ciba Foundation Study Group No. 20. Functions of the Corpus Callosum. London: J. & A. Churchill, 1965.

Trevarthen, Colwyn B. Two mechanisms of vision in primates. Psychologische Forschung, 1968, 31, 299-337.

Twitchell, Thomas Evans. Sensory factors in purposive movement.
Journal of Neurophysiology, 1954, 17, 239-252.

Vereeken, P. Spatial Development. Groningen: J. W. Wolters, 1961.

Walsh, E. G. Perception of linear motion following unilateral laby-
rinthectomy: variation of threshold according to the orientation of
the head. Journal of Physiology, 1960, 153, 350-357.

Walsh, E. Geoffrey. Sense of visual direction in normal subjects and
neurological patients. Developmental Medicine and Child Neurology, 1969, 11, 333-345.

Walshe, F. M. R. The anatomy and physiology of cutaneous sensibility. Brain, 1942, 65, 48-112.

Wechsler, David; and Hagin, Rosa A. The problem of axial rotation in
reading disability. Perceptual and Motor Skills, 1964, 19, 319-326.

Weidenbacker, Rheta; Sandry, Martin; and Moed, George. Sensory discrimination of children with cerebral palsy: pressure/pain thresholds
on the foot. Perceptual and Motor Skills, 1963, 17, 603-610.

Werner, Heinz; and Wapner, Seymour. Sensory-tonic field theory of
perception. Journal of Personality, 1949, 18, 88-107.

Wheeler, Lawrence; Burke, Cletus J.; and Reitan, Ralph M. An application of discriminant functions to the problem of predicting brain
damage using behavioral variables. Perceptual and Motor Skills,
1963, 16, 417-440.

Wilson, P.; Pecci-Saavedra, J.; and Doty, R. W. Extraoptic influences
upon transmission in primate lateral geniculate nucleus. Federation
Proceedings, 1965, 24, 206.

Wilson, Wm. A. Jr. Intersensory transfer in normal and brain-operated
monkeys. Neuropsychologia, 1965, 3, 363-370.

Wolff, Peter H.; and Hurwitz, Irving. The choreiform syndrome. Developmental Medicine and Child Neurology, 1966, 4, 160-165.

Worden, Frederic C.; and Livingston, Robert B. Brain-stem reticular
formation. In D. E. Sheer (Ed.), Electrical Stimulation of the
Brain. Austin: University of Texas Press, 1961.

Yakovlev, Paul I. Motility, behavior, and the brain. Journal of Nervous and Mental Disease, 1948, 107, 313-335.

Young, Richard D. Effect of prenatal drugs and neonatal stimulation on later behavior. Journal of Comparative and Physiological Psychology, 1964, 58, 309-311.

Zangwill, O. L. Cerebral Dominance and Its Relation to Psychological Function. Edinburgh: Oliver and Boyd, 1960.

Zaporozhets, A. V. The development of perception in the preschool child. In P. H. Mussen (Ed.), European Research in Child Development. Monographs of the Society for Research in Child Development, 1965, 30, Serial No. 100.

Zubek, John P.; Flye, J.; and Willows, D. Changes in cutaneous sensitivity after prolonged exposure to unpatterned light. Psychonomic Science, 1964, 1, 283-284.

Index

Aarons — 58
Abercrombie — 33, 88, 168, 173
Abuladze — 34
Adams — 43, 179
Adaptive behavior — 8, 11, 14, 26, 28, 41, 67, 77-78, 87, 114, 244
  adaptive response as treatment — 125-129
Ades — 71, 72, 239
Adey — 50, 193
Adiadokokinesia — 222
Ajuriaguerra — 247, 249
Akelaitis — 142, 144
Albe-Fessard — 30, 44, 48, 69, 213
Alpert — 20
Ames — 5
Andersson — 65, 125, 220
Anokin — 171
Ansell — 33
Arm extension test — 103-105, 112, 254
Armstrong — 179
Aslonov — 14
Athetoid movement:
  see choreoathetoid
Auditory system — 11, 30, 70-72
Aungst — 173
Avoidance response — 228-229
Ayres — 4, 44, 62, 70, 75, 81, 87, 89, 96, 107, 113, 138, 139, 140, 173, 182, 191, 207, 216, 222, 235, 236, 237, 242

Balow — 247
Barlow — 18, 19
Barnett — 213
Basal ganglia — 27, 29, 34, 48-49
Beery — 28
Belmont, I. — 28
Belmont, L. — 28, 94, 139, 249
Bender — 62
Bennett — 19, 199
Benton — 173, 236
Bergès — 173
Bilateral integration: see Integration of function of the two sides of the body

Bilateral Motor Coordination (test)— 97, 111, 138, 172
Biochemical changes due to activity — 19, 20, 21
Birch — 28, 92, 94, 95, 139, 169, 191, 249
Bishop — 43, 46, 54, 63, 175
Black — 36, 143
Blackburn — 93
Blank — 62
Blitz — 219
Bobath and Bobath — 81, 113-114, 146, 235
Body scheme — 57-58, 67, 165-166, 168-170, 196, 223
Bogen, G. M. — 230, 245, 249
Bogen, J. E. — 229-230, 245, 249
Bortner — 92
Brain, Lord — 196
Brain stem — 9, 10, 11, 27, 28, 29, 34, 40-46, 53, 65, 71
  auditory processes — 238-241
  interhemispheral integration — 44
  motor patterns — 45-46
  visual processes — 192
  See also postural mechanisms
Brazier — 15, 32, 51, 128, 178
Breinin — 68
Bremer — 144
Brenner — 92
Bridgman — 144
Brodal — 57, 162
Bryden — 142
Buchwald — 69
Bucy — 194
Burke — 62
Burns — 35
Buser — 29, 37, 199
Buzzard — 161

C fibers (neurons) — 175, 210
Carpenter — 137
Casler — 62, 167, 168, 179, 216
Centrencephalic system — 32, 41, 44, 140, 175, 239, 244
Centrifugal influences — 31-33
Centrum medianum — 213

Cerebellum — 27, 46-48, 57, 58, 69
Cerebral hemispheres — 9, 10, 12, 27, 74
Chambers — 45, 198, 210, 228
Choreiform syndrome — 95
Choreoathetoid movements — 95, 112, 138, 172
Chow — 66
Clements — 102
Coghill — 36, 166, 244
Cohen — 162
Cohn — 62
Colbert — 61
Cole — 92
Coleman — 139
Colliculi — 54, 64, 71, 143, 193
Convergence of sensory activity — 28-31, 37, 40, 48, 60-61
Corkin — 51
Corpus callosum — 140, 143, 231-232, 245
Cortex — 9, 12, 14, 27, 30, 34, 69
   change due to activity — 19
   as converging center — 29, 30, 37
   archicortex — 49
   paleocortex — 49 (see also limbic system)
   neocortex — 52-53
Craddock — 193
Critchley — 247
Crossing the Mid-line of the Body (test) — 97, 111, 137, 224, 252, 254
Culbertson — 92

DaFonseca — 29, 60
Dember — 3
Denny-Brown — 78, 193-194, 195, 228
Deprivation, sensory — 20-21
Design Copying (test) — 97
Deutsch — 139
Diamond — 52
Dinnerstein — 219
Doran — 248
Doty — 43, 44, 141, 194
Double Circles (test) — 112
Double Tactile Stimuli Perception (test) — 97, 208
Dubrovsky — 64

Ebner — 143
Eccles, J. C. — 18, 29, 46, 129, 198
Eccles, R. M. — 123
Egyhazi — 21, 36, 250
Eldred — 69, 84
Eliasson — 46
Ellinwood — 228
Environment, organism interaction with — 10-11, 22-24, 26, 36, 125, 167-171, 196-199, 257-265
Environmental scheme — 196, 197, 223, 227
Epicritic system (of Head) — 211-213
Equilibrium reactions — 82, 111
   as treatment media — 152
   symptom of disorder — 135-136
Ernhart — 92
Evarts — 47
Extraocular muscles — 57

Fair — 125
Fangel — 227-228
Fay — 113
Fessard — 29, 44, 213
Figge — 203
Figure-ground Perception (test) — 97
Finger Identification (test) — 97, 172-173, 208, 252
Fink — 62
Fiorentino — 81, 107
Fish — 216
Fisher — 169
Fitzhugh — 230
Flick — 248
Flye — 62
Fogel — 173
Fox — 42, 73, 179
Fredrickson — 203
French — 32, 40
Frostig — 191

Gabor — 228
Gamma efferent system: (see intrafusal fiber to muscle spindle)
Ganz — 199
Gardener — 33
Garfield — 173
"Gate control" — 214-215
Gavrilova — 14
Gazzaniga — 142, 239

Gellhorn — 43, 68-69
Geniculate body — 54, 64
Gernandt — 85, 197
Gerstmann — 91
Geschwind — 227, 239, 240
Gesell — 81
   Developmental Quotients — 167, 179
Ghent — 169, 191
Gibson, E. J. — 197, 199, 200
Gibson, J. J. — 92
Gidoni — 81
Gillman — 92
Gleitman — 198
Glickstein — 143
Goldberg — 63
Goldenberg — 58
Golgi tendon organ — 30, 60
Gordon, E. — 62
Gordon, M. W. — 6
Gottlieb — 248
Graham — 95
Granit — 34
Graphesthesia (test) — 97, 252
Green, J. D. — 6, 49
Green, M. A. — 62
Griffin — 179
Gunn — 92

Hagbarth — 32
Hagin — 93, 102, 139, 140
Halnan — 173
Halstead — 91
Hamilton — 143
Hance — 178
Hand dominance — 140, 241-242, 247-255
Harlow — 63, 170, 216
Head — 211-212
Hebb — 68, 88
Hécaen — 230, 247, 248, 249
Hein — 197, 200
Held — 31, 194, 196, 197, 199-200
Hernández-Peón — 32, 41, 44
Herrick — 5, 9, 15, 26, 36, 49, 119, 244
Hershenson — 199
Heskett — 107, 182
Hippocampus — 51, 73, 143, 194
Hrbek — 168
Hurwitz — 95

Huss — 146, 147
Hyde — 46
Hydén — 21, 36, 250

Ilg — 5
Imbert — 29, 37, 199
Imitation of Postures (test) — 97, 172
Ingram — 93
Inhibitory processes — 31-35, 41, 42, 47-48, 59, 176
Integration of function of the two sides of the body,
   test for — 111-112
   symptom of dysfunction — 137-140
Interhemispheral integrating mechanisms — 140-143
Intrafusal fiber to muscle spindle (see also muscle spindle) 69-70, 84, 118
Ito — 46

Jaffee — 62
Jasper — 41, 43, 44, 192
Jongkees — 58
Jouvet — 42
Joynt — 173
Jung — 29, 60, 74, 176

Kaada — 227-228
Kabat — 113
Karamyan — 26, 47
Karp — 28
Kasatkin — 59
Kempinsky — 58
Kephart — 36, 56, 112, 139
Kerr — 32
Killam — 178
Kinesthesia (test) — 97, 136, 172, 252, 253
Kinesthesis — 67, 168-169
   enhancement through therapy — 179
King — 213
Kinsbourne — 91
Klüver — 194
Knott — 113
Konrad — 64
Koos — 247
Kornhuber — 29, 60, 203
Kraft — 92, 173

Krauthamer — 48
Kuroki — 45

Lamarre — 69
Landau reaction — 81, 217
Lashley — 17
Lassek — 9, 11, 23, 241
Lebowitz — 61
Lefever — 191
Lefford — 28, 169, 191
Lende
Lesný — 216
Levine — 20, 59
Liebeskind — 69
Limbic system — 29, 39, 47, 49-52,
    72, 73, 123, 133, 227
Lindsley — 43, 74
Livanov — 14
Livingston — 32, 41
Localization of Tactile Stimuli
    (test) — 97, 208, 252
Lowenthal — 219
Lukaszewska — 192
Lundberg — 123
Luria — 14, 92, 141, 174, 197,
    237, 240
Lyle — 92

McCleary — 143
McCurdy — 144, 175
McDonald — 173
McFarland — 75
McFie — 230
McGraw — 153
MacKay — 33, 74
McKinney — 173
MacLean — 49
McNew — 192

Machne — 48
Magoun — 40, 41
Manual Form Perception (test) —
    97, 208, 252
Maslow — 190
Mason — 93, 170
Meagher — 213
Mechanism — 14-16, 23
Meikle — 193
Mello — 142
Melzack — 20, 35, 64, 118, 214, 217
Millani-Compareti — 81

Milner — 51, 229, 245
Mishkin — 63, 231
Moed — 219
Moro reflex — 216-217
Morrell — 143
Moruzzi — 40
Moskowitz — 46
Motor Accuracy (test) — 97, 112,
    172, 222, 251, 252, 253, 254-255
Motor impersistence — 173
Mountcastle —65, 66, 176, 212, 217
Muscle — 83-85
    cocontraction — 83, test of 107-109,
        development of 161-162
    extraocular — 85-88, test of 110,
        122-213, control mechanisms
        135, treatment 162-163
    inhibition through pressure — 125
    tone — 57, 68, 85, 102, testing for
        109, symptoms of dysfunction
        136-137
    type of contraction — 15, 83
    use — 17, 67-69, 123-124
Muscle spindle — 30, 31, 60, 69-70,
    84-85, 107
Myers — 36, 143, 144, 175, 193,
    239, 240

Neff — 63
Nelson — 143
Neurons, convergent — 29-31
Neuropsychotherapy — 133
Noback — 46
Norton — 59
Nucleus — 29
    caudate — 29
    red — 29
    thalamic — 30
Nystagmus — 57, 58, 111, 119, 201

Ochs — 127
Olds and Olds — 50
Olfactory system — 50, 72-73
    converging with other senses — 30
Orback — 66
Orbeli — 210
Orienting reflex — 41, 227-229
Ornitz — 61

Painter — 179
Palmer — 61

Papoušek — 125
Parietal lobe — 9
Pecci-Saavedra — 43
Peele — 228
Penfield — 32, 44, 240
Peters — 102
Phylogeny — 4-12, 16, 27, 28, 36, 38, 54, 60, 61, 62-63, 65, 73, 75, 166, 194-195, 237, 244
Piaget — 5
Plasticity
    of the nervous system — 16, 19, 24
Poggio — 212
Pollack — 62
Popov — 210
Position in Space (test) — 97
Posterior column-medial lemniscal system — 30, 54, 65, 69
Postural background movements—136
Postural mechanisms — 17, 44, 75-88
    See also righting reflexes and intelligence — 114
    treatment of and through — 114, 202, 232-233
    symptom of disorder — 135-136, 222
    interhemispheral integration — 140
Powell — 176, 212
Precautions — 129-132
Prechtl — 95
Prescott — 47, 61
Pribram — 49
Prone extensor posture — 81, 99
Proprioception — 15, 66-70
Proprioceptive facilitation — 86, 162-163
Protective extension of the arms — 136
Protopathic system (of Head) — 211-213
Pyramidal tract — 64, 118

Recruitment — 18
Reed — 236
Reid — 173
Reitan — 230
Rekosh — 31, 191
Reticular formation — 29, 40-46, 48, 50, 52, 64, 68, 72, 73, 130, 227, 238, 242
Richter — 21

Riddoch — 161
Riesen — 35, 36, 125, 130, 131, 199
Rietan — 62
Righting reflexes — 19, 76, 81-82, 87
    symptom of disorder — 135
    as treatment media — 152
Right-left discrimination
    development of — 139-140, 164
    as symptom of dysfunction — 139
Right-left Discrimination (test) — 97-98, 111, 139
Roach — 112
Roberts — 45, 78, 84, 240
Rood — 81, 83, 113, 115, 118, 124, 146, 147
Rose — 212
Rosenblith — 140
Rosenzweig — 19, 199
Ruch — 35
Rueping — 170
Russell, G. V. — 50
Russell, I. S. — 127
Russell, W. R. — 22, 240
Rutledge — 143
Rutter — 92, 95

Saccule — 57
Sandifer — 173
Sandry — 219
Scheibel and Scheibel — 16, 18
Scheid — 203
Scherrer — 42
Schiffman — 199
Schilder — 61, 68, 102, 103, 137, 165, 236
    See also arm extension test
Schopler — 167
Schwartz — 42
Schweigert — 192
Scooter board activities — 146, 148-150, 160, 161-162, 182-186, 220, 223, 232
Sechzer — 141, 231
Segundo — 48
Seizures — 131-132
Semans — 114
Semicircular canals — 56-57
Semmes — 63, 66, 141, 191, 230, 242, 248-249
Sensorimotor intelligence — 5, 8
Sensory feedback — 32-33

Sensory overload — 32, 35, 130-131
Shagass — 42
Sheer — 51
Shenkin — 35
Sherrington — 22, 25, 28, 128
Shimamoto — 48
Silver — 93, 102, 139
Silverstein — 92
Siminoff — 175
Smith, K. U. — 33, 144
Smith, O.W. — 92
Smith, P. C. — 92
Smith, W. M. — 33
Smythies — 51
Snyder — 241
Sokolov — 210
Solomon, J. C. — 58, 61
Solomon, P. — 20
Somatosensory areas of brain — 65-66
    change in cortex following
        activity — 19
Somesthesis — 30
Southern California Sensory Integra-
    tion Tests — 96-98, 111, 112, 138,
    172-173, 222
Space Visualization (test) — 97, 222,
    224, 251, 253
Sperry — 22, 67, 143, 144, 175, 198,
    204, 239, 249
Spinal cord — 9, 10, 27, 28, 39-40
Spinothalamic tract — 30, 65
Sprague — 45, 193, 198, 210, 214
Standing Balance: Eyes Closed
    (test) — 98, 252
Standing Balance: Eyes Open
    (test) — 98, 252
Stellar — 210
Stemmer — 95
Stewart — 209
Stimulation, general sensory — 20-22
Stockmeyer — 83, 115, 130
Synapse, neural — 17-18
Szentágothai — 46

Tactile Localization (test): See
    Localization of Tactile Stimuli
    (test)
Tactile stimulation as treatment —
    115-119, 145, 147, 167, 177-179,
    202, 203, 205, 217-220, 232
Tactile system — 11, 15, 61-66, 167-

171, 175-176
Teuber — 141, 174, 191, 229, 248
Thach — 47
Thalamus — 9, 27, 29, 30, 34, 40-
    46, 53
Thompson — 192, 193
Tonic labyrinthine reflex — 79-82
    symptom of disorder — 135
    testing for 98-102, 106-107
    treatment to integrate — 145-153
Tonic neck reflex — 79-82, 87, 98, 228
    testing for — 102-107
    symptom of disorder — 135, 223
    treatment to integrate — 146-153
Trevarthen — 79, 143, 193, 194,
    199-201
Twitchell — 146
Tyson — 173

University of California — 19
Utricle — 57

Veereeken — 139
Verzeano — 48
Vestibular stimulation as treatment—
    119-123, 202, 232, 243-244
Vestibular system — 11, 15, 46-47,
    48, 55-61
    change in nuclei following activity—
        21
    converging with other senses — 30
    testing — 110-111, 203, 205
Vibration as treatment — 125
Visual system — 11, 15, 30, 73-74
    fields — 142

Walk — 199
Wall — 214
Walsh — 57, 88, 120
Walshe — 212
Wapner — 15, 75
Ward — 58
Warrington — 91
Wechsler — 140
Weidenbacker — 219
Weinstein — 191
Werner — 15, 75
Wheeler — 62
Whitley — 248
Whittlesey — 191
Wilson, P. — 43

Wilson, P. D. — 199

Wilson, W. — 28

Wright — 173

Wolff — 95

Worden — 41

Yakovlev — 22

Young — 59

Zangwill — 247

Zaporozhets — 125

Zubek — 62